T0150065

GENTLEMEN BOOTLEGGERS

THE TRUE STORY OF TEMPLETON RYE, PROHIBITION, AND A SMALL TOWN IN CAHOOTS

BRYCE T. BAUER

CHICAGO REVIEW PRESS

To three great men:
Vic Bauer, Chuck Manatt, Louis Lauritsen

Copyright © 2014 by Bryce T. Bauer
All rights reserved
Published by Chicago Review Press Incorporated
814 North Franklin Street
Chicago, Illinois 60610
ISBN 978-1-61373-522-0

Library of Congress Cataloging-in-Publication Data
Bauer, Bryce T.
  Gentlemen bootleggers : the true story of Templeton Rye, Prohibition, and a small town in cahoots / Bryce T. Bauer.
    pages cm
  Summary: "During Prohibition, while Al Capone was rising to worldwide prominence as Public Enemy Number One, the townspeople of rural Templeton, Iowa—population just 418—were busy with a bootlegging empire of their own. Led by Joe Irlbeck, the whip-smart and gregarious son of a Bavarian immigrant, the outfit of farmers, small merchants, and even the church Monsignor worked together to create a whiskey so excellent it was ordered by name: Templeton Rye. Gentlemen Bootleggers tells a never-before-told tale of ingenuity, bootstrapping, and perseverance in one small town, showcasing a group of immigrants who embraced the American ideals of self-reliance, dynamism, and democratic justice. It relies on previously classified Prohibition Bureau investigation files, federal court case files, extensive newspaper archive research, and a recently disclosed interview with kingpin Joe Irlbeck. Unlike other Prohibition-era tales of big-city gangsters, it provides an important reminder that bootlegging wasn't only about glory and riches, but could be in the service of a higher goal: producing the best whiskey money could buy"— Provided by publisher.
  Includes bibliographical references and index.
  ISBN 978-1-61374-848-0 (hardback)
  1. Prohibition—Iowa—History. 2. Distilling, Illicit—Iowa—History. 3. Whiskey—Iowa—History. 4. Templeton (Iowa)—History—20th century. I. Title.

HV5090.I8B38 2014
364.1'32209777465—dc23
                          2014011191

Interior design: Jonathan Hahn
Map design: Chris Erichsen

Printed in the United States of America
5 4 3 2

CONTENTS

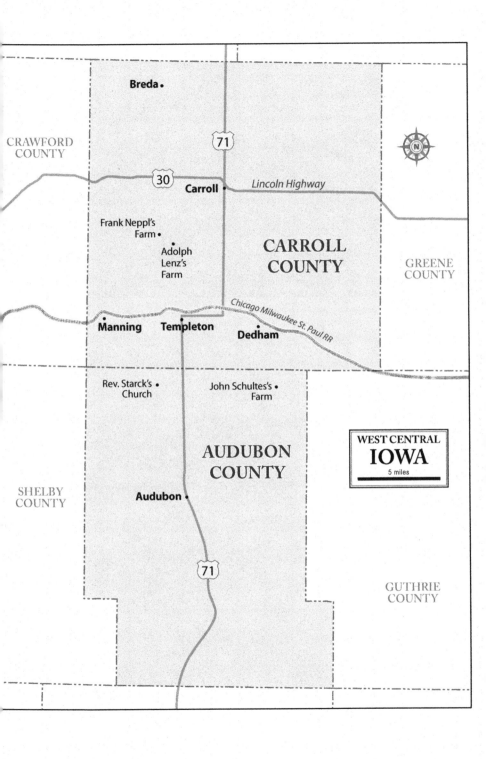

1

JUNE 16, 1931

On June 16, 1931, two bootleggers, both notorious violators of the decade-old National Prohibition Act, which enforced the Eighteenth Amendment's ban on alcohol, fled two different federal courtrooms in a hurry. One hailed a taxi and slid into the backseat as a swarm of spectators thronged inches away; the other sped away in his Ford Model T, trailed by no one.

Their destinations—like their experiences, the shape of their fame, their individual fates—could hardly have been more different. Al Capone, the man in the cab, wended through the clogged, cacophonous streets of downtown Chicago on the way to his splendid floor of suites at the Lexington Hotel. There, the next day, he could pick up the morning newspapers and see his name splayed across the front page, column inches dripping away below, full of paeans to his imminent downfall.

Joe Irlbeck, meanwhile, bounced along the dusty, gully-cut roads of western Iowa. He was headed toward his home in the tiny town of Templeton, Iowa, in the county where he had lived his entire life, Carroll. There he was encircled by neighbors who knew him by name, by sight—as they knew everyone in the surrounding countryside. Some of them were grateful for what he'd done for their community, others perhaps a bit intimidated, a few maybe even disdainful, but still they all supported him. When his crimes hit the paper, the stories were met with amazement more than scorn.

Both bootleggers were about the same age, and though they didn't know each other, they were united. Their last several years had been—and the rest of their lives would be—defined by opposition to the Eighteenth Amendment, the only amendment to ever restrict the freedoms of every citizen.

Its supporters, the drys, were a motley but fierce band of traditional Americans: largely white Protestants, men and, significantly, women, whose ties to America went back generations and who were intensely loyal to the country's English heritage. Some were businessmen, others clergy, yet others professional activists. Politicians were among them, of course. But there were also those who'd never before worked in the public sphere. They weren't all residents of rural America, but it was the values associated with rural America that defined them, that they held dear, that they sought to protect from the sullying effects of alcohol and alcohol's supporters, the wets.

The wets were an even more assorted group, defined, roughly, as everybody the drys were not: Catholic or Jewish, urban and immigrant. To them, Prohibition was nothing but a heavy-handed attempt to legislate morality and an un-American folly. The drys' claim that an era without alcohol would be one of newfound prosperity, in which men would behave as saints and women and children could live in peace, abundance, and godliness, seemed absurd. In the end, the wets would be vindicated—Prohibition would prove to be the most charlatan of laws, one that led the country into temptation and delivered it to evil. But it endured far longer than the wets had predicted. With a century of momentum behind it, repealing it would not be easy. And as long as it remained in effect, the government was obligated to enforce it, no matter how hopeless the fight against its violators appeared to be.

Of medium height and average build, with gray eyes and black hair, Joe Irlbeck nonetheless stood out. His oval face could cut a penetrating stare or a knowing, warm smile. He possessed the attitude of a bartender: companionable, but stern when necessary. He was ambitious and intelligent enough to fulfill his aspirations.

Born in December 1899, he was just eleven months younger than Al Capone. He grew up on a farm near Dedham, seven miles east of Templeton, one of eleven children. His father, like so many early settlers in Carroll County, had been born in Germany, in Bavaria, and came to the newly opened land of western Iowa to find a comfort and safety that was all too elusive in his homeland. Though he found it, the prospect wouldn't last through the second generation. As luck would have it, however, Joe Irlbeck came of age just as a vast new market was opening up: that for illicit alcohol. (Enacting Prohibition, as one astute politician rightly predicted, was tantamount to "legalizing the manufacture of intoxicating liquor without taxation.") He jumped right in.

At a time when asking the provenance of a particular shot of liquor was as absurd—and embarrassingly naive—as asking the origin of the pork in the sausage that rolled off the belts at Swift & Co.'s sprawling processing plant on Chicago's South Side, the whiskey Irlbeck came to make, Templeton rye, managed the remarkable: it established itself as a brand. Newspapers quoted its price independent of other bootleg liquor and discerning buyers ordered it by name.

By 1931, Irlbeck's operation had grown into a sprawling organization capable of producing hundreds of gallons of booze, worth thousands of dollars, a day. To achieve that required the involvement of nearly every one of Templeton's residents, from the town grocer to the church monsignor. As a result of their volume, the quality of their product, and their total commitment to bootlegging, Templeton, population just 428, became known as the "far-famed oasis of the middlewest."

But that same success drew the attention of the federal Prohibition agents charged with cracking down on violators. Leading them was a former blacksmith and sheriff named Benjamin Franklin Wilson, the most respected Prohibition agent in the state. Born in Audubon County, just south of Carroll County, he was familiar with the area.

Aerial view of Templeton looking southwest in 1910. The town's late-Prohibition-era population of 428 would be its highest. *Courtesy of Elaine Schwaller*

The still for which Wilson arrested Irlbeck a few months before his June court date was one of the largest producing Templeton rye. It was located on the land of one of Irlbeck's many partners, a struggling farmer named Frank Neppl. The rent Neppl earned, fifty cents for every gallon of Templeton rye produced, was supposed to buy not just a safe place to run the still but also the promise that if the farm was ever raided Neppl would take the blame and not implicate Irlbeck. For years that policy had frustrated Wilson's many attempts to bust Templeton's bootleggers. But this time, he'd caught a break: he'd found Irlbeck at the still site. The case seemed unbeatable.

The June 16 hearing was just a grand jury investigation to determine whether there was enough evidence for an indictment. As a result, Irlbeck was not allowed to attend. Instead he eavesdropped from outside the federal courthouse, listening from inside his car as the prosecutor's voice drifted down from the second-story courtroom through a window someone had opened to ease the sweltering heat. What he overheard was the government's case falling apart. Neppl kept his word to take the fall and swore Irlbeck had nothing to do with the still. The town banker, subpoenaed to talk about Irlbeck's finances, swore his client was not a bootlegger. And when Irlbeck heard the prosecutor, enraged that his case was not going as he planned, vow to summon every business owner in Templeton and call them to testify that he really was a bootlegger, Irlbeck sped off, confident that if he alerted them to the officers' impending arrival, they'd all stay out of their shops.

Four hundred miles east, in Chicago, things proceeded much differently. There the courtroom was jammed with newspapermen, lawyers, and anyone with enough clout to make their way past the guarded sixth-floor blockade set up to keep all of Chicago from pushing in. They were in "furors," wrote one observer, over the anticipation of seeing Al Capone—the former "cheap Brooklyn roustabout" who through murder, extortion, bribery, and, above all, bootlegging—had earned the title of America's Public Enemy Number One, finally face serious charges and real punishment for almost a decade's worth of flagrant crime.

The complaint against Capone was stunning. As it should've been: it was the work of a two-year-long investigation by a small team of extremely dedicated federal agents, led by George E. Q. Johnson, the unassuming federal prosecutor who'd been born just a few miles from the Iowa courthouse Irlbeck was sitting outside of that day.

For those in attendance who were cheering Capone's downfall, the day appeared a victory.

As soon as the judge entered and everyone sat back down, Johnson's assistant stepped forward to address Capone. He read the first indictment, then asked Capone how he pleaded.

"I plead guilty," Scarface Al replied, his voice scarcely audible to the gallery focused intensely on his every word.

In response to the two other charges, Capone shaved his reply to just "guilty," but his voice remained, by all accounts, meek. Once he did, the judge curtly announced he'd be sentenced two weeks later. Then it was over.

In less than three minutes, the capo of Chicago crime admitted what the entire nation already knew: he was a criminal. The government never even had to present its case, but everyone knew that it was built on evidence from Capone associates who were willing to sell out their boss to save themselves.

As Scarface Al left, he was flanked by his lawyers and a contingent of police officers. Behind him thousands of Chicagoans eagerly jostled for a glimpse of their most famous resident, now at his most downtrodden. They were looking at, a reporter for the Associated Press wrote, "a monarch stripped of his realm."

He would return to his lavish headquarters, increasingly aware that his fellow Chicagoans were tired of the violence he brought to their city, and embarrassed of the corruption his millions had wrought. His heyday, he knew, was over.

His would be a startlingly different fate from that of Irlbeck. For the Iowa bootlegger, the day demonstrated once again just how strongly the citizens of Templeton supported his bootlegging operation, the bootlegging operation that had kept many of their businesses solvent and saved their farms from foreclosure.

But neither man's fate was sealed. Capone would change his mind: he would make the government show its hand and reveal its witnesses. Meanwhile, Wilson would not accept his defeat. Like Irlbeck, he was headed back to Templeton, certain he could gather enough evidence for a new case.

The only question was whether he'd find it before the law changed and Prohibition was repealed.

2

EDEN'S OASIS

That the founding of Templeton, Iowa, and the passage of an absolute prohibition amendment to Iowa's constitution both occurred within a few months of each other in the year 1882 was not a complete coincidence.

Templeton came first. It was announced in a newspaper ad on May 24 that had been taken out by the Chicago, Milwaukee, and St. Paul railroad. Like its competitors, the Milwaukee Road, as the railway was known, was busy stretching train tracks out across the country. For the thirty-six-year-old state of Iowa, those lines functioned like blood vessels, pulsing life into the little towns that sprouted up along the way.

Less than four months later, state prohibition arrived. On June 27 voters approved an amendment banning the manufacture, storage, and sale of liquor, wine, and beer by a margin of 10 percent, foreshadowing the very move the nation would make some four decades later. It was the most ambitious of a long string of liquor control laws (and attempts at their circumvention) that stretched back to Iowa's founding.

From its very beginning, Iowa was at the forefront, along with Kansas and Maine, of temperance activity in the nation. Several times before the state's prohibition amendment, the legislature had enacted laws similarly banning alcohol. And several times those laws were either weakened or repealed as soon as the temperance activists let up in their crusade; even when they were in effect they did little, as they proved nearly impossible to enforce in the places where drinking was already ingrained in the culture. The goal with the amendment was to make the law considerably more difficult to repeal and to elevate its stature and perceived seriousness.

Both Templeton and state prohibition were products of the same specific energies of that place and that time—thrown off by the grand, frenetic engine known as progress, which was then powered by the belief that the frontier was there to be conquered and which was running, in the last decades of the nineteenth century in Iowa, at a rate faster than it had ever run before. Templeton was a stake in the conquest of the place, a new perch of civilization on the prairie. Prohibition was a stake in the attendant idea that such bold new places need not be burdened by the deep-rooted habits of their predecessors but could instead be fertile substrate to try bold ideas anew.

Templeton was founded in a township known as Eden, in southern Carroll County, which was named after Charles Carroll of Carrollton, the only Catholic signer of the Declaration of Independence. In their own ways both names, Eden and Carroll, were apt, providential.

Templeton was perched atop one of the highest points in the state, right along the Missouri-Mississippi divide, which separated the streams that flowed toward the Missouri River bounding Iowa to the west from those flowing to the Mississippi River, which defined its eastern edge. The slope and the gently rolling hills that surrounded it formed an area of exquisite cropland unbroken by soggy divots and further enriched by the band of glacial till and loess soils—among the richest found on earth—that met in the county's center. The debate for decades to come would be whether Templeton was comprised of the best cropland in Iowa, and therefore the world, or merely *some* of the best.

Prior to Templeton's founding, Eden Township was home to 172 of what must have been the hardiest pioneers. By the town's third birthday, that number had surged to nearly 900—a quarter of whom lived within Templeton city limits. At the turn of the century there would be a total of 321 Templetonians.

The town was bonded together not just by the shared experience of building a new community in a foreign place but also by a shared heritage that went much deeper and back much further. As the first timbers of the new town were being lashed together and everyone was still adjusting to the whistle of the trains passing through daily, the citizens of Templeton quickly set about building the community's most important building: a Catholic church. Even as pioneers, isolated on scattered farms set amid still virgin prairie, they had been religious. Pastors from nearby congregations would venture out and hold services in open fields, under the shadow of a quickly erected cross and temporary altar. But with a permanent settlement a permanent place for worship was needed.

By the summer of 1883, they'd completed work on a small temporary chapel. But it didn't take long for them to set about building a church more befitting the spiritual and social importance of one religion, Catholicism, in their lives. The result was Sacred Heart Church, a gothic edifice complete with an imported marble statue of St. Michael, a 150-foot spire—visible across the countryside—and seating for seven hundred. At a time when a pound of butter cost about a quarter, a buggy sold for about $55, and a minister (a relatively high-paying profession) earned about $730 a year, the entire project cost $33,000, including $5,000 spent on the altar alone.

In the beginning the Catholics weren't the only denomination in town; there were also Methodists—Protestants and perennial drys. But their middling numbers had fallen so low by 1903 that their own Templeton church was sold at auction. The buyer: the wife of a leading saloon-keeper.

Templeton wasn't united just by its religion. It attracted a specific kind of Catholic: immigrants from Germany, especially the western and southern provinces of Bavaria and Westphalia, who sought the opportunity of cheap land. Only a few places in the country could claim a higher percentage of residents of German heritage than could Carroll County and, specifically, Templeton.

"Does all of Germany wish to come to America?" asked the regionally influential German-language newspaper out of Carroll, *Der Carroll Demokrat*, in a May 1882 article. "The morning express train left no fewer than sixty-eight families at the local train station who made the trip across the blue waves of the Atlantic Ocean in order to seek a new and happy home here in the distant West in Carroll County. Everyone who has traveled across to Old Germany in the early spring is in agreement that America is the only country where one can have a free and independent life."

So delighted, the paper continued in its report, was one Carroll County man to welcome a new member of his family on that recently arrived train, that he intended to go out and purchase "a small keg, no, a truly large keg of beer."

As the paper indicated, what attracted immigrants to Templeton was the same thing that attracted them to communities throughout the country: that American idea of universal prosperity from universal equality that proved so appealing to the oppressed poor of Europe.

And as the paper also indicated, the German settlers brought with them their traditions, such as a fondness for beer in celebrating family and community. It was just one of many customs associated with people who attached with a hyphen their old identity to their new American one. The German-Americans were hardly alone in their fondness for booze. They'd arrived in a country that already had, by the late-nineteenth century, a well-developed and, at times, fraught relationship to alcohol.

Unless he'd shaven recently, Orlando H. Manning sported what could only be described as a frontier mustache—one so ample that it was not just as wide as his face but half as wide again. Without it, his angular features could have evoked a young Abraham

Lincoln. As it were, he gave the appearance of having pasted a squirrel tail under his nose and let it go bristly.

One of the leading opponents of alcohol in Iowa, he rose to prominence in an unlikely place. Manning was born the first son of a Methodist minister just six months after the state's founding in 1846, and though he wasn't born in Iowa, he grew up with the state. At the age of twenty-one he went into legal practice, locating in Carroll County, which was even then becoming a bastion of anti-dry sentiment. Six years later he opened a bank there and two years after that was elected a state representative, joining the Republican Party, which, though dominant throughout most of the state, had little support from Carroll County's German-American voters, who were more often Democrats. His rise was rapid, and within a few more years he was elected lieutenant governor, the second-highest position in state government. Meanwhile, Carroll County earned a distinction of its own: its voters were one of the few rural counties to vote against the state's prohibition amendment. In the end, they would win—the amendment was quickly challenged by a brewer and a tavern owner and declared unconstitutional on procedural grounds. The law, which for many had represented the pinnacle of decades of effort, was fatally stricken, but the drys vowed not to give up.

At the 1883 Republican State Convention, which was electric with efforts to find a way to keep alcohol out of Iowa, Manning rose to give a speech. It was short, repetitive, and filled with much that had already been said about alcohol many times that day, but to his party's worn denouncements of drink, he added a flourish.

The Republican Party, he declared, "stood for protected homes and firesides; a schoolhouse on every hill, and no saloon in the valley." Immediately he received an "uproarious, long-continued and renewed applause" from the delegates. From the Iowa chapter of the Woman's Christian Temperance Union, one of the nation's most powerful dry organizations, he received an even more florid award: a miniature replica of a schoolhouse covered in tulips and daises from under its window frames up to its little chimney house.

Inside was a statue of the Virgin Mary surrounded by four magnolia blossoms, evoking angels.

For years after, Manning's quote would appear in dry literature across the country. It became so ubiquitous that when Manning died, after he'd left Iowa and made a fortune as a Chicago lawyer, after he took up residence on Madison Avenue in New York and studied the soils of the Nile Delta and Rhine Valley, it would be the almost singular focus of his obituaries, appearing three times in its entirety in one write-up.

Two years before that speech Manning had received another honor, one more permanent than his seemingly immutable utterance: the founders of a new community eight miles west of Templeton in Carroll County decided to name the place after him. Despite the propensities of its namesake, the residents of Manning would go on to boast that their town had "the longest bar west of the Mississippi."

To evoke the saloon as the evil of drink manifest was no sleight of style but a deliberate denunciation of what the drys saw as alcohol's most terrible envoy.

Though they may have been forerunners to the bars that would emerge after Prohibition, saloons in the nineteenth and early twentieth centuries were places far more primitive and debauched. Often they were foul dens, the domain of men and harlots only. Typically their floors were covered in sawdust, to absorb spilled drink and other less pleasant effluents; spittoons dotted their length, but not in every place did decorum demand their use. In some cities officials tried to restrict public drinking to hotels, but the saloon owners just built dingy rooms atop their establishments instead, providing patrons with the convenience of indulging in alcohol and sex under the same roof.

Indicative of the temperance activists' wrathful view of the saloon was a propaganda poster released around the turn of the century. It purported to be an "honest" saloon-keeper's introduction to the community he is about to serve. In it he announces that soon he shall "deal in familiar spirits which will excite men to deeds of riot, robbery, and blood" and "undertake, at short notice, for a small sum, with great expedition, to prepare victims for the asylums, the poorhouses, the prisons, and the gallows." In the illustration a dapper man with a trailing beard and a top hat leans casually against the bar, as a young child, wrapped tightly in an ankle coat, stands in a dark corner, staring, one suspects forlornly, toward the exit.

The image reinforced the drys' key argument: to dawdle at the saloon was to neglect the family at home. The choice was between the life of a degenerate drunk and that of an upstanding family man. And the dichotomy was absolute. Though at the time of Manning's speech, Templeton's founding, and Iowa's attempts at constitutionally mandated sobriety, Americans were drinking only one-third as much alcohol as they had been at their most bibulous—the forty years from 1790 to 1830, when booze was especially cheap—the saloon, to the horror of the drys, was a growth industry.

In 1880 there were an estimated 150,000 saloons across America, a 50 percent increase from the decade prior, and half as many as there would be just twenty years later.

In Chicago around that time, researchers counted 3,500—one for every 203 residents, women and children included. In San Francisco the 3,000 licensed saloons needed hold only 96 people each to sequester the entire city—and that would leave the estimated 2,000 illegal saloons empty. In Des Moines, at a time when such establishments were prohibited by a state law, a local doctor and dry leader reported there were 175, one for each 185 residents. He admitted, though, that the number could be higher—he didn't know exactly. Most of the saloons, after all, were hidden in basements or tucked away in the back of drugstores, and the cops cared little about finding them. They couldn't even manage to shut down saloon-keeper Jim Himes's place, located right across the street from the downtown police station, perhaps because it had the reputation of being the toughest bar in the west.

Des Moines wasn't the only place in Iowa plagued by illegal saloons. With every attempt by lawmakers to restrict alcohol (and they attempted often, even after Iowa's prohibition amendment was overturned in 1883), drinkers would quickly find a way to flout the law. Just a few months after one of the first laws prohibiting alcohol in Iowa went into effect, a newspaper covering the eastern river city of Muscatine complained that "liquor is brought into this city in jugs, flasks, and men's stomachs" and it was known to all.

The citizens of Carroll County proved, as they would under national Prohibition as well, to be especially enthusiastic offenders. Their taverns were built atop skids, so they could be moved by a team of horses as soon as some judge tried to place a lien against the property to cover liquor fines. Bootleggers roamed the streets, pints of liquor hidden in their coats, or—employing the trick from which their profession took its name—tucked in the leg of their boots, offering wares only to trusted customers. An entire side street, running through the city's main business district, sprouted "blind-tigers"—liquor stores, essentially, where the buyer would pass a bit of money and his order through a tiny slat in the door and back out would come the booze, without the seller ever revealing his face. Altogether they helped maintain Carroll County's civic pride as a hospitable stop for travelers parched after a long train trip across dry Iowa.

As wicked as the saloons could seem to the drys, they were, for other Americans, especially working-class immigrants, an important resource that provided a slew of services to make their transition to America a little easier.

Camaraderie and a place to wallow in the mellowing effects of alcohol were the most obvious, of course, but turn-of-the-century saloons also served as employment agencies and check-cashing offices, message drops and temporary residences. In the winter they were warm, and year-round far more comfortable than the dark, dirty, collapsing apartments that qualified as housing in many city slums. For weddings they were banquet halls; for political parties, headquarters. They even provided the era's version of a free lunch (they in fact coined the term, imbuing it from the start with its knowing misdirection) when they offered a full complimentary meal on purchase, of course, of a drink or two.

The trebling of the saloons in the last decades of the nineteenth century could easily be explained by the attendant influx of immigrants, including those from Germany. Between 1880 and 1900, just under half a million immigrants arrived in America every year.

As a result, the saloon, in the decades leading up to Prohibition, became firmly associated in American minds with the poor, immigrant class—men drawn to the city to perform the horrible tasks demanded by the sprawling factories and processing plants of newly industrial America.

To some the saloon was as revolting for serving alcohol as it was for serving immigrants.

Reverend Billy Sunday, one of the nation's foremost foes of that substance known to him as "double distilled liquid damnation," opened his most famous speech (officially titled "Get on the Water Wagon" but known to nearly everyone simply as the "Famous Booze Sermon") by declaring that he was the "sworn, eternal, uncompromising enemy of the liquor traffic." In fact he was so committed to the fight against booze, he said that when he found himself on his deathbed, he planned to call to his wife with specific instructions upon his death. "Send for the butcher and skin me," he planned to say. "Have my hide tanned and made into drum heads, and hire men to go up and down the land and beat the drums and say, 'My husband, Billy Sunday, still lives and gives the whiskey gang a run for its money.'"

But that was only to be if Sunday didn't destroy the whiskey gang first.

Born William Ashley Sunday on November 19, 1862, out on the wilds of frontier Story County, Iowa, he was remarkable for his frenetic energy, untamable passion, and down-home locution even before he was known to everyone as Billy—first as Billy the wickedly fast outfielder for the Chicago White Stockings, who could have been a legend if only he could have learned to hit, then, later, as Billy the reverend. His early life, however, didn't suggest that either occupation was likely.

Sunday's childhood was less than elysian. His father died of disease as a soldier fighting for the Union Army before Billy had a chance to meet him. His stepfather was an alcoholic who abandoned the family before Sunday observed his tenth birthday, and his mother was constantly wracked by poverty. Shortly after his stepfather's desertion he was sent to a branch of the Iowa State Orphans' Asylum. The orphanage provided him with the education and stability he missed at home, but it would also hone his independence to a sharp point—so much so that by the time he turned fourteen, he'd had enough. He fled back home to his grandfather's farm, where his mother was then living. But he couldn't stand it there either, so he set out on his own.

He found early success running in the races held across the state by local fire brigades ever eager, apparently, to prove their vigor. Eventually he was spotted by a star ballplayer from the major leagues, who, impressed by his raw speed, invited him to try out in Chicago, even though Sunday had played little baseball. He made the cut. From there he went to Pittsburgh, playing as a starter, and later, with a reputation as someone who could steal bases and catch nearly anything flying toward him, he moved on to Philadelphia.

Alcohol during Sunday's youth and the beginning of his baseball career never seemed to give him much concern—he had that alcoholic stepfather, but he also counted as his teammates and friends men whose exploits behind home plate were rivaled by their escapades out in the "whiskey-soaked, harlot-ridden world" Sunday would come to rail against. Ballplayer Billy even, as the Reverend Billy would not, drank moderately himself.

His conversion came on a warm summer evening in 1886 in Chicago. While taking a pause from barhopping with his teammates, he overheard the enchanting sound of hymns from parishioners singing out into the street from the nearby Pacific Garden Mission. Tears welled in his eyes and he was so drawn to the carolers that he left his friends to their cavorting, went into the church, and pledged himself to God.

Sunday didn't immediately put down his glove. He continued to play professionally for a couple more years, but his focus was increasingly centered on the church. Eventually religion proved too magnetic. In 1891 he officially decided to give up his lucrative baseball career and enter the much more hardscrabble life of the ministry. As his first assignment, he took a job with the YMCA converting drunks and bums and whores. Sunday believed it was what God wanted him to do.

There was also something else Sunday believed about what God wanted: the Almighty, he claimed, desired the righteous to be rich. And rich Sunday was to become. When he left baseball he turned down an offer of at least $5,000 a year for a salary one-fifth that. No one could have predicted that the move would prove to be as good for his pocketbook as it was for his soul.

Billy Sunday's oratorical skill had always been as awe-inspiring as his speed. In school he could draw a crowd to a debate as reliably as he would later draw one to the ballfield or the tabernacle. But when he set out on his own as a traveling preacher, going from town to town across America holding rallies, which brought Christians of all faiths—and thousands of converts—to his rousing revivals, his appeal took on a dimension unseen before in Christian evangelism.

A writer for the *American Magazine* who traveled from New York to the prohibition town of Fairfield in eastern Iowa in 1907 to watch Sunday in action wrote that "he began by slapping every church tradition in the face," while "his gestures, more vehement even than his words, caused the drops of sweat to fly from his brow and ears as he beat the pulpit and tossed his head until he was hoarse."

Sunday was a biblical literalist, keen on acting out scenes from scripture, onstage, seemingly spontaneously, which captivated his audiences. He did not hesitate to point to attendees and call out

To the Reverend Billy Sunday (left), alcohol was nothing other than "double distilled liquid damnation." Despite his troubled Iowa childhood, he became one of its leading foes as America's most famous evangelist of the era. In his sermons before packed tabernacles, he thrilled his audiences with energetic onstage antics. Here he demonstrates at a visit to the White House. *Courtesy of Library of Congress*

their sins, nor did he refrain from describing in stark terms the hell that awaited the unconverted. Over the course of his career, he was estimated to have preached to a stunning one hundred million people. The number he brought into the Christian fold was reliably a source of amazement, as was the 1,118 he converted in Fairfield. Many of those, in that already religious town, were thought by the local clergy to be eternal heathens. Sunday's revivals were free. At the end of each stay, he would merely ask the community to contribute to him what they thought his services were worth. When he died, he left an estate as rich as his legacy.

Whether those who signed his pledge cards and returned them with a couple of dollars tucked inside remained permanently in the flock was always an issue of debate. But no one could deny that he reached into the heart of the communities he spoke to, urging them to cease at once their sinfulness—and often the sinfulness Sunday was most focused on eradicating was drinking.

When Sunday proclaimed, in one breath, that the saloon was the "sum of all villainies," that it was "worse than war, worse than pestilence, worse than famine," and "the crime of crimes," "the mother of sins," and "the appalling source of misery, pauperism, and crime," he was hoping to scare his listeners sober. And he did. Rum sellers noticed a phenomenon that occurred after Sunday arrived in a town: their orders fell.

After his booze speech in Fairfield, the writer sent by the *American Magazine* reported that three barrels of beer that arrived the next day were ordered returned by their purchasers, the shipping agent giving as the reason "Influence of sermons of Rev. W. Sunday."

But for many Americans, the turn away from booze—or at least the turn toward favoring a ban on booze—came not from the century-old arguments about alcohol's pernicious health and societal effects, but from a modern-day renewal of one history's most powerful rallying cries: jingoism.

It was a cry even Sunday would carry—and be tarnished by.

3

PATRIOTIC MURDER

At 8:35 PM on the evening of April 2, 1917, President Woodrow Wilson, four years in office, stood in front of a tense joint session of the United States Congress. The last claps of the most fulsome applause he'd ever received had just ended. The Capitol steps outside were more peaceful than they had been all day, the mass of "belligerent pacifists" who thronged over them earlier that afternoon quelled by the police.

"The world must be made safe for democracy," he said. To accomplish this, he added, Congress must declare war on the imperial German government. Wilson's insight was that the unremitting submarine attacks against what were supposed to be neutral American merchant and passenger vessels meant that the United States was, in all but name only, in a state of war. Now it was time to make it official.

Over the course of his thirty-six-minute speech, Wilson emphasized that the feud was only with the government of Germany—the political power holders—not its population, and certainly not its diaspora. "We have no quarrel with the German people. We have no feelings toward them but one of sympathy and friendship," he said. "We happily shall have an opportunity to prove that friendship in our daily attitude and actions toward the millions of men and women of German birth and native sympathy who live among us and share our life, and we shall be proud to prove it toward all who are in fact loyal to their neighbors and to the government in the hour of test."

It was hopeful thinking. A pronouncement of ideals. Reality, Wilson knew, would be much different.

About an hour after midnight on the morning before the speech, Wilson had summoned Frank Cobb, editor of the *World*, to the White House. He fretted about the impending war, the consequences for the county, its people, its hard-won society—its sacred Constitution. "Once lead this people into war and they'll forget there ever was such a thing as tolerance," he told Cobb. "To fight you must be brutal and ruthless, and the spirit of ruthless brutality will enter into the very fiber of our national life, infecting Congress, the courts, the policeman on the beat, the man in the street."

He might have added his own executive branch to the list as well.

Not long after receiving Congressional authorization to enter the First World War, Wilson appointed a man named George Creel to lead a newly formed propaganda bureau, the Committee on Public Information.

Creel was a natural pick. He'd once elaborated on his philosophy by adding to the popular phrase that people "do not live by bread alone" the assertion that "they live mostly by slogans." But for German-Americans his appointment proved devastating—for Creel also believed that "fear is a rather important element to be bred into the civilian population." And it was an element the government was banking on.

Unwilling to raise taxes or borrow money on the open market to fund the full cost of the war, Wilson's administration turned to selling billions of dollars of Liberty Bonds at low interest rates to American citizens eager to subsidize the war effort. What motivated them was not just a sense of patriotism but also a fear and hatred of the Germans—a fear and hatred promoted by federal agencies like Creel's.

One man most adept at exploiting this "spirit of self-sacrifice," as he called it, was native Iowan and future president Herbert Clark Hoover, who was tapped to run the wartime Food Administration.

Hoover was born in 1874 to Quaker parents in the thoroughly Quaker village of West Branch, Iowa, on the other side of the state from Templeton. By age ten both his parents had died and he was living as an orphan—first in Iowa, then with relatives in Oregon, where he remained until moving to Stanford to study engineering. From there his success was as immense and wide ranging as the feats of engineering, social as well as mechanical, that brought it about.

By his forties he was already inspiring awe for his quintessentially American, by-the-bootstraps ascent. The orphan boy from provincial Iowa was now a millionaire, a mining tycoon who'd worked in China, Australia, and Africa and had earned a reputation as a master of efficiency for his ability to extract wealth from even the most financially challenging enterprise. He would soon impress the country again when he adeptly supervised the evacuation of 120,000 Americans in Europe and organized the delivery of food aid to the Belgians early in the war's course.

It was no surprise then that when America itself entered the war, it was Hoover whom President Wilson tasked with ensuring that a steady supply of food from the country's fertile heartland reached the dough boys and their allies fighting the Central Powers across the Atlantic.

Working under the slogan "Food will win the war," Hoover decided that rather than forcing farmers to grow more crops while simultaneously forcing citizens to cut back on their consumption of the important staples of wheat, meat, and sugar, he would harness their patriotic fervor to get them to act out of a sense of duty. He sent out a force of a half-million people to go door-to-door urging families to pledge to "wheatless" and "meatless" days to support the war effort. He also encouraged farmers throughout the countryside to streamline their operations and improve their productivity in part by ensuring high prices for their commodities. High prices, patriotism, and a shortage of manual labor due to all the young men who'd been called up for war, encouraged farmers, including those in Iowa, to vastly increase their investment in equipment—and during the war they ordered so many new tractors that manufacturers could not keep up with demand. But crop prices wouldn't stay high, and their tumble would ravage the state.

On the eve of the war, America was, in some ways, almost as much a German country as it was an English one: a full 25 percent of the country's population was of German descent, a number surpassed only by those from Anglophone countries, who made up a mere 2 percent more.

It was during those early years, when the conflict seemed to be little more than an isolated European skirmish, that a prominent British editorialist felt content simply portraying Germany in the "ludicrous" manner of a "fat old bandmaster with a string of sausages hanging out of his pocket." But as the war escalated, and the Allied press began carrying accounts of atrocities carried out by German soldiers, the portrayal shifted. Soon one man became the emblem of warring Germany: Kaiser Wilhelm II, the German emperor, from whom all the nation's destructive power seemed to emanate and whose name and likeness, with his upturned beard and prominent nose, as well as the term "Hun" that he'd previously evoked to describe his country's might, became shorthand for all that was evil or feared of the Germans.

In America, posters from Hoover's Food Department evoked the marauding Huns in order to convince citizens to conserve food. One implored them to EAT LESS WHEAT to DEFEAT THE KAISER AND HIS U-BOATS, and featured a background image of a smoldering ship sinking in the ocean, as the sun cast its last long reddish rays and the Kaiser, steely-eyed and clad in the requisite spiked helmet, looked on. Think of the consequences, it seemed to be saying, of waking up to a bounty of bread steaming on the hearth. To conserve staples, families were encouraged to plant Victory Gardens and eat more of the perishable produce that could not be shipped overseas; they were to, as another poster urged, CAN VEGETABLES, FRUIT, AND THE KAISER TOO.

Other departments also turned to propaganda posters evoking anti-German sentiment to coax out patriotic acts. One read GERMAN SLAVERY OR LIBERTY BONDS in gold type set against black; unpunctuated, the dichotomy was not a possibility but an absolute. In all the propaganda, the message was clear: if Americans failed to support the war, the country would soon be overrun by the German army and made an occupied state, subject to the same horrors as the Belgians.

But, as ambiguous in name as it was nebulous in form and insidious in outcome, unbridled patriotism, called 100 percent Americanism by some, was often best identified not by what it was but by what it was against: disloyalty. With war, disloyalty became a watchword. Opaque and weighty, it could be used to describe genuine acts against the United States and the country's mission in war, but could just as easily be used as an excuse to settle political scores, to intimidate minority groups and those with beliefs outside the mainstream.

At the start of the war many German immigrants still spoke German, and the language was taught in schools throughout the country. Davenport, Iowa, where more than 80 percent of students learned German, broke the school day in half: one part for English instruction, the other for German. But with the war, the German language was added to the heap of things disloyal. In many places German instruction abruptly ceased, and German faculty across the country suddenly found themselves without work—which was fine for one Iowa politician, who considered 90 percent of them "traitors" anyway (meaning that perhaps the other 10 percent had just been bad at their jobs?). In some places, students preempted the school boards in eradicating German from the curriculum, as a cohort did in Denison, Iowa, thirty miles from Templeton, when they broke into the school at night, stole all the German books, and burned them in a great bonfire in protest of a decision by the district to continue dual-language education through the end of term.

Eventually, German was silenced not just in Iowa schools but in all public places. In May 1918, Iowa's wartime governor,

HUN OR HOME?

BUY MORE
LIBERTY
BONDS

"Fear," said the country's chief propagandist, George Creel, "is a rather important element to be bred into the civilian population." To do so Creel and his counterparts at other government agencies produced copious literature casting the Germans as inhuman and bloodthirsty and hellbent on not just defeating the Allies in Europe but crossing the Atlantic and pillaging America as well. "Hun," as used in this poster, was one of their prized watchwords.

Courtesy of Library of Congress

Republican William Lloyd Harding, a political chameleon, fleshy faced with matted hair, and one of the most adept extemporaneous speakers of the era, issued a decree banning the speaking of any language other than English in all schools, public or private, on the telephone, in all public places, and in all public speeches—even church services. Regarding the last restriction, he suggested those who could not understand English could pray at home. As for what they were to do if they needed to make an urgent phone call or ask a train conductor a question, he offered no advice. Though Harding's Babel Proclamation, as it came to be called, was widely considered unconstitutional, it held throughout the war and was used as the basis to punish several German-Americans.

Meanwhile, across the nation, patriots were working hard to purge as many references to Germany from the English language as possible. Supervisors in Keokuk County, in southeastern Iowa, changed the name of a township from "German" to "Plank," in honor of a local boy killed while fighting in France. The German

Savings Bank of Carroll, once slathered in yellow paint for its treasonous name, became the American Savings Bank. Sauerkraut became liberty cabbage. German measles, liberty measles. If measles—measles!—were too pure to be despoiled by association with the Huns, what hope did the German-Americans themselves have?

Anti-German feeling would become more than just popular sentiment—it would thoroughly infect the country, passing beyond intimidation and denigration into actual acts of violence against German-Americans. In Missouri, when officials prosecuted a group of men for lynching a German-American in 1918, the jury deliberated for just twenty-five minutes before returning an acquittal. They agreed, apparently, with the defense team that the murder was "patriotic." What was remarkable about the case was not just the jury's judgment but the fact that the case made it to trial at all. Similar attacks on German-Americans occurred all over the country, often without a modicum of retribution against the perpetrators.

In Davenport, Iowa, anonymous accusations of disloyalty frequently forced German-Americans to go before sham quasi-courts to defend their patriotism and receive punishment for their alleged slights—and when spiteful citizens felt the punishment wasn't severe enough, suspected traitors were forced to kneel and kiss the American flag. In towns elsewhere in the state, German-Americans were forced to parade through the streets, saluting the flag. Once they were finished, they were forced to donate to the war effort.

But one of the most violent incidents happened right next door to the German stronghold of Carroll County.

On the afternoon of Wednesday, December 26, 1917, members of the Audubon County Council of Defense gathered in the offices of what was known as the Commercial Club. The space was chosen because, though the proceedings there that day resembled a court case, their legal basis was slight—hardly official enough to merit a spot in the courthouse, or even the police station.

The council had been called to investigate "murmurings" against several citizens "known to have German sympathies," as one specifics-shy reporter summed up the situation. The presiding judge—for lack of a better term—was Robert C. Spencer, editor of the *Audubon Advocate*, former mayor of the town, an active Democrat and devout Presbyterian, and the grandson of a Civil War veteran. Except, perhaps, for his politics, he epitomized the stalwart American.

In contrast, the loyalty to America of the two men against whom he was asked to lead the inquest would have been questioned even if they had walked around every day wrapped in Old Glory herself. Reverend Ernest J. W. Starck was the pastor of the Evangelical Lutheran Church, a German parish located in the Lincoln Township community of Gray, just across the county line from Carroll. He was born in West Prussia in 1862 before immigrating with his parents at the age of two. He graduated from seminary in Springfield, Illinois, a couple of years after he wed another German native, Elizabeth, whose two sisters were still residents in the land of what was now America's staunchest enemy. Starck was "on trial" alongside a farmer named Fred Tennigkeit. A wealthy bachelor, Tennigkeit was born in Germany but found success in America as a farmer, buying 160 acres of land just a few miles east of Audubon.

The crowd of spectators that afternoon was large and near conniption. The stirring memory of sixty-five young men leaving to go fight just a few days before was still all too present in their minds. If they didn't enter that extralegal tribunal aware they wanted blood, then they certainly did with thirst for a very warped form of justice.

One by one, members of the community, presumably respectable, presumably with bios like Spencer's, recounted alleged instances of disloyalty by the two defendants. Starck, already seen as a traitor by many for simply preaching in German, something he had done prior to the war without raising any objection, was further accused of "inciting insurrection and sedition" for selling

German thrift stamps. Throughout the whole proceeding Starck adamantly denied every charge, defending himself eloquently while "looking into the faces of the determined men before him, refusing to do their bidding."

Tennigkeit was accused of the crime known as "slackerism"—the failure to fully join in the common sacrifice war required. He had never been married and had no children and he was just thirty years old. The Council of Defense estimated his net worth at somewhere between $40,000 and $50,000, yet could find no record of him contributing more than a measly three dollars to the war effort: one dollar to the YMCA and two to the Red Cross. He apparently had yet to purchase a single Liberty Bond. He was further accused of making what were universally termed "pro-German utterances"—either an unspecified critique of a recent Red Cross fundraising drive or a statement to the effect that the United States was fighting on the wrong side, or possibly both. No one seemed quite sure.

After hearing the charges, the members of the council went into a private session to deliberate over what punishment to give Starck and Tennigkeit. It had to be severe, they knew that much. They'd seen the state of the crowd that had come out to see the trial and felt the oppressive tension during the meeting. Theirs wasn't an enviable job. They knew that whatever they meted out would seem soft to the county's most red-blooded patriots who, they worried, might take action of their own.

When they left their private session, their fears were proven founded. They announced that Starck would be forced to leave Audubon County within three days and could never return. Tennigkeit, meanwhile, was threatened with arrest unless he immediately purchased, depending on the accounts, either $1,000 or $5,000 worth of Liberty Bonds—an amount, regardless of the figure, that he claimed was more than he could afford.

The first confirmation that the crowd of onlookers intended more than mere intimidation occurred as Tennigkeit was being led out of the Commercial Club by one of the council's associates.

Instead of continuing to assault him with jeers and accusations, one man decided to make a physical declaration of hate: he leaped forward from the crowd and punched Tennigkeit under the chin, laying him out flat. The blow was powerful enough to shatter Tennigkeit's defiance, and when he recovered he told the mob, which now numbered at least one hundred, that he would head straight to the First National Bank on Main Street. To ensure he could fulfill his promise, someone went to fetch the cashier to reopen the bank, which had already closed for the day. Meanwhile, Reverend Starck took advantage of the distraction and hurried home. He would come to regret not fleeing further.

While Tennigkeit was in the bank, he decided he'd buy $1,000 worth of treasury bonds. As he was doing so, word spread through the shops up and down Audubon's short, steep main street that a German sympathizer, a man believed to be supporting the country slaughtering young American boys, was in the bank receiving his comeuppance. As the mob swelled—it was estimated to have reached between two hundred and six hundred people by then—indignation rose along with it. What fueled their ire was the realization that this "pro-German," a man reputedly worse than thankless for everything America had given him, was about to get away for a mere $1,000. These men and women, wrought sleepless over worry for their sons, grandsons, and nephews sent off to a war they took every chance to support, were likely wondering how Tennigkeit's reluctant and paltry pledge was in any way comparable to their and their families' sacrifices. Their actions next supplied the answer: it wasn't.

At some point members of the mob realized that with Tennigkeit inside the bank, a few hundred men out front, and a contingent of about a hundred sent around back, they had the slacker surrounded. The door to the bank was locked and they weren't about to destroy any patriotic citizen's property, but they could wait. And wait they did. For two hours Tennigkeit paced through the bank lobby, hoping the mob would go away. He would later say he passed the time socializing with the cashier trapped inside with him; the cashier remembered it differently: "I'd just as soon entertain the Kaiser as him," he later retorted. Finally Tennigkeit decided the horde outside had no intention of dispersing, so he called the sheriff—future Prohibition agent Benjamin Franklin Wilson—for help. Wilson arrived quickly and was let inside the bank lobby.

By then it was six or seven at night. The weather was mild, the winter sun had set, and a tiny sliver of moon cast down its light through gaps in the clouded sky. Tennigkeit implored Wilson to protect him against the mob outside and even to deputize a handful of citizens to safely escort him home. But given the numbers, "excited" to "hatred and animosity" against him, as Tennigkeit would later describe them, Wilson claimed that was impossible.

"Give me a gun, then, and I will protect myself," Tennigkeit demanded. But Wilson refused. Instead he told Tennigkeit his only option was to make some gesture that would mollify the crowd. Wilson said he thought that if Tennigkeit agreed to make an additional contribution to the Red Cross the mob would let him leave freely. "I have already done something," Tennigkeit protested. "I just bought a Liberty Bond." As Wilson and Tennigkeit debated about what to do, the bank's cashier began to fret that the mob would try to break in if Tennigkeit didn't soon leave. Eventually Wilson told Tennigkeit he had to go and began escorting the farmer to the door.

As soon as Tennigkeit crossed the threshold, the mob pushed forward. "Come here, you German son of a bitch," a man in the crowd called out. In most accounts, Tennigkeit was reported to have been torn from Wilson's grip, but in the version Tennigkeit would later tell the court, Wilson willingly turned him over. Tennigkeit even claimed Wilson declared "Here is the man you want" as he did so.

Regardless, Tennigkeit, no matter how much he struggled, couldn't possibly escape. He was the mob's prisoner, and they were ready to mete out punishment. First the men in the mob looped a rope around his neck, then they started dragging him up the steep hill of Broadway toward the tree-filled city park about a block away. Some in the crowd thought they should just toss the open end of the rope over a branch and be done with it. Such a hanging, they argued, would surely put a stop to any more disloyalty. But they were dissuaded from such an extreme measure by calmer voices. After the block-long dragging, however, Tennigkeit had fallen unconscious and looked to many as though he might die anyway.

For an hour a doctor worked to revive him. Finally he started to wake, recovering enough to speak. He turned to the crowd, his spirit as beaten as his body. "All right," he said. "I'll give you the money." He found his checkbook and wrote out a check for $1,000 payable to the Red Cross. He was so weak, or so shaken, that his signature was barely legible; a man in the crowd was sent to call the bank and assure it would be accepted. When the reply came back that it would be, the crowd decided to let Tennigkeit go.

Tennigkeit realized, if it wasn't made explicit to him, that this $1,000 donation and the $1,000 bond would merely buy his freedom from the lynch mob and would in no way restore his right to remain in Audubon County and take care of his farm. He was considered a traitor. As the blood returned to his head and the fog of unconsciousness cleared, he vowed to leave Audubon immediately.

Wilson accompanied him home. But before the sheriff would let Tennigkeit enter his own house, he insisted on searching it. As he did, he confiscated a shotgun and two loaded revolvers. Tennigkeit protested little, and as soon as he was free, he set out for Omaha, from which he would take a train that would bring him to Colorado and a new life, one where he wasn't surrounded by neighbors eager to lynch him.

But the mob wasn't finished. Emboldened by their victory breaking Tennigkeit's obstinacy, they decided to find out if the noose would be as persuasive to the Reverend Starck—a man who, in an anthology of the county's prominent men published just two years earlier, had been described as "a very worthy citizen," and "one of the leading ministers of Audubon County."

Not long after Wilson headed back with Tennigkeit, somewhere between 40 and 150 men packed into cars and horse-drawn wagons and set out in a convoy toward Starck's home, next to his church. They had rope. They had guns. And, as no newspaper writer failed to mention, they were determined to show the county's German loyalists, whoever they may be, just what they planned to do to the enemy.

Why Starck hadn't fled farther than the fringes of Audubon County was unclear. Perhaps he was worried that his wife, frail and prone to fainting under stress, would be unable to handle such a hurried exit. Perhaps he was still committed to defending his actions, as he had done earlier that day in front of Spencer's tribunal and earlier that year when he sought an injunction from the Carroll County court against the Audubon County Council of Defense's order that he cease preaching in German. Whatever his reasons, he had taken shelter only as far as his cellar when the mob enveloped his house. First they formed a barricade around the perimeter of his property, then, sending forth a few emissaries to knock on his door, demanded that he show himself.

The answer that came was that he was gone. But the scouts thought otherwise. They pushed past the preacher's family and began searching through his rooms. Starck, hearing the men tearing through his house, worried that he would not only be found, but that once he was he would further be trapped in his cellar with no escape route. So he decided to make a run for it. He broke out a cellar window and climbed through, taking off for the cornfields that surrounded his house. Little snow had yet fallen that winter to impede his progress, but the ground, clear of tall cornstalks, also offered little cover. He made it a few hundred feet at least before he was spotted by the vigilantes, who then fired three shotgun rounds into the air, warning him to halt. According to one account it was those three shots that broke Starck's resolve, as the blow under Tennigkeit's chin earlier had broken his. In this version, Starck began to try to negotiate with his pursuers, promising to hoist an American flag above both his house and his church and to forever be "a true, loyal citizen to the United States" if they would leave him alone. Others in the crowd, however, insisted that Starck remained steely to the end.

In either case, a lynch mob began to close in on him. A few in the crowd called out for the others to stop, to let the reverend speak while they figured out whether they really wanted to go as far as they seemed ready to go. But those calls for temperance were quickly drowned out by shouts to do to Starck what they had just failed to do to Tennigkeit: kill him.

Again a rope came out and members of the mob fashioned a noose. They tightened it around Starck's neck as they led him to a nearby tree. Realizing the men's seriousness, Elizabeth, Starck's wife, came screaming from inside their house. She ran toward her husband, but before she could reach him, she collapsed. Elizabeth's anguish sobered the men in the crowd, who released Starck to let him check on her. As he was doing so, those in the mob who had called earlier for moderation again protested against going so far as to actually lynch the reverend. This time they prevailed and a fellow preacher promised to make sure Starck and his family left immediately. Finally the crowd dispersed and Starck and his family were herded north to Carroll, forced to abandon their home and their parish.

If the true test of a belief's rootedness lies in whether it is still able to swell to passion after the initial outburst it engenders has died down, then the hatred of Tennigkeit and Starck by various members of Audubon's lynch mob ran deep. Neither the attempted murder of the two German-Americans nor a night's rest allayed the outrage of many in the county. Almost as quickly as the mob dispersed that Wednesday night, calls for more severe punishment of Starck began to rise again. This time, however, Starck's whereabouts were unknown. When the word reached Audubon that he was hiding out in a house in Manning, a posse of forty men rushed across the county line and, as they had done at the reverend's home several days before, encircled it with guards before breaking in and searching for him. This time they turned up no one—Starck had managed to escape shortly before by boarding a Chicago Great Western train headed east. But he was still a hunted man.

By February 1918 information had reached Sheriff Wilson from a former Audubon resident that Starck was hiding out in Chicago, prompting Wilson to forward Starck's photo to the police there, requesting their help in arresting the preacher. Apparently unhappy that Starck had been run out of town after all, Wilson told newspaper reporters that he was seeking Starck's extradition back to Audubon, or at least to Iowa if the preacher feared too much for his well-being to again set foot on the ground where he was nearly murdered. He said he planned to have him charged with treason.

Though Starck was arrested in Chicago about two months after Wilson sent his mug shot to the authorities there, court proceedings against him were apparently never brought. The reverend lived in Chicago at least until his wife's death at the beginning of October 1919.

Seeming to be speaking for so many who'd participated in the Audubon lynch mob that day was a paragraph that appeared as a coda to the article about Tennigkeit's and Starck's near-lynchings in the *Audubon Advocate*—the paper Robert Spencer edited when he wasn't serving as chairman of the defense council.

The *Advocate* does not believe in violence. We sincerely hope that in future cases of this kind that the best of judgment will be used in enforcement of loyalty. We believe that the public has stood for about all the shooting in the back that it should be expected to stand for. Our boys are facing the Germans in the trenches. Let us see that none of those in this country goes to shooting them in the back. If there be others besides those of German extraction who attempt to do this, they should be treated in the same way, but let us do it by law, if possible. But let us crush disloyalty in some manner. Let us not just be satisfied with no Kaiser talk, but let us insist upon whooping it up for OUR COUNTRY!"

"If possible . . ."—it was a thin place, more a puncture in the cool veneer of legality that the writer claimed he was advocating. Even his dimmest-witted readers could see through to the threat behind the passage: the vow that such violence as was used against Tennigkeit and Starck wouldn't just be reserved for German-Americans and those who actively worked to aid the Kaiser's army but could be directed at anyone who failed to be patriotic enough. It was an assumption of judgment that led one prominent newspaper editor to declare that Iowa, in the state of such fervid patriotism, was really under a "reign of terror."

Like many celebrities across America, preacher Billy Sunday took up the charge against Germany when the First World War erupted—but he did it, as he did all things, with more vim and vitriol than anyone else. He began promoting Liberty Bonds at the pulpit—demanding that his congregants either purchase them or stay away from his tabernacle. And he decided that if America was God's chosen country—and to Sunday, America *was* God's chosen country—then Germany must be the domain of the devil. The Kaiser and the Huns became Satan incarnate, and he spared them no consideration, even going so far as to state, in a prayer before the United States House of Representatives, "Thou knowest, O Lord, that we are in a life-and-death struggle with one of the most infamous, vile, greedy, avaricious, bloodthirsty, sensual, and vicious nations that has ever disgraced the pages of history. We pray Thee will beat back that great pack of hungry, wolfish Huns, whose fangs drip with blood and gore."

It's surprising he didn't add alcohol to the list. For years Sunday had also been linking alcohol with anti-Americanism. In his Famous Booze Sermon, he declared that he was drawing his sword "in defense of native land," and that he held alcohol responsible for "every plot that was ever hatched against our flag and every anarchist plot against the government and law." But now temperance leaders throughout the country were using anti-German hysteria to take down booze as well. And they were assisted by the indelible connection in popular minds (as well as in reality) between Germans and the liquor trade.

"We have German enemies in this country too," one dry Wisconsin politician stated in early 1918. "And the worst of all our German enemies, the most treacherous, the most menacing are Pabst, Schlitz, Blatz, and Miller."

When Congress officially created Hoover's Food Administration in August 1917 it simultaneously outlawed the production of distilled spirits, ostensibly as a grain-saving measure. Meanwhile, Hoover himself ordered a reduction in the quota of grain allowed for the production of beer, which was also limited to 2.75 percent alcohol, an amount at which he didn't think any man could possibly get drunk.

Around the same time the drys managed to get through the US Senate legislation to begin the process of enacting the Eighteenth Amendment. By December the law had made its way through the House, garnering just enough votes, including all but one of Iowa's delegation, to surmount the two-thirds hurdle required. When it did, it came with a provision that had never before graced a constitutional amendment: the requirement that it be enacted within seven years. The wets thought they'd set the timer for the amendment's self-destruction. But catalyzed by anti-German hysteria, the amendment moved rapidly through state legislatures. By the time the war ended with the Armistice of November 11, 1918, nearly half of the states needed for ratification had already approved it.

Prohibition under the Eighteenth Amendment was coming swifter than anyone had expected. And for the drys in the Iowa legislature it was coming too fast—by the middle of January 1919, with less than ten more states needed to ratify the act, they began to fret that Iowa, long at the forefront of the liquor control movement, wouldn't be able to approve the amendment quickly enough to add its name to the first thirty-six signatories that would bring the amendment into effect. They couldn't let that happen.

At 11:30 AM on the morning of January 15, the Iowa State Legislature approved the amendment, one of five to ratify it just that day. Iowa's dry leaders were right to hurry. The next day Nebraska became the all-important number thirty-six when its house voted unanimously in favor of the legislation, officially putting the number of amendments to the US Constitution at eighteen. The new law would take effect in one year, on January 17, 1920. And to wets and drys alike it seemed that from that date on, America would forever be a sober nation—after all, no provision added to the Constitution had ever before been repealed.

Across the nation, people responded in different ways depending on their temperament. Some set about stocking their personal cellars with as much alcohol as they could fit or afford. Among them were some congressmen who publicly supported Prohibition. But others tried to think of different ways to ready themselves for post-liquor America. In the Carroll County community of Lanesboro, thirty miles northeast of Templeton and tiny, with a population of just 282, a group of citizens worried they'd have nothing to do once Prohibition took effect. As a remedy they contributed fifty dollars each to a fund to buy instruments and hire a conductor to start a town band.

The Eighteenth Amendment added just three provisions totaling a mere 112 words to the Constitution—one provision forbidding the sale, manufacture, and transportation of "intoxicating spirits"; one hopefully assigning concurrent enforcement power to the states in addition to federal authorities; and a third simply outlining the ratification process with its seven-year time limit. They were hardly the stringent details one might expect from such sweeping legislation.

If the United States was going to wipe out what was, at the time of the amendment's ratification, the fifth-largest industry in the country, one that whenever restricted previously had proven its aptitude for moving underground and co-opting public officials charged with its enforcement, it was going to need a legislative arsenal more powerful than nearly any other ever assembled. And the man to whom the responsibility fell was Republican representative Andrew J. Volstead, a lukewarm politician whose most distinguishing characteristic was a mustache bristly enough to suggest descent from a family of walruses. Another son of the rural Midwest—he grew up in Minnesota and graduated from college in Decorah, Iowa—Volstead was temperate if not completely abstinent. But he'd never been an outspoken advocate of Prohibition. It was only because he was chairman of the House Judiciary Committee that he was to have the duty of overseeing the drafting and passage of the National Prohibition Act, the legislation that would enforce the Eighteenth Amendment and forever be better known by his name.

The Volstead Act laid out exactly what constitutional prohibition would mean: Churches could still serve sacramental wine, which could be produced by specially licensed wineries for that purpose alone. Drinkers who had enough foresight and cash to invest in a private cellar prior to Prohibition's arrival could keep it and keep drinking from it. Volstead and the other congressmen and lobbyists writing the bill decided not to make the mere consumption of alcohol in one's own home illegal.

The most significant provision of the tax act was its definition of "intoxicating liquors"—a nebulous term inserted into the amendment's text to avoid dissension from congressmen who wanted some but not all alcohol banned. In reality anything or nothing could be considered intoxicating—was 2.75 percent beer intoxicating even though Herbert Hoover had said it was not, or was intoxicating liquor only hard liquor such as whiskey and gin? The brewing industry had long assumed that the limit would be set high enough to allow the consumption of beer, a conviction that led to a disastrous split between the brewers and the distillers in the effort to fight Prohibition. But the authors of the Volstead Act didn't accept the brewers' argument that beer was a healthful food, nor Hoover's assertion about the level of alcohol needed for one to achieve drunkenness. They decided intoxicating liquor was anything with the slightest whiff of alcohol, anything containing more than 0.5 percent, a limit that proscribed even "liberty cabbage."

Despite all the predictions to the contrary, Prohibition arrived without too great a commotion. For decades, alcohol had been personified by John Barleycorn, a jovial man, perhaps, for the wets; but an enemy as villainous for the drys as the Kaiser. On the night of the country's last wet day, January 16, 1920, drinkers across the country held wakes, often complete with a coffin, to send off their old companion. But the celebrations didn't become the bacchanalian scenes of debauchery many thought they would. In Des Moines police officers even found themselves with enough free time to sit around and reminisce about the days when as many as forty men a night would be jailed for intoxication. "Police say," a reporter for the *Des Moines Register* wrote, "that if the sale of alcohol is regulated, Des Moines will probably have no use for the cells that are now being occupied by drunks."

Fortunately the police didn't auction off the jail just then, for their prediction drastically underestimated how busy they would soon become with liquor cases. Their assumption was a mistake repeated across the country. In the weeks leading up to and following Prohibition, no one really seemed to know what to think—news reports were tepid, uncertainty dominated. People seemed to genuinely wonder whether America was really going dry. Would booze fade to a faint memory, like when a person on a pre-Prohibition night drank too much? Or would bootlegging explode? Would there be riots? Would policemen burst through doors at the slightest sound of clinking glass or even the odor of fermenting sauerkraut?

As the nation waited for Prohibition to become official, the *Carroll Times* captured the mood of the era in a report from the

dry days of wartime prohibition, when residents attempted to hold
a bachelor party missing what was once one of its more prominent
ingredients:

> The party staged an orgy of cottage and cream cheese,
> soda pop, almost-beer, squash pie and other modern ver-
> sions of the cup that satisfies but furnishes no inspiration
> for either mental or physical acrobatics. Sandwiches were
> consumed in volume but somehow the guests all looked as
> if they wanted a drink of water. Of course everybody wants
> to be a law-abiding citizen, and almost everybody is glad
> it happened—the Eighteenth Amendment, we mean—but
> there ought to be some way of "tilting the lid" on special
> occasions when a fellow just naturally gets thirsty whether
> he wants to or not.

The struggle between what the law said about alcohol and
what millions of Americans preferred to do in regard to it would
come to define the next thirteen years. But in that first winter of
temperance it seemed the wets had been decisively beaten.

The drys, too, held their own wakes for John Barleycorn. And
theirs were just as festive as the wets'. But they were celebratory
and forward-looking. Billy Sunday held his in Norfolk, Virginia,
where he was hosting a revival, and as was typical he took the
showmanship and rhetoric of it to a tenor more fervid than did
anyone else. He too had a coffin, but his was twenty-feet long and
ushered by a company of mimes he hired to act as the drunkards
accompanying that old sot to the grave.

"The reign of tears is over," he preached. "Men will walk
upright, women will smile, and children will laugh. Hell will forever be for rent." The Huns were quashed. The brewers and distillers shut down. Sunday could be forgiven for thinking the devil
beaten; a new epoch in America risen.

In Carroll County even the *Der Carroll Demokrat*, one of the
most prominent German-language newspapers in the state, and

one that at one time was subscribed to by more households than any of its English-language competitors, was setting its last type. Barely able to pay its editor and printer a token salary, it was limping along and would soon close completely. An announcement of its passing noted that it had been founded to "foster and preserve the interests of the Germans against Nativism and the temperance fanaticism."

Few defeats had appeared so decisive.

4

STEADY GAZE

During the yearlong intermission between the ratification of the Eighteenth Amendment and the night that the Volstead Act went into effect, drinkers across the country did more than just stock up on all the alcohol they could. Those with a little foresight and a significant disrespect for the law began to prepare for the curtain to lift on one of the biggest new markets ever to be unleashed into the country.

Vast quantities of liquor were shipped to more hospitable jurisdictions abroad to age in storage until they could be smuggled back in. Residents of Windsor, Ontario, took receipt of hundreds of thousands of cases of alcohol to reship over the Detroit River and onto the dry shores of the Motor City, where the cars rolling off the sprawling assembly lines were being snatched up by aspiring rumrunners and refitted with armor plating, faster engines, and better suspensions. And in Cincinnati, George Remus, a pharmacist and lawyer who had immigrated to America from Germany as child, was busy buying up whiskey certificates—essentially shares of distilleries that were denominated in and tied to actual cases of liquor. The passage of the Eighteenth Amendment caused the price of the certificates to plummet, destroying millions of dollars of wealth. (It was a loss, Herbert Hoover remarked, for which the government's failure to compensate was tantamount to "an insult to private property.") But Remus saw in this buyer's market an opportunity to stock up on vast quantities of cheap liquor for later distribution. He would claim in forged withdrawal forms presented to bribed authorities that he was merely distributing medicinal alcohol, which the Volstead Act left legal, in small quantities and with a doctor's script. In reality the only ailment his alcohol was intended to cure was sobriety.

It was also during this time that a sheriff from small-town Iowa got a hint of just how difficult enforcement of the new law would be. Pious, well-meaning, earnest in only the way a man who's wholly given himself over to a cause can be, Benjamin Franklin Wilson managed to survive the First World War as sheriff of deeply divided Audubon County only by compromising law and order to the passions of inflamed patriotism and jingoistic fervor. But he survived. He might not have, had he stood up and defended the county's German-American citizens.

Right or wrong, he later received some absolution for his conduct on the day the Reverend Ernest J. W. Starck and the farmer Fred Tennigkeit were nearly lynched. Late in December 1920, Tennigkeit filed suit against him in federal court at Council Bluffs, Iowa, demanding $50,000 in damages for the altercation. By then Tennigkeit had moved to the plains of eastern Colorado, where he settled on a large wheat farm in Kit Carson County and, according to an investigator sent to Audubon to look into his past, continued to get in trouble. There it was alleged that during a scuffle with a neighbor he was punched in the face and broke his nose. The Colorado neighbor got off a bit better than Wilson: Tennigkeit sued him for only $40,000—an amount he came to less for the damage done to his proboscis and more for the injury done to his ego.

By the time the voir dire finished in Tennigkeit's case against Wilson, on November 8, 1921, it should have been obvious to the former Audubon farmer that the numbers were no more in his favor than they had been that day nearly four years earlier when he was hauled out of the First National Bank and dragged up the main street by an "evilly disposed" mob two hundred men strong. Though nativist violence had died down after the Armistice and

Americans were no longer being asked to sacrifice for the war, there was still a strong anti-German temper in the country. "Hyphenism," the German language, and, of course, German-American ties to alcohol, were still enraging politicians from the highest levels of government on down. In fact, readers of the *Atlantic News-Telegraph*'s report of the trial needed only to look across the page to be reminded as to why so many hated the Germans. Printed three columns away from the article was a cartoon. In it a Hun soldier labeled War was drawn stooping under the weight of a beard nearly as long as his torso, a jumbo-sized, plumed helmet atop his head. He was shown next to a battered and scarred anthropomorphic globe labeled World exclaiming to a magistrate that she deserved a divorce "on the grounds of cruel and inhumane treatment," because "he soaks me every chance he gets."

It bode poorly then when Tennigkeit drew a jury whose last names could have been taken from the manifest of the Mayflower: there was a Woods, a Merritt, a McKec, a Frazier, a Gordon, a Baker, a Lincoln, a Blair, an Eldridge, and even a Wilson; the only two who showed even a tinge of foreignness were J. D. Peterson and Ronald Kier.

Prior to the start of the trial, the jury was "carefully examined as to their feelings relative to pro-Germanism and kindred subjects" and Tennigkeit's lawyer himself tried to remove the ethnicity element by asking the jury in his opening statement to imagine for the purposes of the trial that Tennigkeit was "not a German, but a Lithuanian." What mattered was that Wilson, "in violation of his official duties and the obligations of his office," handed Tennigkeit over to the mob—or "gathering," as the judge tried to insist it be called in testimony—and then "continued to mingle with said mob without in any way attempting to protect the plaintiff or prevent the injuries" to Tennigkeit's physical and mental well-being.

But Wilson's lawyer recognized just how devastating the charge of anti-Americanism was and refused to relinquish it from his arsenal: "We intend to show that this man was disloyal," he declared in his opening statement. That that would matter—that if Tennigkeit did indeed want Germany to win the war, then he deserved to be beaten and nearly murdered—Wilson and his lawyers seemed to accept without hesitation. And the jury seemed fine with it too. The entirety of Wilson's defense consisted of the argument that Tennigkeit so offended the people of Audubon County and drew such a large crowd against him that he was lucky Wilson intervened to the degree he did. In Wilson's deposition he argued that had it not been for his "exercise of much skill, the plaintiff would have lost his life at the hands of said mob."

At 4:25 PM on November 9 the jury began deliberations. Fifteen minutes later they returned with the verdict. Unanimous on the first ballot, they decided Wilson had carried out his duty and was innocent. After hearing the verdict, the judge, Martin J. Wade, assessed Tennigkeit $325.43 in court costs.

Wilson was of average height and weight, fit at five ten and 155 pounds. His features were rough but sharp, reflecting a life, even in his younger years, marked by hard labor. They would combine with his earnest, deep-set brown eyes and head of short but not cropped dark brown hair to give him a powerful "steady gaze"—a much-valued law enforcement trait at the time—and an appearance of seriousness that reflected his austere and frank temperament. Wilson began his working life as a blacksmith, but decided to run for sheriff in 1916. Despite his lack of experience in law enforcement, he had served on the fire brigade, and he won the election. Though the war would dominate his term, Wilson would define himself, and find his passion, with the enforcement of the state's liquor laws. In doing so he would learn a lesson among the most important for any Prohibition agent: when it came to bootlegging, sometimes the good guys were the bad guys.

In late September 1919, as Americans across the country were preparing to celebrate the first anniversary of the Armistice, Benjamin Franklin Wilson was busy gathering information against a twenty-six-year-old Audubon man named Henry Hagedorn who

Law enforcement agent Benjamin Franklin Wilson. Wilson's life was as transformed by the Eighteenth Amendment as that of Joe Irlbeck. Born in Audubon County, Iowa, just a few miles south of Templeton, he became one of the state's most respected federal Prohibition agents. He'd remain in liquor law enforcement his whole life, eventually becoming the top alcohol officer in Iowa.

Courtesy of National Archives, St. Louis, Missouri

had been running a lucrative business selling moonshine to his friends at barn dances held in northern Audubon County.

Wilson learned of Hagedorn's business from a few of the bootlegger's more loose-lipped customers, and the allegations were confirmed when he raided the Hagedorn farm on the afternoon of Friday, September 26, and found three quarts of whiskey. At less than a gallon, the haul was minuscule—a little more than a few nips for a small party. Because of its size Wilson suspected he hadn't pinched a big-time bootlegger. Hagedorn was clearly buying from someone else—someone whom Wilson suspected of being responsible for much of the booze sloshing around the area. And Wilson was determined to dry up his jurisdiction.

Almost immediately after being arrested Hagedorn pleaded guilty. Hagedorn lived in Lincoln Township, where the Reverend

Starck had lived and preached before he was run out of the community. It was a township whose residents, throughout Prohibition, would resemble their neighbors directly to the north, in Carroll County, more so than the rest of their fellow citizens in Audubon in their enthusiasm for violating liquor laws. Wilson began pressing Hagedorn to rat out the source of his booze, just as his customers had done to him. Under pressure, Hagedorn caved. He identified a man in Carroll County who he said imported his supply from Minnesota.

Within hours of the raid on his farm, Hagedorn led a sting against the Carroll County bootlegger (who was never named publicly), taking along several of his friends to serve as witnesses as he went to buy another three quarts of liquor at $11 each. When he returned successfully, Wilson had all the evidence he needed to stop the "bootlegging ring," as it would be called in the press, at its source. But as sheriff of Audubon County, he didn't have the authority to cross the county line and make the necessary arrests.

At first, that didn't seem too serious an obstacle—he simply turned the evidence over to his counterpart in Carroll, Sheriff Henry V. Janssen, expecting that Janssen would be eager to shut down the bootlegger. Instead Janssen ignored it.

Furious at the feckless response, Wilson complained to the *Audubon Advocate*, whose editor, as chairman of Audubon's Council of Defense during the war, was undoubtedly close to the county's law enforcement. In the newspaper's story a few days after the initial raid, readers were informed that it was unknown whether the "Carroll county offender" had been caught. "If the Carroll sheriff did call on Hagedorn's supplier he has not notified Wilson," the paper reported.

Janssen, of course, had not, as the *Advocate* likely knew, and the paper's snide comment did not go unnoticed. Two weeks later the *Carroll Times* ran its own story about the case, defending Janssen and purporting to tell the truth about the alleged connection between Hagedorn and a larger bootlegging ring based in Carroll County. The paper charged that Wilson was the one who bungled the case, because he refused to accompany Carroll County officers on the raid. The *Times* did not make it clear why Wilson had refused. He may have thought it was simply unnecessary for him to assist the Carroll authorities with their job. Or it may have been made very clear to him that he shouldn't be so concerned about what went on across the county border. Nor did the paper explain why Janssen and his deputies wouldn't simply raid the place themselves—but the answer to that question was a bit more clear: as had long been the case, they probably didn't care.

Wilson was left with the smallest of victories: Hagedorn was eventually fined $300 by the court. The *Des Moines Register* wrote a small note about the case, concluding Hagedorn, in the future, "will stick close to the farm" as "he finds it does not pay to take on side industries."

The *Register* would be wrong. Hagedorn would take up bootlegging again; he'd just move across the county line and settle in a place where people were learning that such side industries did indeed pay, and pay very well.

Despite the setback, Wilson wasn't about to stop his pursuit of bootleggers. The case, in fact, had taught him a valuable lesson: just as important as a thorough investigation was finding officials trustworthy enough to carry out the arrests. It was something he would be reminded of regularly over his long career.

Several months later, Wilson made another bootlegging bust, this one considerably larger. On two northern Audubon County farms he found a still each and a combined total of seven gallons of whiskey and 160 gallons of mash (the mixture of water, grain, sugar, and yeast from which alcohol is distilled). His investigation also led him to a farm site just across the Carroll County line. Instead of passing on the intelligence to Sheriff Janssen, he went instead to the officers of the newly formed Prohibition Bureau, who helped him raid the distillery. There they found another still, eleven more gallons of whiskey, forty additional gallons of mash, and a nearly sixty-year-old man named Ulysses S. Beebe, whom they arrested and charged in federal court.

To Wilson this was the way liquor-law enforcement was supposed to work. Honest officers working on honest information, arresting bootleggers. Ever since he was first elected as sheriff of Audubon County, Wilson had shown enthusiasm for the particularity his job demanded—even receiving a bouquet from the state's automobile department for enforcing vehicle registration laws so completely that no other county in the state could compare. But Wilson aspired to a career more exciting and, to him, more morally weighty than making sure drivers carried the proper paperwork in their cars.

Wilson's term as sheriff ended during the first year of Prohibition, 1920. And though he filed renomination papers, he did very little if any campaigning. His reasons for not vigorously pursuing reelection were not clear: he obviously had a knack and a passion for law enforcement. Perhaps he thought his reelection was already guaranteed based on his performance alone, or maybe he really did not want to continue as sheriff but did not want to publicly admit that either. Whatever Wilson's reasons, it came as little surprise to the press when he lost the county Republican Party primary to his eventual successor, Andrew Jorgensen—who had been one of Wilson's witnesses in Tennigkeit's suit against him.

For another man in Wilson's position, such a defeat might have signaled the end of a law enforcement career. Wilson's educational attainment was slight: he had dropped out of school at the seventh grade to follow his father into blacksmithing, becoming a specialist in horseshoeing. But he'd sold that business a long time before losing the election, and he wasn't eager to go back to it. Instead he decided to improve his résumé. In 1921 he set out for the federal government's notorious Leavenworth Penitentiary in Kansas to study the new science of fingerprinting.

When he returned to Iowa, he received a slew of job offers from agencies eager to add fingerprint experts to their staff. But he was holding out for just one job—as a Federal Prohibition Agent. That his desire to join the Prohibition Bureau came from an innate conviction that the country must be rid of bootleggers, rather than from a desire for mere employment, was made apparent by the steep pay cut he was willing to take to get the job.

All the energy that had propelled the passage of the Eighteenth Amendment—all the political pressure brought by the nation's leading dry organization, the Anti-Saloon League; all the rum sellers and drunkards damned by Billy Sunday; and all the bars and beer barrels bludgeoned to bits by the zealous hatchet of temperance crusader Carrie Nation—seemed to take a collective rest the moment Prohibition went into effect.

The staggering implications of Prohibition were obscured by the relatively few words the amendment contained. As a practical matter, banning the manufacture, sale, and transportation of intoxicating liquors would be a massive undertaking. In addition to the countless officers required to perform the formidable task of investigating and arresting still owners and rumrunners across the United States, the Prohibition Bureau also employed chemists to analyze samples of bootleg whiskey, lawyers to advise officers on legal matters, special investigators to conduct undercover operations and probe allegations of corruption, storekeeper-gaugers to monitor liquor kept in warehouses for industrial and medicinal purposes and to supervise its removal, watchmen to prevent liquor theft at those warehouses, clerks to issue permits for the production and distribution of sacramental wine, and a veritable web of directors and assistants, stenographers and file clerks who made up the bureaucracy of any government agency.

To carry it all out, Congress appropriated, in the first year, the grand sum of just over $2 million—a minuscule fraction of the money that would soon be earned by the gangsters ever desperate to protect their ability to exploit the law. In contrast, the United States Department of Agriculture employed twenty-four hundred agents in just its county agricultural extension service and operated on a budget of more than $30 million.

The result was not only a bureau that was hopelessly under-staffed, but one in which the employees were also disastrously underpaid. At the job he was applying for, Wilson could expect to earn no more than the average railway wage laborer—a sum significantly less than what he made as a blacksmith in the years before he became Audubon's sheriff.

Consequently, most people who applied to the bureau did so for one of two reasons: either they were tantalized by the prospect of all the riches that they might earn from bribes or they were motivated by an inborn hatred of alcohol. The bureau would become infamous for the former type of employee. But Wilson, a devout Methodist, would prove to be one of the most outstanding of the latter. In fact, the Prohibition Bureau seemed to have been set up just for Wilson. Employment there didn't require passing the civil service exam required for most other federal employees. And it meant that someone who hadn't even made it to high school, such as Wilson, could scoot in on earnestness, connections, or politics alone. Foremost in consideration was an unwavering adherence, or at least the ability to lie about such an adherence, to the Volstead Act.

"Do you use intoxicating beverages, morphine, or opium?" asked one of the most important, and certainly most lied about, questions on the application to be a federal Prohibition agent.

"No," Wilson wrote.

"Are you member of any organization opposed to Prohibition?"

"No," Wilson again wrote.

Then the final test to determine whether the candidate was suitably dry: "State definitively your attitude toward the enforcement of the Federal prohibition laws."

"I think it should be enforced to the letter," Wilson wrote.

Characteristically, he didn't quite manage the syntax, but his sentiment was spot on.

Perhaps, though, as important as his emphatic answer was US Representative William Green's equally emphatic letter of recommendation—a practical necessity for appointment to the Prohibition Bureau, which had quickly turned into a prodigious font of that precious political resource: patronage.

On the first of February 1922, Wilson took his oath of office in Des Moines and with badge number 6846 in hand, headed south to Creston, Iowa, a small community seventy miles from his home in Audubon, to start his career as a revenuer. His salary was $1,800 a year, plus travel expenses.

Although Wilson's jurisdiction was only supposed to cover a range of counties in extreme southern Iowa, officials at the Prohibition Bureau were already becoming aware of the emergence of what appeared to be an organized bootlegging operation in Carroll County, especially in the area around Templeton. It was a trend Wilson himself had noticed nearly two years prior when he returned to the evidence room with the three stills he'd seized in his cross-county raid and concluded that their designs were so similar that they were obviously made from the same pattern.

With the hiring of Wilson the bureau now had on staff the only officer since the start of Prohibition who'd proven to have any skill organizing successful raids into the wet territory of Carroll County. Shortly after starting his job, Wilson was asked to begin planning another incursion into Carroll. Neither the dry officials in Washington nor Wilson himself could have known how intractable the situation in that lawless county would prove to be, nor how the work there would turn a slightly educated blacksmith's son into one of the most effective and respected Prohibition agents in the Midwest.

The bootleggers first setting up shop in Carroll also had no idea about their role in shaping Wilson's career, just as they had no idea how significantly they'd shape the story of Iowa's experience with Prohibition, and how famous and infamous they would make their beloved little community, so recently scratched from the frontier soil of Iowa. All they knew was that with Wilson out as sheriff of Audubon and supposedly away in southern Iowa harassing bootleggers there, they were rid of the one major threat to their nascent industry. And with demand for illegal liquor booming across America, they got down to business.

5

ANYPLACE BUT THE RECTORY

In many ways, the summer of 1920 was the first normal one in years for farmers throughout the state. The war was over and the soldiers who survived were returning home. Herbert Hoover's Food Administration was slowly being dismantled, its influence over the commodity markets waning. The weather was slightly cooler and drier than average, but that would turn in September when a spate of warm days and brilliant sun invigorated the cornfields, giving them a needed boost in the last days of the growing season and helping to produce a crop larger than any previously recorded. To famers multiplying that bounty by the record-high grain prices of the last several years, the hoped-for windfall could only portend a prosperous decade to come. But such simple math couldn't reveal that the plenitude would be phantasmal. That all the war-era investments in equipment, grain-saving practices, and expanded cropland would continue to lead to season after season of record-breaking crops, that all the toil and risk-taking that farmers had so patriotically taken on in response to the government's—and Herbert Hoover's—war cry against the Huns would lead to the breadbasket overflowing and no one in need of the excess, was unforeseen. For now, despite all the new labor-saving equipment farmers had purchased, there was still a lot of work to be done, and many tiring days and long nights ahead for farm laborers across the state.

One of them was Joseph Irlbeck. Like many young men across the state who grew up on farms, Irlbeck—who would celebrate his twentieth birthday that December—went to work as a laborer on a neighbor's farm after leaving home. The wages were measly— Bill Trecker paid just one dollar a day—but it came with free room and board and the camaraderie of a couple other young farm-hands. At the end of the day, they could relax, sit around and play cards, shoot the shit, and on the weekends attend one of the many barn dances that were such a cornerstone of social life in the area. For those like Irlbeck and his friends who had not been caught up in the temperance movement, such occasions called for a bottle of whiskey, a pint or a gallon, or at least several bottles of beer. Despite so many state laws against it, before January 17 purchasing such necessary provisions was not much harder than purchasing anything else that had to be shipped in from another state. And with legal booze available so cheaply throughout the country, the added cost of smuggling it in had only a small impact on the price. But in the months after the appearance of John Bar-leycorn's obituary—well, as with war-era grain prices, there would be something to learn about scarcity.

One night that summer, Irlbeck and a few of his friends stopped by the nearby farm of Max Kastl. They had heard he was run-ning a small still and a side business selling bootleg whiskey. And they thought maybe they could do a bit of business with him. The whole thing was new to them—they had never bought moonshine before.

Irlbeck asked Kastl if he had a gallon to spare, and the bootleg-ger replied that he did. But when Irlbeck heard the price, he was in disbelief—Kastl said he never sold his whiskey for less than ten dollars a gallon. With every man wanting about a quart to himself, Irlbeck and his friends were going to have to pay more than two dollars each for the booze—nearly a half week's pay and ten times the cost of a pack of cigarettes. Irlbeck handed over the money to Kastl, but he went away realizing that he was either going to have to find a new job or quit drinking. He would opt for the former.

Joe Irlbeck in 1935. From a German Catholic family, he built the Templeton rye bootlegging operation that ran stills throughout Carroll County and produced a whiskey that became renowned all over the Midwest. *Courtesy of Elaine Schwaller*

Irlbeck's experience was no different from that of countless other Americans that summer who experienced what was, depending on a person's sense of adventure and the character of the local petty-criminal class, the thrill or terror of buying from a bootlegger for the first time. Among the many shocks drinkers experienced when alcohol went underground was a magnificent, stupefying rise in price. One of the arguments for Prohibition that resonated particularly well with the wetter group of drys—the wealthy, politically connected, Anglo-Saxon drys who saw in Prohibition a political expediency rather than a moral mission—was liquor's use among working-class immigrants. Since America's settlement, alcohol had been one of the few pleasures of the man who labored hard in the dirty, low-skilled jobs plentiful in the cities. It was so available to the workingman, in fact, that it came to be seen by some as his particular scourge, with the saloon, especially, portrayed as the pit into which the poor laborer tossed his money, his job, his family, and finally himself. Overnight, Prohibition managed to accomplish more to get workers to stop drinking than decades of effort by the industrial titans who turned into temperance crusaders, like Henry Ford and John D. Rockefeller. It did so by turning booze into a luxury commodity.

The country's elite, men and women with lots of disposable income, had countless means to acquire liquor. Legally, they could tap their own reserves, if they'd had the foresight to assemble a stash. Illegally, they could turn to the burgeoning bootleg industry, which was prepared to deliver alcohol, aged or freshly brewed, foreign or local, to private homes and fashionable clubs.

In Chicago, fifteen thousand doctors filled out applications for the right to prescribe medicinal alcohol, no doubt evaluating the treatment's suitability more on their patient's ability to pay the requisite exam fee than on any actual evidence of ailment. To fill those prescriptions, another fifty-seven thousand druggists applied to open up shops, where the medicine would be sold in bottles labeled BOURBON and SCOTCH—after all, if it held that liquor was good balm, then how could it not also hold that one's preference for Scotch over bourbon, Burgundy over Bordeaux was equally critical? And across the country fancy speakeasies began to open up in cities. In them prices for drinks, even water, eclipsed what would be considered normal decades later, and the moneyed and daring clientele they attracted gave rise to the glitterati of what would come to be known as the Jazz Age.

Even drinkers in the Midwest, lacking, at least stereotypically, the glamour of the big city, were willing to hand over munificent sums for a good bottle of booze. A twenty-year-old Ernest Hemingway reporting for the *Toronto Star Weekly* on June 5, 1920, about the new industry for the shipment of booze from Canada into the United States, wrote that he heard of a man from "a small town in Iowa," who spent $2,500 on ten cases of Canadian whiskey.

"He has ordered more," Hemingway concluded.

The markup on that man's order would have been somewhere in the neighborhood of $200 per case—a margin that would allow some rumrunners to employ means far more extravagant than merely shuttling skiffs full of booze over the Detroit River.

A week earlier readers of the *Des Moines Register* unfurled their newspapers to an ecstatic story detailing the new heights bootleggers were scaling in order to slake Iowans' thirst. FLYING "LEGGER" HERE FROM CANADA, read a headline, spanning the entire front page, for a story detailing how a man had flown into a secluded airfield near Des Moines with a cargo of eighteen cases of high-proof whiskey. He concealed his plane in a nearby grove, and waited as a few well-heeled drinkers, who had been tipped off prior to his arrival, drove out one at a time to evaluate his wares. His asking price was also $250 a case. And he sold out in two hours, before the police even learned he was in town. When word reached them, they were unsure whether they would be able to catch him and, even if they did, that they would be able to recover for evidence any of the whiskey he'd sold, so great was the city's thirst.

"If the bootlegger escapes without punishment," the *Register* wrote, "there will probably be many duplicate performances and the work of the 'booze squads' would become very much more complicated."

Airmail alcohol never caught on in Des Moines—or anywhere else in Iowa, for that matter. Drinkers throughout the nation were turning instead to the increasingly diverse supplies produced, at least partially, within the United States. Domestic alcohol would come to cost far less than the liquor imported from Canada during the first dry months of 1920. But few would obtain booze as cheaply as some daring Carroll drinkers did shortly after the start of Prohibition.

Around the same time Hemingway was chatting up rumrunners in Canada, a detective for the Chicago and North Western Railroad was notified that a barrel of wine being shipped from California to New York, ostensibly for export, went missing while the train was stopped at the depot in Carroll. According to the bemused account in the *Carroll Times*, the detective went "traipsing around hill and gully, over bluff and vale, through slime and discouragement," before uncovering the barrel in, of all places, the county dump. He found it still full and apparently drinkable, and concluded that the thief must have just been storing it there, until he, or the barrel's buyer, could stop by and pick it up. Eager to find out who was responsible for the crime, the investigator decided to wait until someone came to retrieve it. For thirty-six "long, hungry, wakeful" hours, he waited anxiously. But no one appeared. Frustrated, he repossessed the wine and sent it back on its way east, having lost, as the *Times* concluded in the snarky tone it was beginning to take in many articles about Prohibition, "a lot of sleep and not a little confidence in that old adage: 'He who loves wine, women, and song will come to the place it is to be found.'"

In Carroll County, increasingly, lovers of wine—or whiskey, anyway—didn't have to go too far or look too hard. Max Kastl, the bootlegger who'd sold Irlbeck booze at a price he could barely afford, was one of several men who'd turned to illicit distilling almost immediately after Prohibition. Soon they would be joined by many more who would produce whiskey not just for local drinkers but for shipment to markets far away. And it was all started, at least according to his claims, by a boisterous man with an improbable name: Herbert Hoover.

Like his world-renowned namesake, Herbert Hoover of Carroll County came from humble origins. He'd been born in Ohio to

Elijah Hoover, a Civil War veteran, a wanderer, and a member of the German Methodist Church who moved to Iowa when Herbert was five, shortly after his wife died. Jocular and carefree, Herbert embraced rather than begrudged the sharing of his first and last name with one of the most famous and powerful men in America. And when during the middle of the First World War he and his wife Mabel gave birth to a baby boy, they decided to make the connection even more prominent. For the child's first name the couple chose that of the boy's father. But for Herbert Junior's middle name, they selected something a bit more auspicious: Clark.

For most of his life, the elder Herbert toiled in various small towns near Carroll, including Templeton, as a blacksmith, like his future nemesis, Benjamin Franklin Wilson. Unlike Wilson, he was committed to the profession. Around the time of the birth of his son, he even wrote a poem about his life, casting himself as the honest and hardworking iron forger celebrated in Henry Wadsworth Longfellow's poem "The Village Blacksmith." In Hoover's version, he buys candy for the children who play by his door and he celebrates his small town, with its fine shops and friendly farmers. "I am the Village Blacksmith / and a Dog-Gone good one too," he concludes, signing the poem "Herbert Hoover Strongfellow."

Hoover knew that all he would need to cook up his own batch of bootleg whiskey were a few small pieces of equipment: a mash tank, a still, and a copper condenser—equipment he, as a blacksmith, could easily build. He also needed just a few handfuls of ingredients: grain, yeast, perhaps sugar, in addition to water—all of which were available for purchase cheaply, and without the slightest arousal of suspicion, at the local grocery store he'd also written about in his poem. The basic steps of whiskey making are simple—so simple, in fact, the process has been modified little in the thousand years since it first began in Ireland.

Hoover spent two years trying to perfect his whiskey recipe, sometimes working in a small frame building behind his Manning home, where he moved from Templeton. The first time he made what would become Templeton rye, he took an old wooden pickle barrel, cleaned it, and filled it with water to check for leaks. Then he drained it and poured into it more water, lukewarm this time. He stirred in a cup of sugar, just a bit of compressed baker's yeast, and the ingredient that would make Templeton famous: a handful of ground rye flour. This was his mash, and for the next ten days he let it sit, watching as bubbles of carbon dioxide rose languorously to the surface through the thick concoction. They were the byproduct of fermentation, of the yeast turning sugar molecules into alcohol.

As he was watching his mash, he also began fashioning a tiny still. He took a copper coffeepot, and to the hole in the tapering top, which he'd made detachable, he affixed a length of copper tubing, being sure to solder only on the outside, so the whiskey vapor eventually passing through the joint wouldn't take on any lead. He then bent the pipe around in circles, forming a coil, which he placed in another barrel, the last bit of copper tubing poking through a hole in the side, near the bottom, which he'd drilled and sealed tight to make sure no liquid could leak past the seam. Finally he made a little notch at the top of this barrel, which he would point to the nearest drain when he set the entire contraption up on his cookstove.

When he judged the fermentation complete—when the froth on top had receded and the bubbles came less frequently and the whole brew smelled right—he began transferring the mash into his little still. When it was nearly full, he turned on the gas and struck a match, igniting the burner. As the blue flame hissed underneath the modified coffeepot, he slowly stirred his mash, making sure none stayed too long at the bottom, where it could scald. Slowly the temperature rose. Hoover waited until the temperature reached what he judged to be just a few degrees shy of 173 degrees Fahrenheit—the point at which alcohol vaporizes. Then he fitted the top of his coffeepot back on, possibly taking a bit of leftover rye flour and water to make a paste to seal the seam between the two.

Occasionally tapping the top of the still to gauge by pressure how much vapor was forming and how close the mash was to boiling, he also began filling the second barrel, the one with a copper tube coiled inside, with cold water. The water would help keep the copper pipe cool enough to recondense the alcoholic vapor swirling through it, so that by the time it reached the spigot sticking out of the bottom of the barrel it would flow out as a liquid, ready to be captured in another barrel, or a tin can, or a glass mason jar. Hoover knew that what he wanted was what seasoned whiskey distillers called the heart, roughly the middle 75 percent of the liquid, which was composed of good, drinkable whiskey. If he didn't throw out the first bit of liquid to come out of the still, the "foreshots," his whiskey would contain the poisonous byproducts of fermentation, such as wood alcohol; if he didn't dump the last bit, the "tails," he'd contaminate it with foul-tasting chemicals that vaporized after most of the alcohol had boiled off.

Whiskey, at least any that most buyers would consider acceptable, had to be at least 40 percent alcohol—80 proof. More advanced stills would have contained a special chamber known as the doubler or thump keg, because of the deep staccato sound it makes when running, to bring the alcohol up to the desired proof the first time it runs through. On more slapdash contraptions—and Hoover's still was nothing if not slapdash, even for a moonshiner—the liquid from the first run had to be distilled a second time to concentrate the alcohol. What came out was strong enough to be called whiskey, but clear and known to distillers as raw or green liquor—a substance closer to vodka but not nearly as pure.

To produce the distinctive caramel color, as well as mellow the harsher notes and develop the whiskey's body, the green liquor would need to spend some time aging in charred oak barrels before it could be bottled. Moonshiners frequently skipped this last step. Waiting for liquor to age not only tied up capital in the ingredients used to make the booze, but it also made bootlegging riskier. The heavy barrels full of whiskey required a large space where they could be stored safely for at least several months and in the event of a raid were difficult to move quickly. They were also absolutely impossible to explain away if found by the feds. Moonshiners could argue, as those in Templeton would become fond of doing, that their still was not a still at all, but, in fact, a livestock feed boiler—a ruse that no one had to believe as long as it provided cover for authorities who preferred to ignore local bootlegging instead of stopping it. But alcohol was alcohol, and unless it was accompanied by a permit designating it for medicinal or religious or industrial use, its manufacture was entirely illegal under the Volstead Act.

Despite the hassle and risk, Hoover introduced his whiskey to the mellowing effects of oak wood. He'd produced only a minuscule amount—not even enough to fill a quart jar—so he'd have no trouble hiding it in the unlikely event a federal agent visited. Nor did he have to worry about a quick return on his investment. Those first few gulps of whiskey, made from a simple recipe of sugar and rye distilled through a jerry-rigged still out back behind his home, was barely enough to fuel a party of one. With that batch, Hoover had no grand plans of creating a bootlegging empire. He simply wanted a good glass of whiskey at a time when there was none to be had cheaply. But so, apparently, did everyone else.

How many batches of whiskey Hoover made in his little copper coffeepot is not known, but if he was the popular, gregarious man he claimed to be in his poem, he almost certainly didn't keep it all to himself. If he gave a few sips to friends who dropped by his shop, they probably asked him for a few more to take home and share with their own guests. As word quickly spread that Prohibition, rather than draining the community of high-quality booze, had given rise to excellent, locally produced rye whiskey, Hoover realized that the opportunity to augment his blacksmith's salary by going into business as a professional bootlegger was practically limitless. The only impediment was his tiny makeshift still. So not long after the last tails of his first batch of whiskey were sent down the drain, Hoover was back at his anvil with loftier aspirations in mind.

By 1922 the coffeepot had become a water reservoir from an old cookstove, the copper coil attached by way of a funnel Hoover soldered over a hole he'd cut into the side. His mash was now allowed to ferment in a much larger barrel, and more importantly, he now had a partner who not only let him use his farm for storage but also helped him keep the still running around the clock. Though the stream of liquor flowing out the coil's end was thicker, and though the amount of mash used in each run was greater, Hoover still found himself turning away customers. But those who couldn't get any of Hoover's rye no longer had to suffer in sobriety—it didn't take long for dozens of other moonshiners to start making their own hooch using a method based on Hoover's—a fact one local automobile dealer surmised when he went one day to take a few cars out of storage and discovered that they had been stripped of every piece of copper.

Anyone who surveyed the nation's illicit booze market wouldn't take long to figure out why so many drinkers in rural Carroll County would turn to making whiskey themselves rather than buying it from a bootlegger.

For most tipplers, options ran a truncated gamut from the questionable to the abhorrent. The worst of it was consumed by the most desperate inebriates who, deprived of their cheap pre-Prohibition booze, scoured their surroundings for anything that could possibly be intoxicating. In the Midwest they found that they could drink the sludge that pooled at the bottom of silos, the drippings from years of rotting and fermenting animal feed. Elsewhere they turned to drinking antifreeze stolen from car radiators or the alcohol gel that provided the fuel in cans of Sterno, which was eventually banned in Iowa because it could be strained through a cloth or piece of bread to produce drinkable alcohol.

Just as frightening were the liquids that more upstanding, better-off drinkers turned to. From their pharmacist, drinkers could purchase bay rum, hair tonic, and toilet water—of the latter, a particularly potent form from France, clocking in at 76 percent alcohol, was popular for a brief period while residents of Carroll County were subjected to state prohibition. But that source dried up too once the druggist became suspicious as to why so many men were suddenly interested in one particular brand of cosmetic. Once he realized they weren't using it to improve their hygiene, he pulled the product from his shelf, embarrassed. Unlike most pharmaceutical intoxicants, the toilet water sold in Carroll apparently contained genuine, drinkable ethyl alcohol, rather than its toxic siblings, isopropyl and wood alcohol.

Just as repulsive, if not more so, was much of the booze actually produced for human consumption. Even in areas of the country with rich moonshining traditions, bootleggers under pressure to supply a steadily increasing demand while maintaining a greater degree of furtiveness cut corners by using faster fermenting ingredients and inferior materials for their stills. Among the most pervasive shortcuts was the use of stills soldered with, or even partially made from, lead, which would leach into the alcohol during distillation, producing a drink laced with the potent toxin. But many bootleggers added other ingredients both harmless and poisonous. To make their alcohol appear to be aged whiskey, some added caramel coloring, others burnt sugar or prune juice. So it would have the smokiness of peated Scotch, they added creosote. To make it hold a bead—produce a bubble after shaking that would remain intact, something many buyers associated only with genuine, undiluted whiskey—more sympathetic bootleggers added glycerin or fusel oil; those less concerned about repeat customers added sulfuric acid. To cover up the fact that alcohol labeled 100 proof was nowhere near as high, iodine was added—as it assaulted the digestive system it created a burning sensation that made some confident they were getting their money's worth. For those not fully convinced, some bootleggers offered a second version that promised an even stronger kick—it was laced with embalming fluid.

But some of the most deadly poisons drinkers risked ingesting were added not by dishonest bootleggers but by decree of the federal government. Regulations demanded that alcohol manufactured for industrial uses be rendered undrinkable by the addition of one or more of several dozen denaturants, including such deadly toxins as formaldehyde and mercury. Skilled chemists could remove most of these chemicals by redistilling the alcohol, and great quantities of bootleg liquor were produced this way, but too often they failed and the alcohol was nearly as toxic as it was before they processed it.

Together the results of liquor poisoned by nearsighted federal rule makers and incompetent and unscrupulous bootleggers made for a series of headlines that contrasted in the most grisly fashion with fawning stories of the antics of the stylish speakeasy set. Already in March 1920 in Des Moines "undertakers' highballs" and "graveyard gin" were accepted slang for the toxic brew. And its effects became well known to *Des Moines Register* subscribers who read stories of drinkers going blind from drinking wood alcohol and teenagers dying after drinking such seemingly innocuous liquors as essence of wintergreen, bought from a pharmacist and containing no indication as to the poisons mixed in.

What led to Templeton rye's early notoriety and lasting popularity was its reputation for quality and, above all, safety.

Among those getting in on the action was Joe Irlbeck. Irlbeck never said exactly where he got his first still, but it was retrofitted from a copper wash boiler, just like the kind Hoover eventually started selling, and could easily have been one of Hoover's early models. The water for Irlbeck's first batch of whiskey came straight from a natural spring. The motivation to start the operation came, of course, from the realization that he wasn't going to get ahead in life spending all his wages on overpriced bootleg liquor.

In the summer of 1921 he went to work again for Bill Trecker. One day after work he and another of Trecker's farmhands lashed a fifty-gallon barrel onto the running board of a Ford Model T and drove to a spring on Trecker's farm. There they filled the barrel full of water. As they started to drive off they ran into their first hitch: when Irlbeck stepped on the gas nothing happened. When he stepped harder, still nothing happened. Under the weight of more than four hundred pounds of water, the Model T wouldn't budge.

So Irlbeck and his accomplice detached the barrel and rolled it into a nearby patch of weeds and decided they'd ferment their first barrel of mash right there, under the open sky. They dumped out some of the water and added in some sugar and yeast, but no rye or grain, and let the concoction sit. As two young men looking for a quick drink, they weren't really concerned with quality, nor had they yet found a copy of Hoover's recipe for rye whiskey.

For a few days, they continued with their farm work, occasionally driving out to check on the barrel when they had a free moment and Trecker wasn't around. That they were using a corner of his farm to contravene the liquor laws was something they'd neglected to tell him. When the mash was ready to be distilled, they finally decided they had to tell their boss. It was one thing to tuck a fifty-gallon barrel of water and sugar and yeast into an overgrown corner of the farm; it was something else entirely to rig up a still and start making whiskey. When they brought up the subject, they had no idea whether he'd be thrilled to have a new source of booze, eager to grab for himself a part of Prohibition's untaxed millions, or indifferent about the whole thing, chalking the idea up to the youthful tinkering of two of his restless employees. As it was, he exploded.

For nearly a minute he screamed at them about how terrible an idea the still was. He was particularly worried about what the owner of the land he was leasing would do if he stopped by and saw what was going on. He'd be kicked off, for sure.

Eventually, though, he calmed down. By then it had started to drizzle. The rain put Irlbeck into a bind: it would make it difficult for him to run a still with an open flame outside. Luckily Trecker offered a compromise.

"Well," he told the aspiring bootleggers, "you can have one building to cook the mash off, but this evening, everything off the place."

"Yes," Irlbeck agreed. "By dark."

Trecker's worries that someone might show up proved correct. In the middle of running the still, one of Irlbeck's friends stopped by. But rather than running to the feds, he sat down next to it with a jar and decided to sample some of the liquor, still warm, that was trickling out. Either Irlbeck's first sugar-and-water mash was particularly tasty, which is unlikely, or his friend was particularly fond of alcohol. Regardless, the visitor didn't stop after his first taste— he kept drinking it about as fast as it was coming out of the still.

As soon as the last drop of booze dripped from the end of the coil, Irlbeck tightened the lid on the jar that contained the liquor his friend had not managed to drink, and took apart the still as promised. But the end of the run wasn't the end of Irlbeck's foray into bootlegging. He'd soon have plenty of places to hide his stills.

It should have surprised no one that Irlbeck and so many other men—and a few women—around Templeton had the skills to make booze, or knew someone from which to learn them quickly. For most of America's history, alcohol production was just another farm chore, as routine as collecting eggs and tilling the soil. Shortly after the first Europeans arrived in America and discovered the new indigenous grain, corn, they set about testing its suitability for beer making. Their results were encouraging. Many of the homesteaders carving out farms from the new land had little choice but to make their own booze if they wanted a drink, so isolated were their original settlements. As those communities developed, many farmers still found it better to distill their excess grain into whiskey and sell that instead. Not only did doing so increase the value of their crops, it also made them easier to transport.

Nor was it any accident that Templeton's bootleggers chose to use rye in their mash. The grain was one of the first distilled by European settlers, and rye whiskey had become the dominant liquor after the American Revolution. It was even made by George Washington on his Mount Vernon farm. Herbert Hoover's inclusion of rye in his original recipe likely had more to do with his fondness for rye whiskey than any surplus of the grain in the area; though it was among the many crops planted by the first settlers of Carroll County, it had largely been replaced by corn before the beginning of the twentieth century. But Templeton's bootleggers would come to praise it for its ability to give even the shortest aged whiskey a quality flavor.

What made Templeton's embrace of bootlegging even less surprising was that it fit right in with national trends. Rapid growth in the illicit production of liquor was a phenomenon that occurred with as much predictability after the barring of alcohol as the flare-up of hatred toward America's enemies following a declaration of war. Prohibition was now national, which only meant that bootlegging would be too.

Within months, the Genna brothers became Chicago's most productive bootleggers by outsourcing distilling to hundreds of slum-dwellers all over the city's Near West Side, imbuing the neighborhood with an indelible odor of fermentation that wouldn't dissipate until repeal. On a smaller scale, thirsty Americans embraced one of the most ingenious products to originate during Prohibition: raisin cakes. Sold by California grape growers, who, despite innumerable predictions of their downfall following the Eighteenth Amendment, experienced an unprecedented explosion in demand, the cakes came with labels attached boldly cautioning that over time the product will "ferment and turn into wine." If potential buyers still couldn't get the hint, salesladies would hold public presentations on what not to do with the cakes if the buyer desired them to stay in their alcohol-free form. Countless Americans desired they not.

The Templeton rye cookers weren't the only ones from Carroll County to enter the new bootlegging industry in a big way.

Henry, Leonard, Claude, and Leslie Chapman, born in 1879, 1884, 1885, and 1899 respectively, were four of the fourteen children of

Albert and Martha Chapman, who were originally from Illinois and Indiana but had settled in western Iowa to farm. Until Prohibition there was little to suggest that any of the boys were anything but upstanding members of the community. But as the ocean of money to be made from violating the dry laws continued to swell, they couldn't keep from jumping in. Henry lived in Glidden, one of the only towns in Carroll where dry sentiment reigned, and there he worked as a chemical salesman. Leonard, who always went by "Len," was a clothing salesman for Hauger-Martin Co. out of Grand Rapids, Michigan. Claude, whom everyone called "Barney," was on track to follow his father, working before Prohibition as a farm laborer.

Leslie, or "Les," meanwhile was just a few months shy of twenty-one when Prohibition began, but even he claimed to have a legitimate occupation: auto finance. Unlike his brothers, that job would come to appear if not spurious, then at least circumspect, with the questions arising in retrospect of not just how he was able to finance those autos, but what, exactly, he was financing them for. Even odder was what he would take on a few years later, after he'd made a good deal of money in the booze industry—he joined the team that designed and built Carroll's very own model of airplane. With one wing but three engines, it was known as the "Triad." Among the other men involved in the project was William Saul, who was Carroll's county attorney when Prohibition began. They'd work on other ventures together as well.

For most of the 1920s the Chapmans were known to the liquor law enforcers merely as small-time bootleggers. But during that time they were busy building a liquor trafficking syndicate that would come to operate in six states. Early on Len moved from Carroll to Spirit Lake, Iowa, a resort town 120 miles north of Templeton. There he bought a cottage and deemed it their new headquarters.

Theirs would come to be an operation that was everything the one emerging in Templeton was not. It was formed not out of a reverence for quality whiskey and the artisanal distilling it required but instead as a purely money-making endeavor, selling nothing more than a barely passable product to the bottom of the market. Sometimes, they failed to do even that. Some of what they sold came from massive stills the brothers set up in Iowa, including at least one in Carroll County that they used to distill pure cane-sugar mash. But when that wasn't enough, they also imported liquor from the suburbs of Chicago and the shores of Lake Michigan. In at least one case, they even turned to a company in New York City that dealt in a particularly potent form of mouthwash.

On October 5, 1923, Len and Barney Chapman were at the train depot in Humboldt, Iowa, one hundred miles northeast of Templeton, loading twenty cases of ten gallons each of the mouthwash that had arrived earlier in the day on the Minneapolis and St. Louis Railway into Barney's REO Speed Wagon. Watching nearby was Benjamin Franklin Wilson. After they'd loaded the seventeenth case into the truck, Wilson and the five other officers assisting him came out of hiding and arrested them. They then seized both the Speed Wagon and Len's car, a Buick Roadster, which he had parked nearby.

A government chemist later analyzed the mouthwash and found that it was manufactured to be undrinkable by the addition of diethyl phthalate, a bitter chemical used in flexible plastics and a coloring derived from coal tar, and was therefore legal. But when officers searched Len's vehicle they found, in addition to a lady's fur coat and several suitcases of clothes, a veritable chemistry set. It included several test tubes, alcohol proofing equipment, three cans of Sterno, and a small glass still, which the officers suspected the men planned to use to redistill the mouthwash to strip out the chemicals that made it undrinkable. They also found three pint bottles filled with a seemingly similar liquid and labeled IDEAL MOUTH WASH. Loose in the bag were additional labels. What was allegedly "ideal" about the mouthwash was becoming clear.

But the Chapmans argued that since the alcoholic substance Wilson arrested them with was still unfit for consumption, they couldn't possibly be guilty of illegal possession of intoxicating liquor. Furthermore, they insisted the officers illegally seized their property, because it had been used to transport nothing but that mouthwash, which, albeit foul-tasting and potentially intoxicating, was not in violation of any law. Perhaps because Wilson had more confidence in the court in Humboldt County than he did in the one at Carroll County, the government let the case be tried under state law instead of federal. Three months later the jury returned with its verdict: Barney was found not guilty, but Len was convicted on bootlegging charges, perhaps because of the additional pint bottles found in his car.

Neither Len nor Wilson were willing to accept the jury's verdict. Len vowed to appeal, to take his case even to the state supreme court. Wilson and the government's attorney meanwhile took another look at the evidence: they had Barney helping his brother load two hundred gallons of alcohol and they had his brother with a car full of all the tools needed to make that alcohol drinkable. Even if Barney fought the charges, they knew it would take an extremely credulous juror to not be convinced that Barney knew exactly what his brother intended to do with that mouth wash once they hauled it away.

A few months after the initial judgment, the US attorney filed a new case against Barney, this time in federal court, charging him with possessing ingredients with which to make intoxicating liquor. Barney chose not to challenge the charges and pleaded guilty. Buoyed by their success, the officers charged Len with the same offense and he too pleaded guilty. All told, Len was fined $300, while Barney was forced to pay $200. But they didn't leave the bootlegging game.

So enthusiastically did the country embrace bootlegging that in the first six months of 1920 alone, the federal government opened 7,291 cases for Volstead Act violations. In the first compete fiscal year, 1921, that number jumped to 29,114. It would continue to climb dramatically for the next thirteen years.

So widespread had bootlegging become that a little less than three years after the *Carroll Times* wrote that, by the paper's prediction, the Eighteenth Amendment would lead to moonshining being "indulged to some little extent," it came back with another opinion piece on the matter. In a series of snarky one-paragraph editorials printed one after another in a column, the *Times* estimated, obviously in jest, that whiskey was produced for sale by a full 20 percent of the people in the state. And lest those remaining 80 percent be thought teetotalers, it added that the rest, while not producing it on a commercial scale, still made booze for their own use. It then proposed to any of its disillusioned dry readers that "if the Anti-Saloon League of Iowa wishes to accomplish anything it must enlarge the scope of its activities and change its name. We propose calling it the Anti-Bootlegger and Home Hootch Society. We propose further that three members constitute a quorum for the transaction of business, on the theory that if more are required it would be necessary to enlist the support of the enemy to transact business."

Despite the ironic tone, the essence of the editorial was, from the dry perspective, uncomfortably close to the truth. Even if the Constitution now said alcohol was illegal, many people still considered it their right to drink. Consumption did fall significantly those first dry years, dropping to an estimated 30 percent of its pre-Prohibition level. But it found its bottom quickly, and once it did, it started on its way back up. For a certain segment of America, at least, the demand for drink was insatiable—as was the desire for outsized profits among those who satisfied it.

Though the cost of illicit liquor quickly fell from the jarring price Irlbeck and his fellow Iowa drinkers paid in the months after the Volstead Act went into effect, the bootleggers never had to offer significant discounts to move their product. Depending on the local market, beer that sold for $50 a barrel netted $15 in profit, even after all the bribes were considered. Meanwhile the markup on liquor was as high as 2,000 percent.

Despite such margins, however, supply could never outstrip demand. In an attempt to fill the void, bootleggers employed untold expedients. Among those was the use of sugar by Templeton's bootleggers. In previous eras, when farmers turned to distilling, they did so to dispose of excess grain. But Templeton's whiskey cookers weren't out to create a new market for their farm products: their goal was to simply augment their incomes. And using local ingredients would have only cut into their profits. Therefore early on they decided rather than using corn from the surrounding fields, they'd mostly use sugar. It was a cutting-edge move. By the start of Prohibition, experienced bootleggers in other parts of the country had only been using it in significant amounts for about a decade. But with its ability to ferment more quickly than grain and yield vastly more, its use caught on quickly.

Soon the bootleggers' demand for sugar and yeast grew so great that it became clear to Templeton's shopkeepers that the orders were not for household use—no family had been overtaken by a feverish compulsion for cake baking; none had decided to take in store considerable stocks of leavening against some unforeseen future calamity. Instead of sharing their suspicions with the police, however, the town's grocers decided to embrace the booming new market. Chief among them were the brothers William and Frank Greteman.

The two were the sons of Otto Greteman, who had immigrated to America from the small German village of Bornholte in the nineteenth century. He arrived a widower; his wife had died on the passage over. But soon he remarried to a woman named Elizabeth, whose parents were immigrants from Germany themselves. The couple then moved west, settling in a small town in the northeastern corner of Iowa, before starting a family.

When Frank was twenty he started peddling religious materials; three years later he moved to Carroll County, where he opened a general store in Dedham and another in the village of Willey, between Templeton and Carroll. When the Dedham shop burned down, he relocated to Templeton and, with foresight that would prove auspicious, expanded into the grocery business in 1917. Soon several train cars laden with hundred-pound sacks of sugar were arriving regularly at the train depot. Consigned, ostensibly, to Greteman, the sacks were unloaded onto the platform, where they sat until nightfall. By morning they would be gone—spirited away by bootleggers keen on hiding their purchases from federal agents. For his services, Greteman charged just five dollars a sack—the same price he'd charge legitimate buyers purchasing from his store. For yeast, the bootleggers turned to the town's bakers, who would pad their orders with a bit extra to sell for a profit, again providing cover against prying police.

Nearby William Greteman and his wife, Catherine, ran one of Templeton's hardware stores, where he was kept busy ordering four-foot-by-eight-foot copper sheets, used to make stills. Though many of them would be purchased by Wendel Hacker—a Templeton blacksmith who claimed his stills were not stills at all, but feed boilers—Greteman himself claimed the copper was for use in making rain gutters. If ever questioned by federal agents about who, exactly, was spending the money to make their gutters out of pricey copper, he could always point to the house of future sheriff Frank Buchheit, which sparkled with them. Joe Kohorst, another hardware dealer, could offer a slightly more plausible explanation: as he was also the town's undertaker, he could say that he needed the copper to line coffins. What he kept secret was that he had a third business: rum-running, for which the discretion accorded to hearses proved to be a competitive advantage.

The ruse used to import oak barrels needed for aging whiskey stood up to even less scrutiny: the barrels simply arrived labeled VINEGAR, though with a quick jostle anyone could conclude they were, in fact, empty.

That Main Street business owners—and in a town as small as Templeton nearly all businesses were Main Street businesses—were willing to knowingly sell bootlegging supplies and in effect become complicit in the lawbreaking showed just how fully all the town's citizens were behind the bootleggers. In addition to ingredients, the bootleggers also employed lawyers to defend them in court and negotiate with judges to reduce jail sentences to fines. They needed bankers to help cover up what was a business with large flows of cash. They needed car dealers and mechanics to retrofit and keep their vehicles well maintained for the rigors of high-speed rum-running. They needed friends in public office to keep the local law enforcement away, and they, of course, needed workers to run the stills, bottle the whiskey, and transport it to buyers.

As the rye industry took off, nearly every household in Templeton was involved in some aspect of its production. Whiskey making so permeated the city, even some of the children knew what was going on: one afternoon, when a stranger arrived in town searching for a drink, he met a boy on the street and asked him where one might be found. "Mister," the boy replied, "see that house next to the church? That's the rectory. Any house but that one."

The boy wasn't being truthful, of course. There was most certainly booze in the rectory, and it wasn't just sacramental wine, either. Like their fellow clergy in Catholic churches around the country, Templeton's religious leaders had little tolerance for the Eighteenth Amendment. But unlike their counterparts, they didn't just tell their parishioners in confession that whiskey making was hardly a sin, they directly violated the Volstead Act themselves, permitting a small still to be set up in the church basement and passing out small sample bottle of Templeton rye to any visitor who showed interest in becoming a customer.

But not everyone was willing to help, or even stand by, as Templeton was transformed into a bastion of outlawry.

Situated in a little office on the corner of First and Main Streets, down the block from the Gretemans' stores, just across the street from the railway depot, and next door to the offices of a number of other prominent Templeton citizens whose fondness for whiskey was well known, one man began to write down a few details about Templeton's increasingly prominent underground industry. He noted who was buying whiskey and supplies, who was known to be running a still, which downtown shops kept a stash of booze to sell on the side, and which town officials were most complicit in letting the bootleggers operate with impunity.

What his notes contained was a surprisingly detailed overview of Templeton's bootlegging industry. He had dozens of names and, he felt, more than enough information to secure search warrants against the lawbreakers. He decided he had to tell someone— someone with enough power to do something, and someone far from Templeton. He pulled out a piece of paper, addressed it to the highest law enforcement official in the country, and started transcribing everything he knew.

6

THIS NEFARIOUS BUSINESS

On March 11, 1920, fifty-four days into America's first dry year, Assistant Attorney General William Little Frierson unfolded a remarkable letter addressed to his boss, A. Mitchell Palmer, America's top cop. Before him were three pages filled with neat if undistinguished cursive script, the first of which was postmarked eight days earlier from Templeton, Iowa.

"Honorable sir," the letter began. "A shrewd government agent will find several illicit 'stills' in this locality. The population here voice their intention of defying the government in this nefarious business. Your men can gather up a nice bunch of birds if they want them."

To start the agents out, the letter named a half dozen people, including Herbert Hoover, alleged to possess stills. It also listed a number of places where booze could be bought, including a butcher shop, whose owner was said to be "pro-German and determined to defy the Prohibition law," and a drugstore, which carried "quite a supply of whiskey and alcohol." Investigators might even "find something of interest in the basement of the Catholic church here, or in the priest's residence," the letter writer suggested. It was signed, "Most Respectfully, H. F. Vermeule."

Fifty-year-old Henry F. Vermeule wasn't a leader of the Anti-Saloon League or a disgruntled police officer upset that he wasn't allowed to enforce the law, but the town jeweler—a dealer in

Town jeweler Henry F. Vermeule was one of the few Templeton citizens to object to bootlegging, and he was so opposed to it that he twice wrote letters (including this page of the second one he sent, on April 26, 1920) to the US attorney general naming dozens of neighbors he thought should be arrested. *Courtesy of National Archives, College Park, Maryland*

luxury goods, with a specialty in watchmaking, whose fortune could only increase if his neighbors' did. The sole clue to the reason for his dissension was his last name, his heritage. He wasn't German. Vermeule's mother was born in Sweden and his father in

New Jersey. The family had arrived in western Iowa before Templeton's founding and came to Carroll County, despite its already established identity as a German settlement. Whether he decided to turn in his fellow citizens because he truly believed alcohol— or at least bootlegging—was evil, out of respect for the law, or because he harbored some other hatred against his neighbors was unclear, but in a community as tight-knit as Templeton, the letter certainly showed that the bonds that tied together the rest of the town did not connect to him.

Even though the attorney general was responsible for law enforcement nationwide, investigations into Prohibition violations were handled by the Treasury Department and its Prohibition Bureau. So Frierson forwarded Vermeule's letter to the commissioner for internal revenue, "for whatever action you deem advisable."

If the department hadn't already heard about all the booze sloshing around Carroll County and wasn't already at work on an investigation, then its swift reaction revealed just how seriously the accusations in Vermeule's letter must have seemed. Within a month a Prohibition agent was in the area, ready to make a dramatic, widespread raid.

The first place he stopped was at the home of a moonshiner near Carroll, but before he could make an arrest, the man ran to his phone to alert his compatriots that the feds were in town. Warning the entire bootlegging network may have been as easy as just picking up the phone. If his line was connected to Templeton's system, the operator on the other end would have been one of the daughters of Frank Greteman—the grocer to the bootleggers also ran the town's switchboard, which became effectively a private warning system for the area's whiskey cookers.

Regardless of whom he first warned, the Greteman girls were soon busy ringing the rest of the families who had stills. By the time the Prohibition agent headed off to the home of the next suspect, it was already too late—everything had been dismantled, what equipment couldn't be hidden was destroyed, and whiskey and

Left to right: Otto Greteman, Barbara (Reicher) Heitman, Coletta (Greteman) Reicher, Mayme Albers, Rose Greteman, and Florence (Reicher) Fox in 1914 at the Templeton Telephone Office owned by Frank Greteman. The phone network functioned as a warning system to bootleggers when federal Prohibition agents came to town. *Courtesy of Elaine Schwaller*

mash that couldn't be moved in time was dumped on the ground or poured into the gutter. The revenuers returned to headquarters almost empty-handed.

Word of the raid reached Vermeule as well—in fact, he was likely one of the first to know of it, as his office was in the same building as Greteman's switchboard. Though the news disappointed him, the defeat didn't weaken his resolve to fight the bootleggers around him, nor did it make him lose faith in the federal government's ability to deal with them.

A few days later, he shot off another letter to the attorney general. "Honorable Sir—Twenty-one stills were in operation here and several hundred gallons of moonshine were on hand at the time of the last raid. It will take at least five good men to handle this bunch of outlaws and carry out a successful raid. Would like to see you bag this bunch of birds, as all have the money to pay.

Trusting that you will clean up this bunch, I am. Most respectfully, H. F. Vermeule."

Vermeule also named eight more men he said were running stills in and around Templeton, including Victor Clemens Schwaller, who was the town's justice of the peace and related to Frank Greteman through marriage.

Frierson replied to Vermeule, asking him to write a letter directly to the revenue department containing everything he knew about the lawbreakers, but he did not promise that another raid was imminent, nor did he urge his counterparts in Prohibition enforcement to take quick action.

In Vermeule's first letter he'd reminded the government that they were dealing with a different flock of bootleggers than they might be used to pursuing in the city. As such, they couldn't just send in an agent armed with a badge, a warrant, and a sledgehammer and expect to smash stills. Instead, for an officer to be successful, Vermeule wrote, he'd have to first start with a little cunning.

"I will say that a well-dressed 'spotter' can do nothing here," he wrote. "He must represent the 'sport' element, that is, to be able to play cards, pool, smoke a cigarette, pretend to drink, whether he does or not, and tell some personal stories of bootlegging and 'moonshining.' Such a one hanging around the north pool hall here will, in my opinion, secure you a cage full of birds." Even though they were everywhere, Vermeule knew the bootleggers weren't sitting ducks.

In a town as small as Templeton a strange face, trim or disheveled, asking too many questions or none at all, would immediately arouse suspicion. Just because the butcher shop and the dispensary ran side businesses selling liquor, people couldn't walk in and buy a drink as easily as they could buy a cut of beef or a bottle of the most recent fad in patent medicine. Especially in the first years of Templeton rye, before word of its fame spread across the Midwest, a thirsty visitor would first need to convince a booze dealer he was not an officer working undercover. Often he would do so by having another trusted buyer—a friend, a family member, or someone with deep ties to the community and known as a straight shooter—to vouch for him. Only then would he be given the opportunity to purchase any of the illicit wares.

Nor were the federal agents likely to find large quantities of liquor stored at the places where it was sold. Instead, Templeton's bootleggers relied on all sorts of elaborate tactics to hide their stock from prying agents. Early on, someone noticed that the moonshiners' favored ceramic whiskey jugs, cylindrical and domed, with a little loop handle on the side, were roughly the same circumference as the fence posts that perforated the rural landscape. That sparked an idea: if the jugs were lowered one by one into the posthole and the fence post placed back on top, they could be stored securely, safe from the less perceptive of the fed's spotters. For those a bit more perceptive, the height of the fence posts around Templeton would come to serve as an easy indication as to how much liquor was available in the community. As whiskey stocks increased, the idea caught on and soon troops of boys earned pocket money by fencing in vacant lots and backyards throughout town.

In winter, when the ground was frozen too solid to dig postholes, many bootleggers turned to hiding their contraband deep under the snowdrifts that piled up in the ditches along the county roads, as well as in the culverts that ran underneath them. The stashes, in addition to providing a place to hide their booze, also provided legal cover—being on publicly accessible land meant that the feds had a difficult time finding someone to charge with illegal possession for any booze they found—though that didn't stop them from destroying it anyway.

Throughout the summer and fall of 1920, Templeton's bootleggers continued to expand their business with little harassment from the authorities. In fact, in those first dry months it seemed that officials—in Carroll County at least—were even less worried about alcohol than they had been before Prohibition, when at least a person who drank too much was arrested. Now, it seemed, since alcohol was not supposed to exist, it was treated as though it didn't.

Carroll County residents learned just how lax Sheriff Henry V. Janssen was in enforcing liquor laws in his jurisdiction when they opened their newspapers a couple of weeks before Vermeule wrote his second letter and found a story so absurd as to almost be unbelievable. It told of a Sioux City man, a salesman of some sort, and possibly a salesman of liquor, who was driving, stupefyingly drunk, early one morning through Carroll County. When he was in the vicinity of Arcadia, twenty miles north of Templeton, he missed a turn and crashed through a fence into a barren field. The accident broke a steering rod, locking his car in a hard turn in one direction, but failed to jolt him from his stupor. Miraculously the car also remained upright, and the man proceeded to tear through the field in circles until morning, when a couple of field hands arrived and called the sheriff for help extricating the "wild man" and his Ford sedan. When Janssen arrived, he managed to take control of the vehicle, but instead of arresting the driver for drunkenness, he helped the man to Arcadia for repairs. Then he let him go on to wherever he was going. Onlookers estimated that before he was stopped he had driven nearly three hundred miles in circles.

"The sheriff insists that if the farmer who owns the field expects to plow it, that it is now unnecessary as the Ford done all the plowing the field would need this season," the *Carroll Times* surmised in its bemused report, before going on to insinuate, with a clever transmutation of the sheriff's middle name, that perhaps there was more to the story than reached print: "The driver failed to mention his name, or the company he represented—but he was a go-getter—and if you don't believe it ask Henry Veracity Janssen." Maybe, in fact, it was all a belated April Fool's joke.

Whatever the real story, the apparently flippant attitude of Carroll County's chief law enforcer toward liquor violations was already clear to those, like Vermeule and B. F. Wilson, who watched appalled as bootlegging flourished throughout the area. Just a few column inches away, in the same issue of the *Times*, the newspaper announced that Janssen was seeking reelection. In a slight endorsement that would seem to ring only more true when his post-Volstead record was taken into account, the paper wrote that "he has a way of handling men that almost makes it a pleasure to the culprit."

More evidence for the truism of that statement arrived a few days after Christmas 1920, when B. F. Wilson and a team of federal agents carried out another raid in southern Carroll County—again with the noticeable absence of support from Sheriff Janssen. They were drawn to a farm, just a half mile south of Manning, not far from the Carroll-Audubon border, after discovering that a large amount of the liquor sold in the two counties was coming from Amos Heuerman, the farm's hired man.

Despite their certainty that somewhere, tucked away on the land, was a still, they struggled to find it. Wilson, in fact, had been to the place several months before to search, but had turned up nothing. It was only when the officers pried up the boards beneath a metal hog oiler—an ovoid contraption designed to coat a pig's back with a slick of oil to prevent insects from biting—did they discover what they were looking for.

From under the boards ran a tunnel that ended at a large subterranean room, electrified and complete with running water, that was hidden below a nearby feed shed. In it they found two stills—one with a capacity of fifteen gallons, the other of twenty-five—and two hundred gallons of mash almost ready for distillation. Not only could Wilson be proud that he helped capture one of the largest and most elaborately hidden distilling operations yet found in western Iowa, but he could also have the satisfaction of knowing that he had, by all appearances, been able to snuff out the bootlegging operation that had first caused him such frustration the year before when he arrested Henry Hagedorn in Audubon County. The farm on which he had just found the two stills was owned by Henry's relative, Herman Hagedorn. And Wilson's success came despite the recalcitrance of Carroll's law enforcement officials—whom the feds deliberately decided not to inform of the impending raid, for fear they'd tip off the bootleggers.

If Herman had been Henry's supplier, it was unclear whether Henry, after his arrest late in the previous year, lied to Wilson when he said he believed the liquor came from Minnesota. Perhaps he did so hoping to keep Wilson from looking for a still in addition to booze if he did raid Herman's farm, or Herman may actually have been importing his booze at the time and only later, with the profits, built the still and excavated its hiding place.

Regardless, it seemed Wilson was on the verge of adding two more names to his roster of foiled bootleggers. Though the agents were able to confiscate the still and destroy the mash during the raid, they weren't able to make any arrests on the spot. Heuerman, the farm hand, was in Manning at the time and wasn't arrested until he returned home later that day. Hagedorn, meanwhile, was in Chicago, selling livestock. For him the officers issued an arrest warrant, with instructions that it be carried out as soon as he stepped off the train from Chicago. In the meantime, they filed a complaint at the United States Federal Court in Fort Dodge, the dockets of which would soon rarely be empty of liquor cases from Carroll County.

As first-time violators of the National Prohibition Act, Heuerman and Hagedorn faced up to six months in prison and a $1,000 fine—a relatively paltry sum for Hagedorn, who was described by one observer at the time as "a substantial and wealthy farmer." Both men were released to await their trial—Henry's father having posted the $1,000 bail needed to free both of them.

Money still seemed to be of little concern when their case came in front of a judge on June 14, 1921: both men pleaded guilty and accepted a fine of $150, with no jail time unless the fine was not paid. Hagedorn apparently paid his fine quickly, but a month later, when Heuerman's fine was still outstanding, another arrest warrant was issued for him. This time it was returned not with the convict, but with a note from the federal marshal assigned to the case.

"I have made a careful search for the defendant and have been unable to find him in the Northern District of Iowa," he scrawled on the back of the warrant. Heuerman would be missing, to the court at least, for several more years. But Hagedorn wasn't about to leave Carroll County. One reason was, of course, because he owned a large tract of land and ran what historically had been a profitable farming operation on it. But the second was that despite the setback of the raid, he was still bullish on the bootlegging market. Not long after the court case against him was closed, he began working on getting back to business.

If Wilson's pride in shutting down what seemed to be such an important source of liquor in the area was eroded any by the escape of Heuerman, it was sure to be injured further by the realization that would come eighteen months later—that the still, in all likelihood, wasn't, in fact, responsible for much of the booze sating the drinkers in Carroll and Audubon Counties after all. By all evidence, Hagedorn apparently came to bootlegging by his own volition, not as part of the emerging liquor ring in Templeton. He lived several miles from town, his family rooted in Manning and to the south, in Audubon. His liquor also posed little competitive threat to that produced by Hoover and the other Templeton rye bootleggers.

"The raisin market in Manning must have experienced an unusual strain recently, judging from the quantity taken last week by federal officers," began the *Carroll Herald*'s article on the raid, which revealed that in addition to the stills and mash, officers found four hundred pounds of raisins in Hagedorn's liquor bunker. Like sugar, the main virtue of using raisins was that they fermented quickly and easily and produced a high yield. But by not adding any grain at all and not aging his product, Hagedorn was making what came to be known during Prohibition by a catch-all generic: "alcohol." It was not whiskey, it was not rum, it was not gin. It was not bought for its aroma, its flavor, or its reminiscence to pre-Prohibition tipples. Instead it was bought for its only defining characteristic: that it was potent enough to get a person drunk, quickly. Essentially it may have been vodka, and it certainly found its way into numerous cocktails as well as many bottles of what was colloquially called "near beer" and officially all other names that did not include the word "beer," because the federal government didn't want it to even allude to its previously intoxicating iteration. Regardless of what it was called, it was made exactly like old-fashioned beer, but with all the alcohol distilled out and discarded before bottling. Many people found it necessary to correct this deficiency before they could be bothered to drink it. But once they did they drank it in Iowa in such vast quantities that it was regarded as the most popular Prohibition-era befuddlement.

Proof that Hagedorn was hardly the only one making booze in Carroll County came just a week after his bust. Over two days, the same federal agents who'd carried out the earlier raid with Wilson returned to Carroll County and nabbed fifteen more stills. For an agency better known for incompetency and corruption, it was an amazing showing.

As fierce a stranglehold as dry organizations such as the Anti-Saloon League had on the United States Congress, the congressional drys' grip on the federal purse was even more tightfisted. Though the Prohibition Bureau's budget for 1921 had significantly increased from its paltry outlay the year before, it was still a mere $7.1 million. For most of the rest of the decade it would come nowhere close to approaching what many thought was adequate. Nor would it ever reach a tiny fraction of what the vociferously dry rebel Iowa senator Smith Wildman Brookhart proposed: a truly munificent $240 million.

What made the raid in Carroll even more miraculous, however, was that at least at first glance of the following day's newspaper, the officers somehow managed to convince Sheriff Henry Janssen to help them with their seizures. But the particulars of the raid seemed to suggest at just what price they secured his assistance. Despite finding so many stills, they failed to implicate a single bootlegger. Someone had clearly tipped them off. And election returns for the next year provide a bit of hint as to who might have done so: up for reelection, Janssen beat his Democratic primary challenger easily, buoyed by the nearly four-to-one margin he earned in the townships that included Templeton, Manning, and Dedham. The general election was even easier—no Republican even stepped up to oppose him.

Republican Iowa senator and notorious dry Smith Wildman Brookhart so rankled his fellow legislators with his numerous proposals to toughen Prohibition and his constant chastisement against drinking in the Capitol that one of them inserted a limerick about him into the Congressional Record. It read: "I come from way out in Iowa / The home of corn and many an art, / Where bootleggin's so bad / It makes all of us sad / That everyone knows it but BROOKHART." *Courtesy of Library of Congress*

But the steadfast support that Janssen and his lax attitude toward liquor earned from Carroll's citizens wasn't entirely a byproduct of their dislike of the Eighteenth Amendment. It also stemmed from their recognition that illicit booze was now vital to their local economy. If bootlegging had started out as simply a way to ensure a supply of good booze for local use, it had, by the country's second dry year, taken on a far more important role: increasingly it was the only way many rural families could earn enough money to pay their mortgages and feed their large families.

Every year for at least the previous two decades, the president of the Iowa Department of Agriculture had published the address he gave at that year's state convention of agricultural leaders. Accompanying each speech was a compendium of statistics titled "Iowa's Source of Wealth," listing the value of various commodities—corn, oats, swine, milk cows—that underscored the vibrancy of the state's farm economy. And in nearly every one of those years, the statistics were as predictably impressive as the address was mundane, the latter mostly a patter of the encouraging insights about rural Iowa's strong future.

This optimism held throughout the two decades from the start of the new century to the end of the First World War, a period that would come to be known as the "golden era of agriculture." It was an era when many thought rural America stood on the same level of economic prominence as its urban counterpart, and when rural life was considered blessed with abundance, space, and clean living—virtues thought to be lacking in the cities. By all measures, that prosperity should have extended into the first few years of the 1920s as well. Spurred by the government's exhortations during the First World War to invest heavily in new equipment, expanded acreage, and grain conservation, farmers were now routinely harvesting bumper crops. But with the advent of Armistice, the government dismantled its price supports, and demand for all that food evaporated. Even before the war was over, corn prices had plummeted on mere rumors of peace. When the end of the war actually came, land prices crashed as well—leaving many owing mortgages far higher than what their real estate was actually worth.

Historically, farm communities, notably those in Ireland and Appalachia, had turned to moonshining as a means of survival during difficult economic times. By the time residents of Templeton did so, $13 billion in farm wealth had already evaporated. And the rural economy had become so bad so quickly that during the early 1920s hundreds of thousands of people were leaving the farm each year, many taking work in the city, where the economy was booming and wages were far above what one could earn working in the fields. No longer was the tone of the annual report upbeat; by 1922 it was almost desperate. In that year's address, president C. E. Cameron summed up the dire situation: "For the last two or three years the farmer's lot has not been a pleasant one. Because of the severe reaction from war-time prices and the depreciation in values which followed so rapidly, the farmer was caught holding the sack, without ability to meet his obligations from the diminished proceeds of his own and his family's labors." Cameron then called on the federal government to extend support to the nation's farmers by guaranteeing that commodity prices stayed above the cost of production. His pleas went unheeded.

Bootlegging wasn't the only response to the tough economic situation in America, however. Rural Americans, and those who held rural values but had been displaced to the city, who were unsettled by the economic upheaval of the increasingly urban, cosmopolitan, socially permissive America, saw a new organization rise to embrace them—and to fight the very people that called Carroll County home.

Whether the Reverend J. M. Lowe knew it or not, the tailwinds that deposited him before a large crowd in Audubon County a few years after the start of Prohibition had first started whipping up far earlier. Some of them were the product of the First World War and of the rural economic collapse that followed. But others had started building many decades before, with the vast changes then transforming American society. The last few decades of the nineteenth century saw a great influx of immigrants from Catholic Ireland and Germany, industrialization and the rise of the city, and the declining importance of rural America. It was no small sign that when the results of the 1920 Census were released, Americans learned theirs was, for the first time ever, an urban country.

The August day on which Lowe had come to preach had been uncomfortably hot, if not downright sweltering, a day that would have made many consider staying under the shade of their porches. But by later that afternoon the temperature had begun dropping toward what would turn out to be a surprisingly comfortable evening. As it did, people began filling the city park in Audubon. Some did so with genuine curiosity to hear what the reverend had to say, others purely for the entertainment and the possibility of spectacle, of excitement. A few may even have gone with a feeling of disgust, ready to challenge anything he said that they thought was too far out of line.

The most striking sight was not the swelling crowd, nor, certainly, Lowe himself, who was never famous and never would be, but the pointy white hoods that stuck above the throng like beacons. Milling about, standing in groups close to where Lowe would speak, the men under the shrouds that draped down past their knees constituted a shallow mystery: no one knew exactly who they were, but everyone did. They were some of the allegedly four hundred or more members of the Invisible Empire, the second coming of the Knights of the Ku Klux Klan, who resided in Audubon County. Their membership was alleged to include the town marshal and the night watchman, while the mayor, perhaps not officially a member, was suspected of at least being a sympathizer.

Those civic leaders may have evinced that the Audubon klavern, as the local organization was called, had a modicum of political power. But support, or even tolerance, for the group didn't appear to be universal. Lowe's defensive tone seemed to suggest that the Klan, in fact, was facing considerable criticism in the area.

"The Ku Klux Klan is a pro-American organization, the most strictly American organization in existence today," he said. "The Ku Klux Klan stands for freedom of speech, schools, press, religion, government, and ballot. Why, then, should we, a truly American organization, standing for all the things which should be near and dear to every American citizen, be criticized, while the colored people of this country, the Jews, the Catholics, all have their organizations and they are not criticized?"

Lowe's reasoning wasn't quite clear, but he was implying that the Klan ultimately stood for that phrase last employed with such vigor during the First World War: the "100 percent Americans."

In the opinion of the Klan, blacks, Jews, and Catholics were part something else—part something un-American, old world, immoral. Like the first incarnation of the Ku Klux Klan in the mid-nineteenth century, which directed its violence against blacks and their white allies and died out by the 1870s, the second Klan arose in the south, in Georgia in 1915, but quickly spread across the country, fanned as much by the avarice of its organizers—who earned part of the ten-dollar initiation fee in addition to a cut of the profits from the robes—as by its ability to tap into the insecurities of its target membership: white, Anglo-Saxon, middle-class Protestants who feared for the future of their hegemony.

William Joseph Simmons, who founded this second coming of the Klan, did so fully aware of the inherent appeal of secret societies with secret rites and novel nomenclature. But what proved most attractive to recruits was the Klan's seeming offer of empowerment against the broader forces of change that many members saw as undermining the traditional, pure, American way of life—the same forces of change that seemed to be undermining rural America in favor of urbanization, agriculture in favor of industry, hardworking middle-class citizens in favor of stock-market-minted plutocrats, English-speaking Anglo-Saxons in favor of foreign-language-speaking immigrants. In short, the Klan provided a tonic, however illusory, to the malaise rural Americans were feeling after the end of the "golden era of agriculture," a tonic strongly spiked with that always nefarious nostrum of nativism. In the specifics, its agenda differed by region (once those dues were paid, the Klan's leaders didn't seem to care much what the local klaverns did). In Iowa the Klan directed most of its hatred toward Catholics and those who flouted the Eighteenth Amendment, whom they mostly saw as one and the same. *Who else would be bootleggers but Catholics?* their assumption appeared to be. When rural America realized something fundamental had shifted, Carroll County's bootleggers sought a way to survive in the new environment; the members of the KKK just wanted the old ways to return. The difference threatened blood.

A Ku Klux Klan rally in 1924 in Cherokee, Iowa, eighty miles northwest of Templeton. The resurgence of the Ku Klux Klan in the early-to-mid 1920s spread throughout Iowa and the Midwest. Instead of targeting blacks, this KKK movement went after Catholics and immigrants and also sought to enforce the liquor laws, employing vigilantism if necessary. *Courtesy of Cherokee Area Archives*

The Klan reached Iowa in 1920, but didn't really take off until after it launched an aggressive membership drive in 1923. Recruiters that year fanned out across the state, extolling the Klan, stressing to people the threats to American values all around them, and collecting their ten-dollar initiation fee. Soon the club claimed nearly one hundred thousand members in dozens of klaverns throughout the state. Though their members' activities varied from hosting Fourth of July celebrations and parades to campaigning for increased funding for schools, which the Klan considered one of the most important local institutions, the most visible were the actions they carried out while hidden behind the white robe.

One Klan member in the small town of Marathon, Iowa, eighty miles north of Templeton, wrote to his girlfriend, who was in the

Klan's women's auxiliary group, about his and his fellow klansmen's efforts to intimidate Catholics, whom he derisively referred to as "fish" because of their practice of abstaining from meat on Fridays. Sometimes the Klan would burn crosses in front of the homes of Catholics; other times they'd ride through town on horses, dressed in full regalia, as a reminder of their hate. The members of the Marathon klavern pinned the blame for all of the local bootlegging in the community on the Catholics. To try to rid their community of moonshiners, they passed along the location of stills to local law enforcement, purchased liquor for use as evidence, and even considered going directly after the stills themselves. Their turn to vigilantism may have been spurred in part by that complaint, ever common across the country from those who genuinely thought the Volstead Act should be enforced, that local law enforcement was corrupt. "We have a Klan sheriff but our prosecuting attorney is a fish eater and he will do anything he can to fish the Klan," the Marathon Klan member complained in one of his letters.

Catholic public officials, whether they actually protected bootleggers or not, weren't the only force that opposed the Klan in its march to promote its version of Americanism. A local chapter of a backlash organization, national in scope, the Knights of the Flaming Circle—an allusion to the Klan's flaming cross—was active around Marathon in intimidating the Klan there. The Marathon Flaming Circle seemed largely to respond to the Klan's provocations in kind, proffering public displays of their presence, but not attacking the Klan directly. Elsewhere, though, many of their members did escalate the conflict significantly, rounding up KKK members and beating them.

If the Flaming Circle's members hadn't been so quick to resort to violence, the group would have seemed almost like a parody of the Klan. Instead of only admitting white, native-born Protestants as the Klan did, the organization vowed to accept anyone who was anything other than that. Instead of being the white knights, they were the red knights. Instead of fiery crosses, they burned fiery circles. Their mission against bigotry was one that would be fought, they announced, "intolerantly."

The Flaming Circle joined an increasingly powerful opposition that included politicians, labor leaders, and immigrant groups who sought to restrict the Klan's ability to organize and worked to publicly shame its members. By 1925 the Klan in Iowa had lost half its members; nationally it entered a rapid decline, almost disappearing by 1926.

But in some places it never even managed to get started. In September 1924 the Klan planned to hold a large meeting in a field in thoroughly Catholic Carroll County, after which they were going to found a new klavern. But, unlike in Audubon County, they never even had a chance to gather. Someone had reported them to the fire department.

In July 1920 one of the state's ten new Prohibition agents, a fleshy and dog-eyed man named Ben Koolbeck, updated a reporter on the bootlegging situation in Des Moines. He admitted that though some pre-Prohibition beer drinkers—especially in "beer-loving foreign settlements"—were turning to whiskey to sate their thirst, most people were following the law and had given up on booze. "People are finding out that they can get along without any sort of alcoholic drink," he said. He even rattled off a statistic to prove his point: 90 percent of former drinkers had completely forgotten about alcohol, he claimed. It was divine amnesia on a massive scale, no doubt.

More reliable evidence, however, suggested that either he was wildly delusional or the remaining 10 percent were on one wild bender. What would become apparent was that, in reality, it was a mix of the two. The slump in alcohol consumption was not quite so deep nor quite so persistent as many of the most committed drys wanted to believe. Within a few years it had mostly been reversed—either more Americans were drinking again, or the appetite of those who never quit was increasing.

More drinking meant, of course, more money for the bootleggers. A year and a half after Prohibition's advent, bootlegging had become a $1-billion-a-year industry. By the middle of the decade, it was worth $4 billion. The upward trend was matched by the whiskey cookers in Carroll County. Just how pervasive bootlegging had become there, just how many residents had set up stills since blacksmith Herbert Hoover's first experiment with rye whiskey and Vermeule's letter to Attorney General Palmer, would be revealed when B. F. Wilson returned to the area as an agent of the Prohibition Bureau.

Though his original appointment had been to investigate Volstead Act violations in southern Iowa, far from the area where he'd had his first successes busting stills, he was soon sent back north to work. Perhaps the Prohibition Bureau was frustrated by the showing of its agents there, but Wilson was also gaining a reputation within the dry force for being proactive—someone willing to work long hours to develop his own cases. Soon that reputation would be known by everyone across Iowa.

By May 1922 he was busy working his old contacts for information about bootlegging in his old stomping grounds of northern Audubon and southern Carroll Counties. It took him several weeks, but he managed to amass allegations strong enough to secure search warrants against a score of bootleggers. More importantly, he was able to keep the details of his investigation secret from unsympathetic residents and officials eager to tip off the lawbreakers. Wilson finally had the authority to do what he'd always wanted: to take care of the job himself. In a few weeks he'd be ready to strike.

7

STORMING EDEN

Late in the morning of June 26, 1922, B. F. Wilson and more than two dozen other men, including three other federal Prohibition agents, a minister from the Methodist church in Audubon, the superintendent of the town's schools, and Andrew Jorgensen, Wilson's successor as Audubon sheriff, met at a secret location in Audubon County to review their strategy for what would be the biggest raid ever carried out in Iowa. At eleven o'clock, once everyone was certain of their role in the attack, they split up into groups of five or six, each with their own vehicle, and took off simultaneously for targets across what one of Wilson's colleagues would later tell reporters was the "heart of the liquor belt" in Iowa.

Among them they had thirty-eight search warrants, most of which had been issued by Manning mayor Orrin W. Emmons and town constable W. J. Brandhorst, the only two Carroll County officials Wilson and the other agents deemed trustworthy enough to inform about their plans. Sheriff Jorgensen and the local police officers and mayors of the other towns that were targeted for raids were left entirely in the dark. The unprecedented police action would be as much a surprise to them as it was to Wilson's targets.

Armed with sawed-off shotguns, the officers and their deputies spent the next three hours making busts in and around Dedham, Templeton, and Manning in Carroll County and Lincoln Township in Audubon County. To prevent their targets from destroying any evidence as soon as they showed up, their first action when arriving at each of the suspected still sites was to detain the owner, confining him to the vehicle in which they had arrived.

But they quickly realized they'd made a dangerous assumption: by only taking into custody the men whose property they were raiding, they had left the men's wives free to fight the invaders and destroy the evidence themselves. And fight and destroy they did. The women, one raider later told the press, "put up a good deal more resistance than their husbands."

Once they finally had a property secured, the officers began to search it for whiskey, mash, stills, barrels, and ingredients for alcohol production. Though few were as well hidden as the setup they'd found a year and a half earlier on the farm of Herman Hagedorn, who'd excavated a chamber under a feed shed and connected it to a disguised entrance by a tunnel, the feds did find stills in a number of unlikely places. On more than one farm the distilling equipment was hidden in the chicken coop. They also found bootlegging operations tucked away in barns and storm cellars, and a few were even located in the actual family residence.

In some places the last-minute rush to dispose of the evidence succeeded: on the farm of Peter Thielen, the son of immigrants from Germany and Luxembourg, raiders found nothing more than an empty eight-gallon whiskey barrel, but when they stuck their nose inside, they got a good whiff of moonshine. Whether Thielen had dumped the liquor out at the last minute, hidden it in another container, or simply drunk what was left, the raiders didn't bother figuring out. They just tossed the barrel onto their ever-growing heap of contraband. On the Dedham farm of Jake Duwell they had better luck ascertaining the fate of the booze they almost found. There they discovered that not only had he dumped all of his bootleg liquor on the ground, but that he'd then proceeded to set it alight, in the process helping prove the officers' case that his booze was certainly over the 0.5 percent alcohol threshold needed to be considered intoxicating under the Volstead Act. Nevertheless, they did find one hundred gallons of rye and corn mash in Duwell's possession.

Among the still sites raided, the officers found operations in a considerable variety of sizes, styles, and types. Some of the moonshiners' operations were tiny, with one still measuring just three gallons. Others didn't seem to be in the bootlegging business at all: at the Templeton home of Clarence Bengford, Wilson's men found four gallons of corn whiskey and nothing more. It was hardly enough to host a decent Fourth of July party, let alone stock a rum-running operation.

But most of the bootleggers raided that day were clearly in it to make booze to sell. In addition to the thirty-gallon still and four hundred gallons of mash found on the farm of Herman Lang, one mile west of Carroll, officers also found nine and a half gallons of white moonshine whiskey, one quart of caramel coloring, a funnel, and a pint of the amber-colored finished product. Even if he wasn't planning on aging his product, no moonshiner would go to the trouble of making his raw whiskey look like premium-grade booze unless he was planning on selling it, and selling it to customers whom he didn't have too serious qualms about deceiving. Meanwhile, demand for the rye whiskey coming out of the copper still of Dedham resident John Steffes was apparently so high that he no longer precisely fit the definition of a moonshiner: when officers arrived not long after noon on that hot, cloudy day, they discovered a steady stream of evidence flowing out of his fired-up still. Operating under the cover of moonlight he was not.

By far the operation that most impressed the officers and the newspaper writers alike was the one found on the farm of Max Kastl near Templeton. There Kastl had built a thirty-gallon still below ground, and kept the tanks and condensing coil cool with a steady stream of chilled water from a large, elevated tank erected nearby—saving the still operator from having to haul water in whenever he needed to distill off another run of liquor or mix up another batch of mash. Someone in the party remarked that it was the most complete distillery ever found in Iowa, by which he apparently meant it nearly resembled the above-ground distilleries from the pre-Prohibition days.

Altogether, in nineteen successful raids the agents confiscated $50,000 worth of loot—including 2,500 gallons of mash, a little of which was saved for samples, the rest of which was dumped on the ground, and 125 gallons of alcohol—and implicated twenty-two people, including one woman. But despite all their efforts to keep the raid silent, they returned to Audubon County fuming that their raid had not caught every bootlegger they knew to be working in Carroll County.

At seven of the homes officers raided they found nothing. But they didn't attribute their failure at those places to bad information; rather, they suspected that whoever was running or cooking whiskey there had been tipped off—as had Peter Thielen and Jake Duwell—far enough ahead of time to hide their still and dispose of their liquor and mash. Moreover, they returned to Audubon even more certain that law enforcement officers in Carroll County were actively working to protect the bootleggers.

In the middle of one of the busts, at a place owned by the relative of a Carroll County official, officers were interrupted by that official, who tried to intervene and stop the raid. Wilson refused and threatened to report him to the state attorney general. Even more evidence came during the raids that netted both Rupert Kasperbauer, constable of Eden Township, and Victor Clemens Schwaller, Templeton's justice of the peace.

Schwaller's arrest was the one that most shocked those unaware of just how pervasive bootlegging was in Carroll County. But of all the men in Templeton to hold public office, Schwaller was perhaps the least surprising to also be involved in bootlegging. Born in 1857, Schwaller was the only son of a couple from Bern, Switzerland, who immigrated to the United States in 1850, when they were in their twenties, and settled near Templeton two decades later—arriving before the town was even founded. Victor Schwaller's parents were farmers. He was about everything but: in addition to being a bootlegger, he'd been a traveling salesmen,

V. C. Schwaller and his son John in 1905. Both men would become important Templeton rye bootleggers. *Courtesy of Elaine Schwaller*

a grocer, a lawyer, Templeton's postmaster, an insurance agent, and an auctioneer. More generally he was a mild rabble-rouser, quick-witted, clever, tenacious, and a bit strong-headed.

It was in late November 1876, when he was only nineteen, that Schwaller expressed the first and last of these qualities dramatically. Shortly after midnight at a saloon operating in the tiny settlement of Hillsdale—which had popped up on the map just a few years before, had almost been wiped out the prior autumn in a massive hailstorm, and would come to reach the height of its population, about fifty souls, a decade or so later—Schwaller was yearning for a turn on the floor at a dance held by the German-Americans who comprised nearly the entire population of the area. However, either it was not his turn yet or he hadn't paid for the dance, and when he tried to walk out into the ballroom, the floor manager asked him to leave. At first he refused, then he and the floor manager started arguing and fighting and drawing other attendees into the fray. Eventually the fight spilled outside and Schwaller pulled out a revolver. First he fired into the air, hitting no one, but the argument continued and again he fired, this time blowing off a bystander's thumb. After the second shot, a twenty-one-year-old man named Frank Hoelker tried to wrestle

Schwaller's gun away. Schwaller fired a third time, hitting Hoelker in the upper left side of his torso. The bullet passed through Hoelker's lung, grazed his heart, and stopped in his spleen. Hoelker managed to take away the gun anyway and then dashed back into the saloon before anyone noticed he was bleeding. As he did, the fight continued, and Schwaller, now defenseless, was badly beaten.

Once everyone finally calmed down and managed to assess the situation they realized just how grave it was. Someone called the sheriff and then, unsure whether Hoelker would live, called both the nearest doctor and the priest. Hoelker survived the night, but his wound would continue to fester for the next five weeks. In January it killed him. A trio of doctors performed an autopsy and agreed that the bullet had been his sole cause of death. A panel of another three men then decided that Schwaller had acted maliciously, and voted to bring the case to a grand jury that was to meet several months later. In the meantime Schwaller was released on $3,000 bail.

Despite the doctors' finding and the panel's certainty that the shooting was premeditated, Schwaller's neighbors were divided about his fate. His case was further helped by his counsel: almost immediately after the incident he'd retained one of Carroll's top lawyers, the indefatigable dry Orlando H. Manning, who was then at the very beginning of his bright career as a lawyer and politician. In retrospect, the choice would seem ironic, but at the time it was clearly wise: when the grand jury convened in April, Manning argued that Schwaller had pulled the gun in self-defense. Taking into account Schwaller's substantial injuries as well as the varying accounts of the struggle, the grand jury agreed and refused to indict him. As he would many years later in another high-profile case, Schwaller prevailed in court despite significant evidence against him. In his murder case, he also learned a key lesson: the value of an intricate understanding of the law. A free man, he set out to learn as much as he could.

During the raid on Schwaller's residence, Wilson, his fellow agent Sumner J. Knox, and two Audubon men found a ten-gallon copper still and fifty gallons of mash. As they did at all the other places they raided that day, they took a sample of the mash and seized the still. They then prepared to file charges against Schwaller in both the mayor's court in Manning and the United States Federal Court at Fort Dodge, Iowa. While all of Schwaller's compatriots accepted their fate—accepted, in fact, the inevitable fines of a few hundred dollars as simply the cost of doing business—Schwaller wasn't keen to let Wilson win.

On July 13 Mayor Orrin Emmons of Manning called a hearing in his chambers to decide a question that had been pondered across Carroll and Audubon Counties for the past two weeks: what authority, exactly, did Emmons have to issue warrants to search and seize property outside his town's jurisdiction? Of the sixteen bootleggers called in front of him, fifteen demurred, choosing not to challenge Emmons's warrants. But Schwaller was incensed, not just at the fact that Emmons issued warrants that, the bootlegger thought, he had no right to issue, but also at the idea that the mayor would hold the hearing into their legality in his own court. Emmons, Schwaller declared in court, was prejudiced against him. He demanded a change of venue. And Emmons himself granted it—Schwaller's case was reassigned to the justice of the peace for Warren Township, which included Manning.

Twelve days later, in front of the new judge, C. J. Eden, Schwaller and his lawyer argued that not only were Wilson and the other feds operating on an illegally issued warrant, but that the details of the property described within it were wrong as well. Despite being represented by its own stellar counsel, County Attorney William Irving Saul, former editor of the *Carroll Herald* and grandson of one of the community's earliest settlers, the government couldn't come up with a reasonable argument to refute Schwaller's claim. Eden declared the warrant invalid. Then he went even further: Schwaller's property, including his little copper still and the mash seized for evidence, were to be returned to him. Not only was Wilson being told that his raid, the largest ever conducted in Iowa, was illegal, he was also being forced to return the very item that most made a bootlegger a bootlegger and that most made Schwaller his enemy: his still, complete with the mash needed to draw booze from it.

Throughout his fight for the return of his still and mash, Schwaller denied that that was even what the seized property was. That ten-gallon copper apparatus, he argued, was hardly for the distilling of illicit liquor; it was simply a small boiler for, well, boiling things—what, exactly, he didn't bother to reveal. He concocted an even less creative cover story to explain away the mash, lumping it together with "considerable other personal property" he said the agents stole. He further blamed a missing can of kerosene on the raiders' trespass.

His complaint was worth little, however, in the federal court, where Wilson had soon listed the thing he claimed to be a still as evidence. As such, the feds weren't going to just hand it back over to Schwaller. As for the mash—or "swill," as the *Audubon Advocate* decided to call it—"the Prohibition department will probably be glad to turn the barrels over to Vic," the paper concluded. After all, a state chemist had already determined a month before that it was a tepid, if still felonious, 7.34 percent alcohol. By now it was also rank.

Schwaller's fight against the liquor charges won him little other than notoriety. Since his arrest, he'd been out on bail of $500, secured, partially, by a bond from John Kaus, the butcher, whose shop jeweler Henry Vermeule had called a "notorious joint for the dispensing of booze" in his letter to the attorney general. On November 14 Schwaller and the rest of the bootleggers caught with him were finally arraigned in Fort Dodge. When he had left Carroll, Schwaller had vowed to fight the charges. One by one the others pleaded guilty and learned their sentences: Max Kastl was fined $300, as were John Steffes, Herman Lang, and nearly everyone else. And by the time Schwaller was called in front of Judge George C. Scott, he'd changed his mind. He pleaded guilty. Scott fined him just $100—tying for the lowest penalty with the brothers Alphonse and Ed Kerkhoff, who'd been found with nothing more than fifty gallons of corn mash between them. It wasn't exactly a triumph, but Schwaller's legal wrangling may have worn enough on the feds to make them cut a deal, lowering his fine to get him to stop fighting the charges.

The real victory was clearly Wilson's. Within his first ten months as a Prohibition agent, he had not only orchestrated the largest bootlegging raid in the state, he had also managed to do something that had eluded his fellow agents for more than two years: he had finally given Vermeule the response he'd wanted. Wilson had managed to confiscate stills from about half of the men Vermeule had named in his letter.

Wilson's partnership with Manning officials even seemed to spur them to go after their own local bootlegger. A month after Marshal Brandhorst issued Wilson his warrants, he dropped in on Herbert Hoover. What he found tucked away in the little shack behind Hoover's house was a "very crude affair"—a twenty-gallon still "all steamed up and running." He also found a barrel of Hoover's mash, disguised with brush, in a pasture near town owned by Rosalia Lang, Herman's wife. Instead of trying to convince the raiders that his equipment was used for something other than making booze, instead of arguing that he was not a bootlegger, Hoover informed them "very confidently" that "he was the first man in Carroll County to manufacture hootch." If the case went anywhere, it didn't cause any more sensation around Carroll County, and Hoover continued working as a blacksmith in Manning.

By that time Vermeule cared little. He'd left Templeton in 1921, settling forty miles away in Lake City, a community not known to be infested with bootleggers. Wilson knew, however, that his work in Carroll County was not finished. There were still many whiskey cookers he had not yet caught. He may have even suspected that his job was about to get a lot harder—before his raid, Carroll's bootleggers had faced so little pressure from the law that they all but operated in the open. Now that they knew someone in law enforcement was actually after them, they would be more careful.

Templeton rye production was about to undergo a radical change. Not only was it to become more secretive, it was also to become much larger and much more famous. And it was a change that would be led by that young man who, only a few years earlier, had struggled even to afford a drink: Joe Irlbeck.

But in the meantime, Wilson could enjoy his success. A few weeks before Christmas he was even able to raise something of a toast to his first year as an agent. With all of the cases closed on the bootleggers he'd arrested earlier in the year, he and his successor as Audubon sheriff, Andrew Jorgensen, decided it was time to destroy the evidence for good. They took twenty stills and hacked them apart, saving the copper to later sell to a junk dealer. The confiscated mash and liquor they poured out. Gossip around Audubon was that there was so much of the stuff that the town's gutters overflowed with it. But that was a lie. The two men dumped it straight into the sewer.

8

"THE TREASURE CHEST"

The alley, a dead end in the shadow of Sacred Heart Church's towering spire, was dark, especially in the corner where the semi truck was parked, but also closer to the street, where Steve Smith sat in his car with a nervous tension born not so much of fear as of a state of hypervigilance. He knew that at any moment something terrible could happen, and if it did he was the one responsible for stopping it. In one hand he gripped a revolver, a .22 special, loaded with up to nine rounds of ammo. The other hand was free, but perched a few inches from the switch for the headlights. They were his first volley of attack—he could turn them on and hope for a few-second advantage while the hijackers or the feds or whoever was after the booze or the money were temporarily blinded. Hopefully he could get a few shots off. Hopefully he could get enough shots off.

Short, with a generic name and an all-around usefulness, Steve Smith was second in command to Joe Irlbeck, who, after B. F. Wilson's large 1922 raid, had begun to consolidate Templeton bootlegging under his control. Smith was not only his driver, he also helped deliver whiskey to retail customers, oversaw the aging of whiskey in a Templeton garage, and hauled equipment and ingredients to Irlbeck's dozens of illicit stills surrounding Templeton. He was one of Irlbeck's earliest employees. The two men had become almost like family, so much so that when Irlbeck and his wife, Lauretta, hosted a family Easter celebration, they invited Smith—which was good, because he probably had no other place to go. He'd arrived in Carroll County a bit of a drifter and had no relatives in the area. And unlike so many others in the illicit alcohol business, Smith was also someone whom Irlbeck could trust, which is why he found himself sitting in a car that night with a gun, on guard against an ambush.

In front of him was the truck, a couple of workers, 320 ten-gallon barrels of Templeton rye, at least $16,000 in cash, Joe Irlbeck, and, facing him, Iowa's most prominent bootlegger, Kenneth Sonderleiter. Five foot nine and a little heavy at 175 pounds, Sonderleiter's classic good looks—his thick eyebrows and full lips and high cheekbones just barely visible behind his fleshy cheeks—cut the profile of someone who seemed better suited to life as a company man, someone in sales, perhaps, someone quick-witted and always ready with a friendly joke and an order slip—a benign fellow, in other words, rather than a guy who led the cutthroat, clandestine life of a gangster. It was the square life he might have been expecting to lead when he, the oldest of eleven children, left school after the seventh grade at the age of twelve to help out at his father's beverage business. He even showed a measure of his own ambition when, at the age of twenty, he started a beverage business of his own. But by the time Prohibition arrived about two years later, that enterprise was finished and he was out of a job. And so it was the cutthroat life that he got—literally, it would later seem, when, as he was being booked at Leavenworth Penitentiary for the serious crimes bootleggers often end up committing, it was noted on his inmate report that he had a 2½-inch scar across the lower front of his neck. As for the clandestine part, he never really would seem to figure that out.

Sonderleiter was busted for his work in the bootlegging trade almost as soon as he entered it. In September 1921 he was fined $300 for Volstead Act violations, but claimed he was too poor to pay and spent thirty days in county jail instead. After he was released, his luck seemed to change. And for the next several years he and his wife, Faye, set about consolidating the bootlegging business in Des Moines. They bought liquor in bulk and plied the retail trade, much like any pre-Prohibition booze dealer. Kenneth even passed out business cards to prospective customers (DIAL 5-6350 OFFICE HOURS FROM 8:00 A.M. TO 8:00 P.M. ONLY, his name around the border, the only indication of why one would want to do what the card instructed) and printed up a brochure titled "The Treasure Chest," complete with illustrations of the liquor he was prepared to deliver, which included bottles with labels purporting to be Old Dan Tucker Bourbon Whiskey, Old Crow Whiskey, Old Smuggler Whiskey, and Gordon's Dry Gin. Whether they contained any more genuine booze than did other alcohol available from bootleggers across the country was a question better not asked, but Sonderleiter's customers didn't seem to have enough complaints to keep him from doing a booming trade. Perhaps that was because his more frequent patrons knew that their best chance for a good drink, a drink not endlessly adulterated by a long, hopelessly opaque chain of bootleggers, was to order a product for which Sonderleiter was the exclusive dealer in the city: Templeton rye, hauled in straight from the source.

Sonderleiter's and Irlbeck's first business meeting had been anything but friendly. But as far as those meetings went, it could have been worse. Though Des Moines was the heart of Sonderleiter's realm, it was also one of Irlbeck's biggest markets, one that he had started out supplying directly. His Templeton rye was found in Hotel Fort Des Moines, the state's preeminent hotel, which was completed in 1919 at a cost of $1.3 million and was notorious for its booze-fueled parties. Templeton rye from Irlbeck's operation was also found behind the bar at many of the city's best speakeasies.

But Sonderleiter wanted a cut of what Irlbeck was selling to customers in Des Moines. When the two men met, Kenneth was straightforward: "Joe," he said. "I want you out of Des Moines. It belongs to me."

"It does?" Irlbeck asked.

"Yes. I want Des Moines."

Yet Sonderleiter also wanted Templeton rye. So instead of pushing Irlbeck out completely, he said that his only demand was that Irlbeck sell directly to him and that he reduce the wholesale price a quarter, from $5.50 a gallon to $5.25. In return Sonderleiter offered to transport the booze himself.

Irlbeck decided to let him have what he wanted and accepted the agreement. But that didn't mean he trusted his new associate. Smith was posted to watch the transaction not just in case of a raid, but also to intervene if Sonderleiter tried to hijack his own load by sending in a squad of men, guns blazing, to take the truck and drive it away before Irlbeck was paid. Standing a little farther down the street and providing additional protection was Ed Reicher, known by everyone in the community as "Brownie," and especially appreciated for his work as the town's night marshal—a position he would eventually use to launch a long career in law enforcement.

Smith and Reicher watched through the night as small trucks laden with whiskey barrels pulled up to the semi. Each time a barrel was heaved onto the truck, the bung—the stopper that closed the hole in the side of the barrel where whiskey was poured in and out—was taken off and Sonderleiter stuck his little finger down. If he felt whiskey, the barrel was considered full. Then he took a small syringe, sucked up a bit of whiskey, squirted it into a glass flask and twirled around to see whether the proof was high enough to hold a bead. As long as it did, the barrel was loaded onto the truck.

Before the next keg was brought up, Sonderleiter peeled off $52.50 from his fold of cash and handed it over to Irlbeck. The idea was that if something happened and everyone had to flee, Irlbeck would be able to take off with the money he already had and Sonderleiter could try to make it out with the booze already in his truck.

Though the operation was routine, Irlbeck and Smith and Reicher were, most likely, more nervous than usual loading those thirty-two hundred gallons that night. Sonderleiter had called earlier saying he needed the booze for a special order—this load of Templeton rye was not destined for its usual market in Des Moines but was instead headed to Chicago, where gangsters far more powerful and far more crooked than Sonderleiter worked. That Sonderleiter would have business with bootleggers in Chicago was not unusual—he routinely bought alcohol from them. In fact, Sonderleiter imported far more alcohol from Illinois than he sent there. What he brought in was sent by a well-established network of rumrunners in the border cities of Davenport, Iowa, and Moline and Rock Island, Illinois, and, at least occasionally, hauled over by members of Al Capone's own gang, whose influence had seeped across state lines. But he didn't, at least to Irlbeck's knowledge, routinely send Templeton rye or any other liquor in that direction.

Though it took all night, Irlbeck and Sonderleiter's men managed to load the semi without any problem, and when it was finally full, it pulled out of Templeton and Irlbeck heard no more of it.

If the truck's drivers had only looked at a map, the trip to Chicago would have seemed like a straight shot along a path marked, with no degree of humility, the "Lincoln Highway." Inaugurated in 1913, the Lincoln Highway had the grand ambition to link the nation from coast to coast, starting in New York's Times Square, ending in San Francisco's Lincoln Park, and all along its 3,389-mile route cutting through hundreds of the little towns and big cities that made up the country's interior. Among the places it touched was the town of Carroll.

Though the highway didn't actually pass through Chicago, its planners did include a spur that jogged to the Windy City. But, in reality, the bootleggers' path to their destination was far from direct. The term "highway" didn't then indicate the same thing it would a few decades later. During most of the Prohibition era, it was more a moniker of aspiration than a promise of a certain level of service. In many places, especially in western Iowa, the road was impassable when covered in giant snow drifts or after a heavy rainstorm, when unpaved sections took on the qualities of a tar pit and drivers unlucky enough to be caught in it returned home with stories horrifying enough to make the front-page news.

One of those was Henry A. Wallace, publisher of the must-read agricultural journal *Wallaces' Farmer* and future vice president of the United States, who returned with his own all-too-typical account one day in April 1929 after trying to travel the highway through Carroll County in the middle of a spring thunderstorm. At first, frequent stops, whether altruistic or necessary, to help pull out all sorts of stuck vehicles blocking his way, made for progress that was, at best, halting. Then he chose the wrong ruts. His car sank all the way down to the axle as his halting progress turned into one unbroken overnight stop. Caked with mud, exhausted, and in need of a new fender, he finally returned home sixteen hours into his five-hour trip.

Wallace was not the only prominent person whose travel plans were upset by that stretch of highway. Three years earlier, at the end of January, when the road was frozen solid, two men were traveling at 45 miles per hour from Denver to Chicago when they hit an ice patch six miles outside of Carroll. Their car flipped onto its top, slid off the road, and down a ten-foot embankment into a ditch, where the crash was cushioned by a bank of snow. The passengers weren't seriously injured, but they were trapped until someone came to rescue them. Once they were, the car's driver gave his name as Ed Schmidt, while his passenger said his was Peter Willis. When news of the accident reached Chicago, however, the *Chicago Tribune* corrected the record: Willis was in fact Louis Alterie, hit man for Capone, and the person some credited (or blamed) with introducing the tommy gun into the bloody world of Chicago gangs. Neither the *Tribune* nor the *Carroll Times* in its own report of the incident, however, mentioned whether Willis/Alterie found the need to pick up any Templeton rye for the medicinal purpose of relaxing any bruised muscles before he left town.

Hazardous road conditions weren't the only, or even the most serious, threats rumrunners had to watch out for, of course. There was the occasional honest cop eager to grab headlines by apprehending a large haul. There were their big-city counterparts, who could be just as ever-watchful for lawbreakers, even if the only punishment they handed out was in the form of an on-the-spot fine that went straight into their own pockets. Beyond the lawmen there were also the fellow bootleggers who found road-blocks and ambushes as effective a source of booze as copper stills and mash tanks.

To disguise their shipments, rumrunners hauling from Templeton would try to make their vehicles appear just like all the rest that bounced along the rutted rural roads. Irlbeck's cousin William Englebert, whom everyone called "Speed," was known around the area as an expert breeder of Spotted Poland China hogs, so no one found his frequent trips to Nebraska in a livestock truck suspect. But for a while his brother Anselm couldn't figure out why he only ever took a single hog, rather than a full load of ten, with him. That was until he realized that the truck was mostly filled with Templeton rye; the lone pig was just a decoy along for the ride. Anselm shouldn't have been so slow to catch on, however—he was running booze himself to Des Moines. But his own strategy to avoid suspicion was a bit more subtle: he bought a Chevy and puttered down the road as if he were just a hayseed from the sticks who knew not a thing about cars and was in no particular hurry to go anywhere in particular. Men who had places to go quickly bought a more powerful, more reliable Ford. And rumrunners in particular drove only Fords. Everyone knew that. At least that was what everyone who knew Anselm knew—or at least that was what Anselm thought.

But the most notorious ruse was one that sought not to appear prosaic but to exploit propriety. The hardware dealer Joe Kohorst, who had moved to Templeton from Carroll the year before Pro-hibition went into effect, soon found himself selling, in addition to top-of-the-line phonographs and sewing machines, sheets of copper for use by bootleggers. But he desired an even bigger cut of the profits. So shortly after starting at the hardware store, he also opened a funeral home, which he ran out of his house. Bodies were embalmed in his basement. Wakes were held in his parlor. And the second floor of his four-bedroom house was given over to casket storage. If all that seemed strange, it wasn't exactly odd for Kohorst, who never really conducted his business in a way that made all that much sense. For one thing, he occasionally ran ads for the funeral home in the Carroll paper promising a "lady attendant," alongside the boast—one that would seem much more appropriate on the front of one of Sonderleiter's brochures—that "A Trial Will Convince You." Perhaps his caskets really were that comfortable. But Kohorst also had an interest in keeping the new hearse he bought in 1926 empty of cadavers, as his wife, Mary, used it frequently to transport Templeton rye.

But it wasn't the hazards of transporting Templeton rye that prevented it from being shipped regularly to Chicago by the truckload. What kept it closer to home was simple supply and demand. No matter how much rye Irlbeck managed to produce, he could barely satisfy Iowans, let alone supply a significant portion of the drinking market of America's second-largest city. If Des Moines residents were drinking at a similar rate to people throughout the country, they were collectively consuming more than six hundred gallons of 40-proof liquor a day and could have soaked up Irlbeck's entire production by themselves. At his high point, Irlbeck had the distilling capacity to produce about a thousand gallons of liquor a day, but he rarely managed to come close to that mark. Even at a fraction of that amount, however, he still ranked as one of the largest bootleggers in the rural Midwest, especially since he was also operating outside the control of any urban gangsters.

His syndicate was so loosely organized, so diffused across so many farms throughout southern Carroll and northern Audubon Counties, made up of so many stills of vastly different sizes—from just a few gallons of capacity to several hundred—that few if anyone other than Irlbeck, his wife, Lauretta, and perhaps Steve Smith had any idea just how much Templeton rye was being produced. Irlbeck thought even his neighbors had no clue. And the closest the federal government was able to come was to describe his stills as "numerous," producing "large quantities" of booze—generic terms that would give his lawyers handholds with which to tear apart the government's case.

Irlbeck's success stemmed as much from the demand for booze and the need of Iowa farmers for additional income as it did from the system he devised to produce it all. For the young man who took the few dollars he earned as a farm laborer to one of Carroll's early bootleggers and learned that he didn't earn nearly enough to afford a drink at the era's new prices, a career as the kingpin of a large bootlegging empire didn't seem a likely path. Unlike Carroll County's other bootleggers, Irlbeck didn't own property on which he could hide a still. He didn't have a job that he could use to explain away large orders of sugar and yeast. And he had no reason to travel frequently, something necessary to make connections with big-city buyers and rumrunners. In fact, the only thing he seemed to have was a bit of money from selling his stake in his father's farm and, in nearly unlimited quantities, ambition and the cunning ability to persist beyond the law's grasp.

After Bill Trecker evicted the still Irlbeck had built in 1921 as a farmhand for fear that the property's owner would discover it and, in turn, evict him, Irlbeck decided to become more than a poorly paid farm laborer. That fall after harvest, two of Trecker's neighbors approached Irlbeck and asked him if he wanted to come to work for them. They were recruiting him not for his agricultural skills, but for his knowledge of whiskey making. He agreed. Over the winter he helped them set up a still in their basement and started cooking whiskey for them. At some point, he started using Hoover's recipe and learned that adding a bit of rye to this mash improved the whiskey's flavor. At another point, he had an epiphany—he figured out how he could overcome the problem of not having property on which to run his own still. When he finished working for Trecker's neighbors, he moved to a rental house in Templeton.

First he approached people in town whom he trusted and knew to be amenable to violating the Volstead Act. Then he went to farmers throughout the area, and, as word spread about the amount of money that could be made, some began coming to him directly. Irlbeck's offer was simple: all he needed was space. In exchange for a place to set up a still and some mash tanks and to store ingredients and barrels of liquor, Irlbeck would pay the property owner fifty cents for every gallon of whiskey produced there. Irlbeck would supply the equipment, bring in the ingredients, and take out the finished Templeton rye, and would hire the men to do all the work. The owner didn't have to do anything but agree to one key provision that almost every person who partnered with Irlbeck was strictly required to follow: if the feds, or state, or even local officers raided the still site, they had to claim the still and all the ingredients were theirs and theirs alone. They could not even suggest Irlbeck was involved. In return, Irlbeck promised to pay for any lawyer they wanted to represent them and also to cover whatever fine was necessary to keep them out of jail.

In Carroll County, even after Wilson's massive 1922 raid, that didn't seem like a clause that would be very frequently invoked—the place was starting to look like an oasis, sloshing with bootleggers who didn't dare cross into the desert surrounding it.

Despite its rebellious northern township of Lincoln, Audubon was still, as it had been when Wilson was in charge of law enforcement there, one of the places that stood most in contrast to Carroll in terms of how vigorously it went after liquor-law violators. Just a bit more than a year after Prohibition began, Audubon's county attorney L. Dee Mallonee made it clear that stills and rumrunners would not be tolerated in his jurisdiction and considerable pressure would be put on drinkers to reveal the source of their booze. He also had stern words for any of the county's police officers who might take a sympathetic position toward whiskey making. If they knew of anybody bootlegging, or found any evidence that someone might be, they were required to begin an investigation. If they didn't, he vowed to fine and then fire them.

Mallonee arrived in Audubon right before Prohibition began with a degree from the University of Wisconsin. He was a Republican and a Methodist, and his family's ties in America went back at least to his great-grandparents. It wasn't a surprise that he was a dry. But Mallonee was given a chance to show just how serious he was about upholding his beliefs the following year.

In March 1922 two men approached Fred Ceranek, a thirty-eight-year-old bootlegger in Audubon County, and asked whether he might have some booze to sell. For some reason Ceranek trusted them, or had no reason not to, and sold them a small quantity of liquor. It was a mistake. Before the two men had approached Ceranek, they'd been approached by Andrew Jorgensen, the man who'd replaced B. F. Wilson as sheriff and inherited his hatred of booze. Jorgensen asked them if they were interested in working undercover as informants. There was money in it, he said. They took him up on the offer and were given their new assignment: to go find Ceranek and return with evidence of his guilt.

When the case came to trial in February of the next year, Ceranek's lawyer called Jorgensen's case weak and argued that the jury couldn't possibly come back with a guilty verdict based just on evidence that was simply purchased from some amateur detectives. Either Mallonee, who prosecuted the case, had done a poor job weeding out wet jurors, or at least one of them agreed with Ceranek's lawyer—either concluding that the evidence was insubstantial or feeling uncomfortable that Jorgensen had paid for it. After twenty-four hours, the jurors' deadlock appeared to be intractable and the judge declared a mistrial.

Less tenacious prosecutors might have moved on. There were plenty of other bootlegging cases on Audubon's docket that could have used the county attorney's attention. But Mallonee vowed to try the case again; he vowed, in fact, to keep trying the case until he got a verdict. Ceranek's second trial began three months later and was no more successful for Mallonee than the first—again the jury found itself hopelessly divided and the judge was forced to again declare a mistrial.

In December 1923, nearly two years after Jorgensen's informants returned with their evidence, Mallonee dragged the accused bootlegger into the courthouse one more time. Again it looked as though he might get yet another hung jury. But after nearly twenty-two hours in deliberations, the jurors sent a note to the judge: they had a verdict. When everyone filed back into the courtroom, the foreman stood up and declared that their unanimous decision was that Ceranek was guilty. On December 21, the Friday before Christmas, Judge J. S. Dewell ordered Ceranek to pay, despite all the trouble he'd given the court, $200. It was the minimum fine. The *Atlantic News-Telegraph*, doing some quick math, estimated that the entire trial had cost the county six times as much.

What was perhaps most amazing, however, was that Mallonee had even managed to get the case to trial three times at all. In many jurisdictions that would have been nearly impossible. From a logistical perspective, prosecuting Prohibition violations was a little like trying to bail a sinking ship with shot glasses. The sinking ship was the justice system, the shot glasses the hopelessly overburdened judges.

In one day in late 1924 in Cass County, adjacent to Audubon and with a population of nineteen thousand, the grand jury returned thirty-one indictments, a record high. More revealing: every one was for liquor violations. Half a decade later, in an effort to counter assertions by Des Moines clergy that Iowa was parched, the director of the state fingerprint lab revealed that 75 percent of the cases sent to him dealt with alcohol.

To prove his point, he pulled an illustrative list of cases for a reporter. "In Des Moines fingerprint records received for this one particular day from the police department, for example, are dripping with gin," he said. "Sometimes one would imagine this bureau was run for the purpose of receiving the fingerprints of people involved in crimes pertaining to intoxicating liquor alone."

The situation on the federal level was worse, where the courts had no option but to bring to trial every liquor case in which the defendant pleaded not guilty. In many places, the legal machinery either seized up or started operating in a way that made a farce of the law.

After Emory Roy Buckner, the Iowa-born son of a rural Methodist minister, graduated from Harvard University, he moved to New York City, where he likely expected to be overwhelmed by the crush of overcrowded streets, the unrelenting putrid odors from fermenting summer garbage, and the nonstop cacophony of a city that was already twice as populous as his home state. But nothing could have prepared him for the flood of fifty thousand Prohibition cases annually that would inundate him when he went to work as the US attorney for the Southern District of New York. Even if every judge in the district worked on nothing else but liquor prosecutions, the court wouldn't have managed to clear even 10 percent of its caseload. Despite his Protestant upbringing and Republican politics, Buckner drank through most of Prohibition—stopping only during his time as US attorney, when he felt duty-bound to uphold the Eighteenth Amendment, however much he disliked it.

Under Buckner the court resorted to an enforcement method popular in so many other federal courts, where across the system liquor cases represented nearly half the workload: rapidly adjudicating complaints by setting fines so low that most defendants would simply plead guilty rather than bother to fight the charges in court. In doing so the government was essentially acknowledging what many bootleggers already understood, that the fines were just another cost of doing business—a line item alongside expenditures for tommy guns, goons, and graft. "To call such fines 'convictions' is grotesque," Buckner said. He suggested instead the defendant be considered to have "escaped on the payment of money."

Nonetheless, officers committed to the dry cause kept pressure on the bootleggers. In June 1923 Glen A. Brunson, the Prohibition director for Iowa, claimed that the state was one of three with the most successful enforcement efforts in the nation, a condition he attributed in large part to the willingness of state and local law enforcement officers to cooperate with federal agents. Brunson's boast may have been as much about politics as statistics, however. Just a month earlier the Prohibition Bureau had concluded an investigation into an accusation about lax enforcement in Iowa's southern judicial district. Though the accusation proved unfounded, the investigation revealed one reason at least Brunson found state and local officers so agreeable: they were willing to issue search warrants without any supporting evidence that the person the warrant was directed against was selling intoxicating liquor.

In a letter critical of Brunson's tenure, the assistant attorney general in charge of Prohibition enforcement, the fiery Mable Walker Willebrandt, wrote that the agents obtaining evidence under such warrants were "treading on dangerously thin ice." Predisposed to viewing the Prohibition Bureau as floundering and reprehensible, she concluded the practice was the result of either ignorance or incompetence. "It is very evident that proper instructions have not been given these agents," or Brunson "is lax in not insisting that his orders are carried out," she wrote.

Despite the scrutiny, committed local law enforcement officials didn't let up on the pressure on the bootleggers in their jurisdictions. Seven months after Brunson's boast, Sheriff Charles C. Kennedy of Guthrie County, which bordered Audubon to the east and stretched up to touch the southern corner of Carroll, announced he'd busted his thirty-sixth moonshiner.

"Apparently the supply is attempting to meet the demand," the *Audubon Advocate* noted when reporting Kennedy's record, making a point that many dry officials weren't quite willing to confront. The truth was that alcohol, just as had been the case under state prohibition, flowed to wherever there were drinkers. And even in counties with especially dry law enforcement, there were still people willing to turn over quite a lot of money and undergo no small degree of risk to obtain it.

In a state conference earlier that year called by the governor to work out a coordinated response to liquor prosecution, the delegate from Greene County stood up and addressed the delegates from his neighbor to the west, Carroll. What, if anything, he wanted to know, was being done about the rampant bootlegging in Carroll County? As the four hundred other delegates looked on, Carroll's mayor shot back an accusation, likely as absurd as it was juvenile (the *Jefferson Bee* out of Greene County called it "too ridiculous for denial"): that most of the booze in his city came in from Greene County.

After the uproar settled, Carroll County Attorney T. J. Drees offered a more measured response. "I always get an indictment before I take action against criminals," he said. "If you will join me in telling where these stills and bootleggers you talk about are, I'll go out with you and bust them."

As the tiff threatened to escalate, the lieutenant governor stepped in and dully suggested that the men meet at some later time and figure out how to go after the moonshiners together. But the debate continued for several more weeks in newspapers across the state, until even the *Carroll Times* decided it had to respond to the "mean" accusations. The best the paper could offer, however, was to say that the intoxicating liquor situation in Carroll was better than that in St. Louis or, well, at least, Chicago. After its response, the *Jefferson Bee* decided to raise a few more interesting questions. Why, it wanted to know, was it that so many former county attorneys had taken up the business of defending bootleggers? And what exactly was meant by one citizen's statement, quoted in another Carroll County newspaper, that if local officers were violating their oath to uphold the law by ignoring liquor violations, then they were clearly just bending to the will of the people who elected them?

Carroll, clearly, was gaining a reputation. But even if local officials wanted to go after the bootleggers, even if Drees could get his indictments, actually punishing the lawbreakers was something else altogether. Even in comparatively dry Audubon County, when Mallonee was prosecuting Ceranek, he ran into the roadblock that Willebrandt had acknowledged when she cautioned that "juries will not convict if the punishment does not fit the crime."

No matter how tight the Volstead Act's regulations were (and not a single one of them was overturned), no matter how stark was the line that made 0.5 percent alcohol the standard of officially intoxicating drink, no matter how much the Volstead Act and even the Eighteenth Amendment seemed to be unimpeachably direct on the point that nonmedicinal and nonsacramental alcohol intended for consumption was flat-out illegal, the law's power still came almost exclusively from the twelve citizens who made up the jury that ultimately decided who, if anybody, would be guilty under it. They had the final say. And if they found a bootlegger not guilty, he was not guilty—even if he'd been caught with enough hooch to fill a paddy wagon.

For Ceranek, the jurors who held out in his first two trials seemed mostly resistant to the use of paid informants in his indictment, but in Carroll County jurors seemed to resist the idea of enforcing Prohibition altogether, which made prosecution of violators by anything but federal courts almost impossible, especially when the county also lacked a prosecutor with as tenacious a drive against alcohol as Mallonee. Throughout Prohibition, Carroll's county courthouse was remarkably absent of bootleggers—hosting far fewer criminal cases against them than most other counties. In fact, the first major liquor case didn't open in Carroll until 1925, and its outcome proved just how futile such trials were.

Three days before Christmas 1924, a veritable army of forty-five men, commanded by George Atkins, an agent with the state bureau of investigation, invaded Carroll County with the mission to search out and destroy every form of vice they could find. Slot machines, moonshine, stills, even black market cigarettes—they were after it all. And they even managed to find some.

In the city of Carroll their march against vice took them into not only clandestine casinos but also to places where the only apparent gambling paraphernalia were the Advent calendars set out on the counter, which were hardly games of chance, filled as they were with a piece of candy for each day. Dutifully, the agents confiscated them anyway. But their real haul came from the area surrounding the town of Breda, located on the other side of Carroll County from Templeton. There they found seven or eight caches of booze and managed to seize enough liquor to fill more than six carloads—even after one of the bootleggers managed to flee with his stash in his Ford truck, ungrazed by the two or three shots officers fired his way.

That the officers would find so much booze in Breda was no surprise. Plenty of farmers there, eyeing the success of their counterparts in Templeton and living under the same permissive jurisdiction, decided to set up stills of their own. Though their product would never be as widespread, as popular, as famed as Templeton rye, the bootleggers in Breda still kept many home bars stocked during Prohibition.

So much loot was taken in the raid that even the *Carroll Times*, in no way oblivious to the whiskey cookers and casino owners that made up an influential part of its readership, was a bit stunned, calling the agents' haul "astonishing." Piled together in the county jail, the paper reported, it reached the ceiling. Yet the raid wasn't nearly as successful as it could have been. For all the places busted in Breda, countless others in Templeton and Dedham were dismantled before any officers—or at least any honest officers—showed up. Though they had enough evidence to secure search warrants against several places there, they found no stills, no barrels of mash or bottles of whiskey, no illegal loot at all.

Over the next several days arrest warrants stemming from the raid were issued to dozens of men throughout the county. And as the cases against them were filed over the subsequent weeks, Carroll County's courthouse became busier than anyone could ever remember it being before. In January a few of the men charged with gambling pleaded guilty, taking a fine of just fifty dollars. But most of those arrested on liquor charges entered pleas of not guilty, preferring to take their cases in front of a jury.

The first of these opened two months later on March 16, 1925, a Monday. As a boisterous crowd of onlookers pushed into his courtroom, Judge R. L. McCord gaveled open the trial. At the

CARROLL COUNTY
COURT HOUSE SQUARE
CARROLL, IA. 12

The Carroll County Courthouse, where the first big bootlegging case in the county was tried a full five years after the start of Prohibition. Sympathy for the bootleggers was so widespread in Carroll County that prosecutors tried nearly all their cases in the federal court in Fort Dodge, Iowa, seventy-five miles northeast of Templeton. *Courtesy of the Carroll Historical Society*

defendants table sat Will Heires, a thirty-one-year-old Breda man, whose father was from Germany and mother from Kentucky. From all over Carroll County people came to watch the drama of the county court's first major bootlegging trial, to hear the government's accusations against one of their neighbors, and to hear the rhetoric of Heires's highly regarded defense lawyers: the team of William C. Saul and his son William I. Saul, who had left the post of Carroll's county attorney after prosecuting V. C. Schwaller to take up the job of defending its bootleggers (the *Jefferson Bee* was on to something, after all). But mostly the crowd seemed to be there to cheer on Heires.

Over the next day and a half, McCord's gavel continued to ring out frequently, a staccato warning to what was one of the largest crowds to ever attend a court case held in Carroll County. With each tap, he was admonishing spectators that it was unacceptable to applaud all the points made by the two Sauls. It was of little use.

By Tuesday evening, both sides had rested and the case was handed over to the jury, which would spend the next several hours in fitful disagreement. Throughout many of the early ballots the jurors took, the vote split eight for acquittal, four for conviction. Among themselves, the jurors continued to argue about how strong the state's evidence really was—and about how much of a crime bootlegging really was. By midnight, after hours of debate, one of the men who'd originally voted to convict flipped and the tally became nine to three in favor of an acquittal. But the remaining three held out, and by Wednesday afternoon, McCord was given a note that the deadlock was impassable. He declared a mistrial.

Unlike Audubon County's hung jury of a couple of years earlier, there was no effort made to retry the Heires case—it appeared to have been quietly dropped, as were all of the charges against the other bootleggers arrested in the state's raid. Carroll County's wetter citizens had sent a message to both the bootleggers and the officers considering going after them: they'd stand pat against the state and try to stop any bootlegging case brought in district court. As it had done decades earlier under the state liquor control laws, Carroll County signaled its intention to opt out of the anti-liquor laws. In doing so it joined jurisdictions across the nation where juries effectively nullified local liquor laws. Even so, they could do little against the Volstead Act and the prosecutions held at the federal courthouse in Fort Dodge. Again, the task of enforcing Prohibition in Carroll County fell almost entirely on B. F. Wilson. Yet even he seemed to be losing ground.

The summer before the state agents busted so many stills around Breda, Wilson had gone out to collect evidence against a few bootleggers near Dedham and Arcadia. He and a few other Prohibition agents traveled through the county on what the *Carroll Times* later referred to as a "smelling committee," trying to catch a whiff of fermenting mash on the air currents wafting past hedgerows and onto the public roads. How much such evidence actually helped him, Wilson never said—he also had local informants directing him where to sniff, figuratively, if not literally, speaking.

When they returned on June 6, 1924, they hit four places and collected nearly 110 gallons of booze, much of it buried along a right-of-way. They also found over one hundred gallons of wine, over forty gallons of beer, and two men Wilson had arrested before: Ulysses S. Beebe, nabbed while Wilson was still Audubon County sheriff, and John Steffes, who had been caught in the huge 1922 raid.

Prosecutions against the two men were almost as swift: by the end of the month, Steffes was already facing thirty days in jail, the judge refusing to let him off with just a fine. Beebe's case took significantly longer, but before the end of the year, he was ordered to pay a $250 fine.

It would be nearly half a decade before Wilson would make headlines for another large-scale raid in Carroll County; until then his victories would be smaller but no less significant. In fact, Wilson was beginning to learn from his informants that all those stills in Carroll weren't the work of a bunch of rebellious farmers acting alone, but actually formed an organization controlled by one man: Joe Irlbeck.

Whether the slowdown in federal raids in Carroll was partially the result of Wilson's decision to focus his attention on bringing down Irlbeck instead of his subordinates, or whether it had more to do with the fact that Templeton's whiskey cookers had really become so adept at alerting each other and avoiding imminent raids, it was undoubtedly also the result of forces that had nothing to do with Wilson, or Irlbeck, or Templeton, or even Iowa.

Throughout the mid-1920s the Prohibition Bureau, if not exactly in turmoil, was at least floundering. Corruption was endemic: the number of agents fired every year for proven or suspected involvement with the very criminal enterprises they were supposed to be investigating and shutting down numbered, by some counts, in the hundreds—a majority of the force. So deplorable were the conditions that sometimes when honest agents like Wilson actually tried to enforce the law, the public, taken aback, complained directly to the Prohibition Bureau.

Such was the case when Fort Dodge lawyer Beltram J. Price began a letter dated April 4, 1925, to Wilson's boss, Glen Brunson, in Des Moines. "You need not be assured that I have no respect for bootleggers," he wrote rather obtusely. "But the thing I despise above all things is an officer of the United States government sinking to the level even beneath that of the ordinary bootleggers in his efforts to make a showing with petty violators." Translation: Wilson should not devote himself so much to doing his job, especially when his job was going after one of Price's clients.

What had aroused Price's hackles was a case that began earlier in the year, when Wilson and a local sheriff's deputy were tailing a man already twice convicted on liquor charges. Once they'd stopped the bootlegger's car, the deputy walked up to the vehicle and found the door locked. As he was asking the driver to open up the door, the driver slid across the seat, threw open the door opposite the deputy, and tossed out two half-pint glass bottles, which shattered when they hit the sidewalk.

Acting quickly, Wilson ran up to where the bottles hit the pavement, pulled out of his pocket two handkerchiefs, and pressed them into the puddle, soaking up as much of the bottles' liquid as he could. After the two officers arrested the vehicle's driver, Wilson took his handkerchiefs back to the local Sheriff's office and squeezed them dry, collecting the liquid dripping out into a bottle, which was sent to a lab for analysis. The chemist's report showed it was at least 100 proof. Confident in the officials from Webster County, where Fort Dodge is located, Wilson let them try the case, but when the grand jury refused to indict the bootlegger—as it did with a few other men accused of liquor violations that session—Wilson, with the sheriff's urging, decided to take the case on in federal court instead.

Whether Price thought Wilson was too adept at collecting evidence or too persistent in making sure the case—his client's third liquor violation—proceeded through the courts, he didn't say, but he concluded his letter by threatening to file charges against

Wilson and, in fact, the whole of the Prohibition Bureau's Iowa division. His threat did little.

In Wilson's rebuttal, he actually invited an investigation into himself (and even included a few other incidents for which he'd been criticized), but his superiors at the bureau did not think that was necessary. They had several letters of support, including one from the sheriff of Webster County, who wrote that Wilson "is the best federal man that has ever set his foot in Fort Dodge," and that he would "most assuredly like to see Wilson remain in this territory." In case Wilson's bosses didn't fully understand the sheriff's wishes, he revealed that he'd even once offered Wilson a higher salary than he was earning with the federal government if he'd come to work full time on the Webster County booze squad.

Price's complaint was doomed. After it had a generated a few pages of paperwork, Iowa Prohibition director Brunson wrote in a letter to the commissioner in Washington that "it does not appear that Mr. Price has any grounds whatever for complaint" and that he had always regarded Wilson as "one of my best men." Wilson, he said "is one of my most active agents" and carries out his work without "fear or favor." The federal commissioner agreed and the case was dropped. A year later, Wilson was promoted—his salary increased to $2,400 a year. Meanwhile the bootlegger, Price's client, opted not to fight the government.

But the bootleggers would still get some relief from Washington. As it had done since the start of Prohibition, Congress continued to refuse to appropriate anything more than a token amount for enforcement—for most of the 1920s, the bureau's budget hovered between just $9 million and $13 million and between 1925 and 1926 even fell by more than a quarter-million dollars. In September 1926 Brunson announced that the number of Prohibition agents in his district, which also included South Dakota and Nebraska, had fallen from forty-two to twenty-seven. To make up in part for the shortfall, Brunson hired additional undercover informants or, as wets derisively called them, stool pigeons.

Despite his lack of resources, Brunson had the support of many state and local officers; elsewhere in the country, the federal agents couldn't even get that. Starting with New York State in 1923 and cascading throughout the more urban parts of the country as the decade wore on, state legislatures and city councils began repealing, or completely defunding, liquor law enforcement—effectively nullifying the Eighteenth Amendment's provision for concurrent enforcement between the fifty states and the federal government. It was with the support of those local officers, however, that Wilson was finally able to find a crack in the seemingly impregnable wall of hands-off deniability that Irlbeck had erected around himself. And it was only through the support of the local officers that Wilson was finally able to start building an investigation that would eventually form the basis for an ambitious conspiracy indictment against Irlbeck.

Over several days during the first half of June 1927, Audubon County sheriff Andrew Jorgensen snuck around the periphery of a farm in the northeast corner of the county, just over a border road from Carroll. What specifically, if anything, aroused Jorgensen's suspicion this time is unclear—but the ever-vigilant anti-alcohol man might have just been checking in, making sure one of the more notorious bootlegging venues in his county was still dry. The farm, large at over 250 acres and owned jointly by a few men, had played host twice before to tenants whom Jorgensen had nabbed for bootlegging—the last, two years earlier. Since that raid, a new tenant had settled there, one who fit the profile of a bootlegger in the area, namely that he was through-and-through German. Thirty-five-year-old John Schultes had arrived in America from Germany just before the outbreak of the First World War; he initially settled in Carroll and spoke very little English. Jorgensen probably thought he'd been born drunk and had been at least slightly soused ever since.

Whatever drew him to the place, Jorgensen was onto something. In February of that year, Irlbeck had approached Schultes about setting up a still, promising that if he agreed to let Irlbeck run one in the second floor of his house he could "make a lot of money." More money, potentially, than many of the other farmers Irlbeck partnered with, because Irlbeck, either desperate to add capacity or unable to negotiate a better deal, agreed to pay him half the profit on the whiskey made at his place, rather than the standard fifty cents per gallon. It was a terrible idea. Irlbeck probably thought Schultes would be a good partner—he wasn't a total stranger, after all. But why he would choose to cross the county line, even slightly, into Audubon County, was a mystery. He certainly knew of Audubon County's ambitious still-busting program and of the fact that juries there were willing to convict bootleggers. Maybe he thought the isolation of Schultes's farm site would provide enough cover. Or maybe he was just cavalier—he was still relatively young, relatively new to the bootlegging game. It could have just been a neophyte's mistake.

After Schultes agreed, Irlbeck hauled in a sixty-gallon still in a Ford Model T truck, one thousand pounds of sugar, and ten mash tanks, and set up his distillery. Though Irlbeck quickly ran his first batch, producing about 150 gallons of alcohol, he seemed in little hurry to run another, or even haul away the booze he'd already produced. It wasn't until several months had passed that he refilled some of the mash tanks, and by then he had not taken away more than half the liquor.

On June 17, Jorgensen led a procession that included his deputy, the county attorney, a couple of trusted citizens, and federal Prohibition agent Sumner J. Knox. When they turned south down Schultes's long driveway, the wet county receded behind them. When they reached the farmhouse, they knocked. No one answered. So they broke in. Upstairs they found Irlbeck's still, seventy-two gallons of liquor, and five hundred gallons of mash.

As they hauled all the evidence down the stairs and into their cars, they waited for Schultes to return. Once he did, they placed him under arrest. And then he said something that no bootlegger had ever said before. "It's all Joe Irlbeck's. He just pays me. The still, the liquor, it's Joe's."

Schultes didn't indicate why he decided to turn on Irlbeck— maybe Irlbeck hadn't made him promise to never disclose his name, maybe Schultes thought things weren't on the straight and narrow, maybe the officers made him think things were not on the straight and narrow. Irlbeck, he thought, had said the still was only fifty gallons. And why had Irlbeck run it so infrequently? And why would he leave nearly half his batch of booze lying around for several months, anyway? Regardless of why Schultes flipped, as soon as he did, officers were off after Irlbeck. When they found him and arrested him, they dragged him to Audubon County and threw him in jail that night.

Over the weekend and during the Monday of the following week, Irlbeck and his lawyer were locked in negotiations for a plea deal, terrified that Irlbeck would be sentenced to significant jail time. No matter what, Judge Halleck J. Mantz insisted that Irlbeck would not be able to settle with just a fine. "Joe is in a very awkward position here," he explained to Irlbeck's lawyer. "We don't want the Carroll County bootleggers slopping over into Audubon County, and we are going to use him as an example."

Finally they agreed on terms: both Irlbeck and Schultes pleaded guilty and were fined $300 and sentenced to one year in prison; Mantz also placed them under permanent injunction, prohibiting them from ever producing liquor again; and furthermore the farm itself was enjoined from ever being used again for bootlegging. Immediately after sentencing Irlbeck and Schultes, Mantz suspended their jail terms, provided they stayed out of trouble.

As soon as Irlbeck was released, he fled back to the safety of Templeton. A week later, he drove to Des Moines and saw a baseball game. While there, if he also happened to drop in on Sonderleiter, he would have been able to reassure the Des Moines rumrunner there was nothing to worry about in regard to supply— despite the injunction and the suspended sentence, Irlbeck had no intention of leaving the bootlegging business. If he didn't have any stills running that night, he'd have more up soon.

A common criminal based elsewhere—in Chicago or New York or, probably, even Des Moines—may have reacted violently to a betrayal as dangerous as Schultes's. But Irlbeck didn't dwell on it—and there wasn't a whole lot he could do about it anyway. If he had attacked Schultes, he would obviously have been implicated, and to have done so would have immediately lost him the support of Carroll County officials and citizens and even the relative sympathy of their counterparts in Audubon. Instead, if he took anything away from the incident, it was that he'd have to better choose his partners.

Despite his best efforts, he would be betrayed again. And Schultes wasn't done talking either.

9

CLOSING IN ON THE GOLDEN GOOSE

Nineteen twenty-nine was the year when everything seemed to pivot. It was the year of instabilities, tragedies, and flickerings of desperately conjured hope.

No single thing set the tone for the last year of the 1920s. The decade had begun so auspiciously, with a number of events that seemed to herald a great new American era: the country's triumph after the First World War, the ascendant urban economy and the still-wealthy and rapidly industrializing rural one, the advent of Prohibition with its promises to strengthen the home and clear the way for wealth and peace to triumph widely throughout the nation and deeply throughout the classes. But little of that optimism now remained.

The first time that, perhaps, the contours of that pivot became hazily visible was late in 1928. Election Day of that year, November 6, was the culmination of one of the greatest contests for the American presidency. The match: Alfred A. Smith, candidate for the Democrats, governor of New York, urban, Catholic, fiery, and adamantly wet, versus Herbert H. Hoover, Republican, hero of the Great War, Quaker from the tiny Iowa village of West Branch, multimillionaire engineer and businessman, and spongy—he could be dry or wet depending on where he was. And in 1928, spongy was what the nation wanted. Not ready to give up on Prohibition quite yet, Americans were well aware that, in its current form, it was failing.

In his acceptance speech after he was nominated at the Republican National Convention, Hoover praised the productivity of the small American farmer and called farm relief the nation's "most urgent economic problem." Ever the engineer, he proposed to make transport of agricultural products more efficient by commencing a vast development of the country's waterways that would exceed in scale and cost the development of the Panama Canal. He promised to keep the country on the path of an ever-expanding economy that had marked the previous two Republican administrations and even predicted that the elimination of poverty was near.

On Prohibition, he famously called the law "a great social and economic experiment, noble in motive and far-reaching in purpose," and said that "crime and disobedience of law cannot be permitted to break down the Constitution and laws of the United States." He credited the "abolition of the saloon" with contributing to economic prosperity and stated directly that he did not support efforts to overturn the Eighteenth Amendment. The solution to the problems caused by Prohibition was not dismantling Prohibition, he said, but reaffirming the government's commitment to its enforcement. His proposals earned him the support of many drys—including Iowa senator Smith Wildman Brookhart and the Justice Department's head of Prohibition prosecutions, Mable Walker Willebrandt.

But as soaring as his language was, the content of most of those statements was equivocal. Hoover wasn't actually saying that Prohibition was good or that it would work. He personally didn't appear to believe in it fully—often taking, while serving as the United States secretary of commerce from 1921 until his nomination, two evening cocktails at the Belgian embassy in Washington, which was technically on foreign soil and not under Prohibition's strictures.

Smith predictably tacked differently on the liquor issue. In his telegram accepting the Democratic nomination, he called

Prohibition "entirely unsatisfactory to the great mass of our people" and gladly took up the standard of the anti-Prohibition candidate. But even he wasn't willing to advocate for the wholesale return of liquor throughout the land. Instead he spoke of returning the decision to the states or sending it to a popular referendum. "The cure for the ills of Democracy," he said, "is more Democracy."

To the drys, to the leadership of the Anti-Saloon League, to the ardent Protestant clergy who'd worked so hard to bring about constitutionally dry America, Smith was abhorrent. One temperance leader said, if elected, he'd be a "cocktail President." But where Smith's opponents really excelled in their hatred was not directly on the issue of his wetness but on all those qualities they saw as the attendant evils of wetness.

Just as it always had been, the debate over Prohibition wasn't entirely pure—it also served as a proxy war of racism and bigotry, over ideas of what America was and should become, and who was allowed to participate. And as had happened during the First World War and with the rise of the Ku Klux Klan, the rhetoric was horrifying and vile and directed simultaneously at Catholics and the waves of immigrants filling the country's urban areas.

The KKK, always a reliable source for the most inane manifestations of racism, managed, in its *Fellowship Forum* publication, to sum up the sentiment against Smith perfectly when it wrote that if elected he would create an America that would become "a vassal state of the Vatican and stink-slide of booze and corruption." But it didn't take as extreme and backward an organization as the KKK to spew such racism during the election.

Methodist bishop James Cannon Jr., whose long career advocating against alcohol had brought him to the forefront of the movement by the time of the Hoover-Smith race, claimed that Smith wanted to welcome into America "the kind of dirty people that you find today on the sidewalks of New York," while "Cotton Tom" Heflin, a US senator from Alabama and a vicious white supremacist, announced on the Senate floor that Catholic priests killed their babies and that Smith planned to annex Mexico for its Catholic population.

Over vast swaths of America, the anti-Catholic, anti-immigrant, anti-urban demagoguery influenced voters in favor of Hoover far more than did the issue of Prohibition, about which many were starting to have serious doubts. This attitude especially held sway in the country's rural areas, which had outsize influence in both the House and the Electoral College because of Congress's repeated failures to reapportion representation along the lines of the urban shift that was revealed in the 1920 Census.

On Election Day, Hoover overwhelmingly trounced Smith, taking twenty-one million votes to Smith's fifteen million. Hoover's margin of electoral votes was even more impressive: he won 444 to 87, buoyed by a giant homogenous mass of Republican counties throughout all but the Southeast, which was punctuated by a few urban strongholds of Democratic support.

But not every northern rural area supported Hoover. On April 20, 1928, a few weeks after the Carroll County Democratic Party held its nominating convention, eighteen Carroll County citizens arrived in Des Moines to cast their vote for Smith at the state Democratic convention. Among them were some of the most prominent men in the area, including county sheriff William Schmich, who'd taken over for Janssen a few years earlier and who was a favorite of Eden Township voters, and Charles E. Reynolds, a former county attorney who'd soon find himself fighting Prohibition beyond the ballot box.

Smith enjoyed far more support than just that of the county's Democratic leadership. When the votes from the general election were tallied, they revealed something remarkable: not only had Carroll County voted against Iowa's native son by 20 percentage points—propped up by Eden Township's 447 votes for Smith versus just 23 for Hoover—it led a small, four-county cluster of rural districts, Audubon among them, that did so—one of just a handful of such agglomerations in the nation. Outside of that pro-Smith enclave, only two other counties in Iowa voted against Hoover:

the German stronghold of urban Dubuque County and Plymouth County, which included parts of Sioux City. But Carroll and Audubon, Dubuque and Plymouth were just anomalies. By measure of the Electoral College, Hoover's victory was one of the largest in history. The nation, or so it seemed to some, had opted for more of the same—the temperance crusaders celebrated their ninth dry holiday season, confident there would be decades more of them; the nativists prepared for the century's third Census confident that, even if the statistics weren't on their side, the country's political power, at least, was; and, with the exception of the farmers, Americans everywhere included in their New Year's hopes that 1929 would continue the decade's remarkable prosperity. By the end of Hoover's first term, each of those hopes would prove a fantasy. And the first signs were a series of shocks.

At first it was called a "broom for sweeping trenches," a weapon that was supposed to change the dynamic of the First World War, capable of firing several hundred rounds a minute but light enough to be operated by one person. But the Thompson submachine gun came too late to aid America's doughboys, and when the war ended, surpluses piled up. It was a gun that seemed useless for civilian needs, what with the way it sprayed bullets everywhere, almost at random, that could pierce a quarter-inch of steel and leave jagged-edged bullet holes in everything. It seemed better fit to terrorize the public than to protect them. And in its second life—when it came to be called variously "the tommy gun," "the chopper," "the Chicago typewriter," "the Gat," and "the Ack-Ack" as the country's mobsters used it to settle scores with a fusillade of a thousand bullets on open streets under the light of day—that's mostly what it did.

Throughout the 1920s, the blaring headlines of gangland murders shocked, fascinated, and increasingly disgusted the American public, especially in Chicago, which was widely regarded as the capital of the slaughter. As the turn of the decade approached, businessmen there started to worry that the violence, long dismissed as a threat mostly to the criminal element, was giving the Windy City a reputation as a place too dangerous to visit, to shop in the stores along Michigan Avenue, to stay in one of the glamorous Loop hotels. They were concerned, in other words, that all the killings were bad for business.

Their fears were confirmed the day after Valentine's Day 1929, when Americans across the country opened their newspapers and came face to face with booze-fueled organized crime at its most gruesome. The images they saw were from a shootout the day before in a Chicago garage, the direct product of the tommy gun's destructive power: seven bodies in various contortions sprawled out across a gore-soaked floor. One man had come to rest on his back, with a stream of blood from his nose flowing over his forehead and through his hair before meeting up with a larger flow from the back of his head. Another photo showed a hunk of brain lodged beside a man's cracked skull. In all of them, it was obvious the victims—five known gangsters, one innocent mechanic, and a gangland groupie—had been lined up and executed.

For most Americans, these were the most graphic images they had ever seen in their newspaper, and the uproar following the St. Valentine's Day Massacre quickly developed into a backlash against Prohibition itself and the government's lax response to its violence.

President-elect Hoover announced the next day that once he took office he'd press for an additional $2.5 million for liquor-law enforcement and that he wanted to see the Prohibition Bureau's force increase by four hundred agents. Meanwhile, a pair of businessmen recruited and paid for ballistics experts to help in the investigation. Despite the attention and the money and no shortage of theories, the crime went unsolved. It was just another gangland murder case the Chicago police failed to close.

On Hoover's inauguration day, Monday, March 4, radios throughout most of the nation crackled with a live broadcast from the

East Portico of the White House, where a steady rain fell on a crowd that included, among other dignitaries, the 250 Iowans—the "home folks"—who'd left for Washington two days earlier on a fourteen-car special train out of West Branch.

Wearing a plain black overcoat and striped trousers, Hoover addressed the nation and the crowd, the creases in his round, fleshy face revealing all his life's fifty-four weighty years, his thin hair becoming increasingly matted by the rain. He hit on the themes so common in such orations, speaking of the need for fiscal prudence, the promotion of justice worldwide, and the coaxing of private enterprise, but he also addressed Prohibition and the abundance of illegal liquor and the violence accompanying it. In doing so he castigated state and local officers for not adequately doing their job. He lamented that the justice system was vulnerable to manipulation, and he called on citizens to stop flouting the Volstead Act. To the shock of some wets, he was apparently serious about his election-year rhetoric. But he also held out an invitation for change.

"There would be little traffic in illegal liquor if only criminals patronized it. Our whole system of self-government will crumble either if officials elect what laws they will enforce or citizens elect what laws they will support," he said. "If citizens do not like a law, their duty as honest men and women is to discourage its violation; their right is openly to work for its repeal." Until then, "to those of criminal mind there can be no appeal but vigorous enforcement of the law. Their activities must be stopped."

The address should have registered a direct hit among the people of Templeton, and perhaps forewarned them that over the next four years they would not be able to operate with the same latitude that they had in the previous ten. But it was understandable if no one in Templeton thought about the long-term implication of Hoover's speech that day.

Shortly before seven o'clock that morning, Rosa Galloway, a widow in her midforties and mother of five, woke up in her Templeton home. Frost still clung to the window from the frigid winter air, and the sun had just broached the horizon. Perhaps thinking she'd ask her oldest son, twenty-two-year-old Benjamin Franklin, whom most people called just "Franklin," whether he wanted breakfast or a cup of coffee, or perhaps just wanting to wish him good morning, she walked to the door leading down to her basement, where she thought he was at work, and opened it. She froze. It probably took her a short second or two to process the scene before she screamed and dropped to her knees, bringing her closer to her son as he lay on the top landing, unconscious. The air wafting up from the basement was slightly warm and smelled strongly of whiskey mash, and though she couldn't have known, it also contained toxic levels of carbon monoxide. Quickly she pulled her son off the landing and up into the kitchen, where he lay in her arms for a few more minutes until his breathing stopped. Before help could arrive, he'd died.

The *Carroll Times* that came out two days later printed a story about his death on the front page, and though it accurately reported his asphyxiation, it placed the blame on a "laundry stove," rather than the true culprit. But everyone who rushed to Rosa's house that day to comfort her knew: he died tending a whiskey still hidden in the home's basement. It would be the only death that resulted from the manufacture of liquor in Carroll County. Afterward, the bootleggers who kept stills in the town of Templeton itself seemed to move most of them out to the country, which not only provided better protection from the feds but also allowed them to operate in larger spaces with better ventilation.

As Hoover stood in the rain in Washington, he portrayed bootleggers as a tiny, undesirable element of the population. Patronage of them contributed, he said, to "crime and outlawry." In fact, they undermined the very basis of the nation. In spite of them, though, Hoover said the country had "reached a higher degree of comfort and security than ever existed before in the history of the world." This was an America where the "questions before our country are problems of progress to higher standards; they are not the problems of degradation." For those who were listening in

Templeton, the rhetoric would have been as infuriating as it would have been foreign.

Statistics from the fiscal year that ended on the first of March, a few days earlier, showed that three out of every one hundred farms went into foreclosure or some similar proceeding during that period. This was certainly a "problem of degradation"—indeed, a sign of an outright crumbling of rural America. And with few other opportunities, how was a widowed mother of five supposed to survive?

Funeral services for Franklin Galloway were held on March 7, alongside that of another Templeton resident who had died the same day, forty-seven-year-old Josephine Reicks. Galloway's service came first and Reicks's was held afterward, and undoubtedly nearly everyone in that small, tight-knit community who could come out for the funerals did so, joining family members who arrived from all over the state.

Among those who also traveled to Templeton that day were more than a dozen men whom no one had invited and who weren't there for the funeral anyway. March 7 was the same day—ill-chosen, as he was rapidly realizing—that B. F. Wilson had picked for another large raid in Templeton. Not only was he preparing to round up whiskey cookers in a town mourning the loss of a young man who died making that very product, but on the list of their places to raid was the Reicks house.

No one noted whether the agents, a team of state and federal officers, knew of the funerals that day or had heard any of the whisperings about how Galloway had died. They certainly didn't go into Sacred Heart Church to see what information could be gained from the eulogies. Instead they proceeded to conduct their raids. When they stepped onto the Reicks's porch, however, they stopped. Tied on the door was a black ribbon—a reminder to all of the death that had just struck the family that lived inside. On the porch, the agents debated whether to go ahead with the raid, some arguing that no death absolved illegal activity, while others were adamant that an intrusion at such a time was callous.

Finally, one of the agents against the raid angrily told those in favor of it that "if you want to raid it under conditions like this you go ahead," but he wasn't going to participate and walked away. Eventually the others followed. Had the agents gone ahead, they would have found in the Reicks's basement one of Joe Irlbeck's stills. Instead, they just hit the rest of the homes on their list.

"The federal and state agents swooped down on Templeton, the attacking army led by General Frank Wilson, federal agent, with Sheriff Frank Buchheit second in command," the *Coon Rapids Enterprise*, a newspaper out of a town about fifteen miles east of Templeton, wrote after the raid. "A large truck was required to bring the stills, liquor, and other stuff to Carroll, where it was cached in the court house. Twenty gallons of liquor was bottled and labeled 'Templeton Rye,' being the kind they bring out when you order prewar stuff in Chicago. The only prewar thing about it is that a couple of drinks always brings on a fight."

The *Enterprise* was clearly going for sensation—and referring to Buchheit, who'd replaced William Schmich as sheriff the year prior, as Wilson's "second in command" was certainly a stretch. Though Buchheit had a special still-busting outfit, it mostly consisted of a hat—the only occasion for which he wore one. To the others in the raiding party, it probably seemed like a sensible addition. To his constituents, however, it meant far more: it was a clear beacon, warning them they'd better dump their booze and hide their stills.

Nevertheless, the raid was the most comprehensive sweep of Templeton marshaled by Wilson since the one he'd led in 1922, seven years earlier. Though his agents only captured three stills and eighty total gallons of liquor, they still managed to nab some of the most important bootleggers in town, including Joe Kohorst, from whom they also confiscated two new vehicles; John Schwaller, the son of bootlegger Victor Clemens Schwaller; Leo Kuhl, pre-Prohibition saloonkeeper and former city councilman; Albert Greteman, co-owner of one of the family's general stores whose relative, Lauretta, had married Joe Irlbeck earlier that year

Lauretta Irlbeck in 1929, the year she married Templeton rye kingpin Joe Irlbeck. Her father was grocer and telephone-system operator Frank Greteman.

Courtesy of Elaine Schwaller

(they honeymooned in Kentucky's bourbon country); and John Bierl, who had been Templeton's mayor from 1922 to 1928.

Unusually, Wilson decided to let the cases proceed against the bootleggers in county court, under state laws. But this time, he didn't have to worry about a jury nullifying the law: each of the men pleaded guilty. Judge R. L. McCord, who'd presided over the failed trial against Will Heires, assessed them a fine far harsher than usual—$400—and sentenced each of them to three months in jail.

Though the sentences were tougher than those typically given to Templeton's bootleggers, they could've been a lot worse. A few days before, President Calvin Coolidge, in one of his last acts before turning over the Oval Office to Herbert Hoover, had signed one of the more audacious—and last major—pieces of legislation pushed through by the drys. The Increased Penalties Act, or Jones Law as it was popularly known, did just what its name purported to do: it toughened the punishment for convicted bootleggers. Misdemeanor violations of the Eighteenth Amendment were made felonies. The maximum sentences for first-time lawbreakers were increased tenfold to up to five years in prison and a fine of $10,000. Voters, who'd never really intended the election of 1928 to be taken as a sign that they supported tenacious enforcement of Prohibition, were generally appalled at the law's harshness, but it stayed on the books until repeal.

Despite Wilson's success, however, his victory was short lived. The same afternoon of the raid, before the kegs had even been loaded in the truck to be hauled up to the Carroll County courthouse, two bootleggers the raiders had missed were busy running their still, producing Templeton rye to fill the void left by the seized contraband. Worse, Wilson again failed to catch Irlbeck, or even gather any evidence against him. In the year 1929, Irlbeck, in fact, seemed stronger than ever.

The summer of the year before, Irlbeck had even gone to his lawyer in Audubon, former county attorney L. Dee Mallonee, to see if something could be done about the injunction explicitly barring him from bootlegging that was brought against him following his arrest after the raid on John Schultes's farm. To get it lifted, he needed approval from several county officials, including the sheriff and the new county attorney, both of whom intended to show bootleggers that Audubon was not as welcoming as its neighbor to the north by coming down hard on Irlbeck to make an example out of him. Predictably, they at first balked at the idea, fully aware that the river of rye whiskey flowing out of Templeton had not ebbed a drop since the arrest. "Sign that? Hell no," one of them told Irlbeck's lawyer. "I know he went back to operating a still the day he got out."

At first, Mallonee didn't know what to say, so he just passed their opposition along to Irlbeck. But Irlbeck saw an opening: they apparently believed he was still bootlegging—and of course he was—but what evidence of it did they actually have? Mallonee asked, and the answer he got back was that they had none. He then pressed them about whether it was right to leave such an injunction in place based solely on hearsay and conjecture. Eventually all the people whose signature Irlbeck needed relented, and the injunction was lifted. On August 14, 1928, Mallonee enclosed a copy of Irlbeck's pardon, along with a short note to him. "Dear Joe," he wrote. "You are a free man once more. Respectfully, L. Dee Mallonee."

Not only was he a free man, he was an increasingly popular one as well. The decades-long downslide in the financial health of the state's farms continued. Many were already under pressure to meet mortgage payments taken on when land prices had spiked during and immediately after the war, when farms had been far more profitable. With the land now worth less than the amount of those mortgages, farmers faced the dilemma of either losing the land or scrimping on necessities—like clothing, or adequate health care, or, even store-bought food like flour and sugar—to make payments.

Thousands of other farmers struggled in an even less secure position. Along with land prices the amount of capital—for equipment, for seed, for breeding stock—needed to even start a farming operation spiked dramatically after the war, but it didn't fall nearly as steeply. As a result, the 1920s saw a dramatic rise in the number of tenant farmers, whose situation, on the land and in the community, was even less secure than that of their mortgage-holding neighbors, who were at least working toward owning land of their own.

To both groups, Irlbeck's "rent" money—comparatively extravagant sums that could be made with little labor and no investment on the farmer's part—seemed like a godsend. Even in the late 1920s, many were still forecasting an imminent agricultural recovery and predicting that a man who owned some land, who had some money in the bank, would be a man poised to earn a real good living once that recovery came.

Monsignor F. H. Huesmann standing with his dog on the steps of the Sacred Heart Church rectory with an assistant priest. Huesmann not only gave Templeton rye's production his doctrinal blessing, he promoted the product by passing out samples and even permitted a small still to be housed in the church basement. *Courtesy of Elaine Schwaller*

But bootlegging not only helped people in Templeton save their farms, it also allowed them to live in some semblance of the material abundance enjoyed by the better-off dwellers in the country's economically booming cities. With liquor money, their lives could be enriched by music from a new phonograph or eased with the help of a washing machine, while their children could have a few cents to buy candy and enough to get new shoes for school. What people really aspired to own in Iowa in the 1920s, however, was a new car—and it was to that item that many Carroll County bootleggers directed much of their earnings. Car culture was taking hold across the nation, but few places embraced it with as much enthusiasm as Iowa. The state boasted among the highest rates of automobile ownership in the nation—by one measure coming in second only to California—and also had more miles of paved roads than anyplace else.

In 1928, after years of driving used Ford Model Ts, John Schwaller, one of the bootleggers who would be arrested on the day of Hoover's inaugural speech, had surprised his family with a new Chevy and a trip to Michigan to see some of his wife's family, who were also related to the Gretemans. Others bought top-of-the-line Ford Model As, which had been released in the late 1920s as a stylish upgrade to the humdrum Model T, or splurged for an Oldsmobile.

In 1929 the townspeople also found enough extra cash to spend on a lavish and extraordinary party for one their most popular and respected citizens: the Reverend Frederick H. Huesmann, Catholic pastor at Sacred Heart Church. Huesmann had arrived in Templeton in 1917, already fifty-four. He'd spent his first eighteen years in Oldenburg, Germany, where he was born, and the remainder in America, first studying in Ohio and Indiana and then serving in parishes throughout Iowa. But it was in Templeton that he stayed the longest, and it was there that he came to be beloved by the townspeople. Round-faced and jovial, he was known for his honesty and integrity, and shared with the community not just ancestry but also the belief that the Eighteenth Amendment was a law that went too far.

In early May 1929, Pope Pius XI granted Huesmann the title of "Monsignor." Several weeks later, on the sunny and warm day of June 25, his parish dedicated a day to celebrating the honor. By ten in the morning, over one thousand guests—former parishioners, public officials, at least 130 other clergy—had already arrived. The events began with the reverend traveling in procession from the Catholic school to the church, which had been festooned with white and purple ribbon. He was led by two of the school's pupils, one of whom was Madeline Schwaller, John's daughter. At the church he received his purple robes, which had been donated by the local chapter of the Knights of Columbus—an organization that counted among its members several of Templeton's prominent bootlegging families.

After services, everyone headed to a large banquet, where they kept busy with toasts and speeches, as well as the presentation to Huesmann of a large monetary donation from the community. The meal was concluded with an address from another student of Sacred Heart, the daughter of rumrunners Joe and Mary Kohorst. Afterward, informal festivities continued into the evening with a thirty-five-piece band from Breda. The *Carroll Times*, in its detailed, front-page story the following day, never mentioned how much, or even if any, Templeton rye was consumed during the celebration. But without a doubt, many of the visiting clergymen and friends of Huesmann's went home with at least a small pint bottle in their pockets.

The monsignor was one of the earliest supporters of Templeton's booze industry—Henry Vermeule had even mentioned the connection in his letter to the attorney general a couple of months after the start of Prohibition. Parishioners remembered how he'd pass out bottles to visitors and let them know there was plenty more to buy if they wanted to go into the rum-running business. And in a pinch, he even helped the bootleggers hide their booze from the feds, one time even allowing them to stow some of it away in a coffin that was in the church awaiting the arrival of its more permanent occupant. But the feds never busted Huesmann or attempted to raid church property. Even if they knew he was hiding liquor there, they also had to know that such an incursion would create a fantastic outcry. The church, after all, was one of the few institutions that was allowed to buy alcohol under the Volstead Act, albeit in the form of wine.

Huesmann may have gone further than many Catholic clergy in actively promoting Templeton rye, but he wasn't alone in blessing his parishioners' bootlegging. Catholics had not only opposed Prohibition from the very beginning on grounds that it was both an intrusion and bigoted, but also because the church had a long history with alcohol: many monasteries brewed their own beer and distilled their own liqueurs.

In all likelihood, the support of Huesmann as leader of the Sacred Heart Church, the social nexus of Templeton and the town's most cherished institution, did more than anything else to make bootlegging acceptable in the area. Law enforcement could more easily overlook something that may have been in violation of temporal laws if it was just fine under spiritual ones. And residents could feel more comfortable protecting their neighbor's liquor operations because they all shared a moral belief in which distilling was acceptable.

But the influence of Huesmann and the church only went so far. As the more committed revelers in Templeton continued to celebrate Huesmann's honor, Audubon sheriff Fred Clemmensen— who'd been promoted from a deputy in 1928 after the previous sheriff, Andrew Jorgensen, died suddenly—along with his deputy, cajoled Carroll County sheriff Frank Buchheit and another officer to raid a distillery south of Templeton, three-quarters of a mile from the Audubon County line, that same night. They captured twenty-five hundred gallons of rye mash and two fifty-gallon stills in operation and arrested the farmer, John Buelt, operating them. They also nabbed Buelt's distributor: Fred Stueve, who had the poor fortune of driving in with ten empty kegs and a quart of liquor right as the raid was underway.

"Stueve's big mistake was that he hadn't been in business long enough to recognize the officers' cars," the *Audubon Advocate* reported two days later. "The theory of the officers is that he knew that the place was doing a thriving business and when he saw their cars in the yard he merely thought that business was good."

And Sheriff Buchheit, apparently, was not wearing his hat.

Though 1929 had started out with so much promise—a new president, a still-booming national economy—it receded with a particularly unpleasant form of uncertainty, an uncertainty spiked with fear and dread.

For most of the decade politicians and farm activists had struggled to find a way, through organization or government intervention, to put agriculture back on equivalent footing with industry as it had been during the war, and for most of the decade they failed. But over the course of several weeks in the fall of 1929, parity seemed to be drawing nearer—only it wasn't that agriculture was finally surging, it was that industry was collapsing.

Over its most destructive days in the last week of October, the week of Black Monday and Black Tuesday and Black Thursday, the fall in the stock market wiped out billions of dollars of wealth as the volume of sell orders surged and the ticker tape bringing news of the rapidly eroding prices to traders in Des Moines fell so far behind that it was useless. With the telephone and telegraph also clogged, many in Iowa's capital just stood around, nervous, anxious, waiting for the markets to close so they could finally figure how much they had lost.

Individual Iowans reported paper losses in the tens of thousands, a few even in the millions, while the most popular stock in Iowa, that of the energy concern Cities Service, lost two-thirds of its value. Early one evening a few months later, William Day Jr., at one point the state's richest man with more than $10 million invested, shot himself at his office.

But not everyone met the crash with panic. During the start of the biggest slide, President Herbert Hoover—who had been warning about dangerous speculation since the middle of the decade, when he was commerce secretary, and who had pulled a portion of his fortune out of stocks months before the crash—announced his opinion that "the fundamental business of the country, that is production and distribution of commodities, is on a sound and prosperous basis."

Many saw the crash simply as the urban equivalent of the deflation in Iowa land prices that put so many farmers in debt at the start of the decade. Others even speculated that the crash would be a boon for the state, sending capital back to Iowa land and Iowa farms as investors sought out safer and saner places in which to put their money to use. But no one really knew.

That December, in the weeks leading up to Christmas, children across the country, at least, appeared to have remained confident—writing down, as they had done so many winters before, their hopes for the new year and their more immediate desire for new things under the Christmas tree. They addressed their letters to Santa Claus and asked their parents to stick them in the mail. But for so many, those wants would go unmet, a harbinger of the neglected needs to come.

Among those in Templeton who sent off their wishes were the youngest Bierl sisters, Irma, seven, and Lillian, nine.

"I want the goose that lays the Golden eggs," Irma wrote.

"And please don't forget mama and papa," Lillian added.

Among the rolling hills of Carroll County, unlike in so many other places, such optimistic requests remained a possibility. As their uncle John, who had been pinched in Wilson's spring raid, knew well, the town already had a source of gold far more real than a storybook goose. And over the next few years, that source would seem just as miraculous.

10

WILSON GETS THE BECK

For Frank J. Neppl and his family—his wife, Anna, and the five of their eleven children who still lived at home (Alonzo, the oldest at nineteen, Walter, the baby at eight, and the girls, Verna, Ludwina, and Mildred, in between)—the night of March 3, 1931, didn't seem like the one they'd all been dreading for nearly two years.

For the Neppls, the dread wasn't the panic Americans across the country were feeling as the economic crisis of 1929, rather than abating, pushed into its second year. For them, that panic had long before set in as a way of life. With so many children to feed and clothe, and with the 160-acre farm, complete with a mortgage and the expense of all the equipment needed to run it, Gilded Age wealth was never in sight, but they had expected a little more from all their hard labor. Neppl, blue-eyed and stocky at just five feet seven, would have been proud to raise his family in agrarian comfort, rich in space, purpose, community, and self-sufficiency, if not material abundance. That was the contract: America's offer in exchange for hard work and thriftiness. It was why Neppl's parents had immigrated from Bavaria sixty years earlier. But ever since the bottom had fallen out of the farm economy, that contract seemed like a joke. And Neppl was desperate to escape the deathly spiral of money-losing harvests. So one day in 1929 he approached Joe Irlbeck and asked if he would be interested in running a still at his place.

Neppl's farm was four miles northwest of Templeton and tucked into the intersection of two county roads that met at the top of a hill. At its bottom, at the base of the two long, gentle slopes coming off either byway, there was an old hog house. The building, nothing more than a low-slung wooden shed, was set back several hundred feet from the fence line and situated behind a number of larger barns. It was secluded, in other words, and perfect for an illicit alcohol distillery. For Irlbeck, the deal was a rare opportunity: an ideal space and an eager partner. He quickly took Neppl up on the offer and filled the building with two 250-gallon stills and enough barrels to hold 5,500 gallons of mash. The operation was one of the largest in Irlbeck's empire, and the bootlegger never let it idle long. For Neppl, the rent he received, forty or fifty or sixty dollars a day when the still was running, was a windfall, more than enough to relieve the panic of impending destitution, the panic of possibly losing the farm. But it came with a worry all its own: the ever-present possibility of a raid. Irlbeck required of Neppl what he required of all his employees, after all: that they claim the still, and all the whiskey, as their own, if revenuers came.

In the two years since his 1929 raid, when B. F. Wilson had arrested four bootleggers and seized three stills and eighty gallons of Templeton rye, that beverage had only increased in popularity. Though he'd failed to find enough evidence during that raid to arrest Irlbeck, he continued to hear rumors that Irlbeck was still involved—including information from an informant who had managed to purchase booze from Irlbeck and his associates multiple times. Wilson was eager to finally take him down. In February 1931, if not before, Wilson decided to devote nearly all his effort in Carroll County to doing so. And it was one of the contacts he made during that period who suggested that if he poked around Neppl's farm, he might find the evidence he was looking for to nab Irlbeck once and for all.

On March 3, while Neppl's family sat at home and Irlbeck's still hands cooked up another batch of whiskey not far away, Wilson and his partner, Agent F. H. Burris, crawled through a ditch behind a grove of trees and toward Neppl's hog house. The structure specifically piqued Wilson and Burris's interest when they noticed a light on inside. Knowing it was not a residence, they surmised the light could only be illuminating one thing: a team of illegal whiskey cookers at work. Their suspicion was confirmed when they crawled a bit closer.

The sun had set an hour before the two men set off down the ditch, which ran off one of the adjacent roads. But a nearly full moon added to the light coming from the hog house and Neppl's home up the hill, giving Wilson and Burris a clear view across the surrounding farmland from which they crawled. They had little risk of anyone hearing them; by midnight the temperature would have reached a low of twenty-two degrees—not the bitterest of Iowa nights in early March, but still a good reason to stay indoors, close to the stove, with the doors and windows shut tight. They kept their heads down and their bodies prone, however. Planting season was still a few months off, so the fields were fallow and sheer as they undulated across the Carroll County hills. Any movement would have stood out—even the deer and pheasants sheltered tight to what little cover there was.

Wilson and Burris weren't trying to see the illegal distillery anyway—they just needed to smell it. Three hundred feet from the hog house, Burris took a big whiff and knew he had enough evidence for a search warrant. The yeasty odor of fermenting mash, tinged with the slight sting of alcohol vapor, filled his nose. The redolence of the place coupled with his two years on the Prohibition force busting bootleggers made him "positive that a still is being operated in this said building." So positive, in fact, that US Commissioner H. M. Pratt, after hearing Burris's testimony, amended the preprinted text of the search warrant he filled out the next day. In the blue font of his typewriter he added "and is certain" to the line normally stating that the complainant "has reason to believe, and does believe" his hunch was true.

Perhaps the two agents were motivated by a desire to prove that the bureau was still strong, despite its tumultuous last few years.

Federal Prohibition agent F. H. Burris. Originally from Wisconsin, he assisted B. F. Wilson in many of his raids. He was castigated by the police chief of the sopping-wet city of Sioux City for being "too serious about liquor violations." *Courtesy of National Archives, St. Louis, Missouri*

With the Depression ravaging the Treasury, President Hoover had been forced to cut more than a half million dollars from the Prohibition Bureau, which, as the country increasingly turned against the Eighteenth Amendment, was only becoming more despised by the day.

Search warrant in hand, Wilson and Burris returned to Neppl's farm the following night with a force built to show that the bureau still had some power. Moonlight crested and the air temperature receded to fourteen degrees. March 4 was the coldest night in nearly three weeks. At 11:35 PM Wilson and Burris turned off the road north of Neppl's farm and started down his driveway, toward the hog house.

There would be no crawling through fields for this visit. The two officers were accompanied by Prohibition agents R. R. Lubbers from Sioux City, Oscar Hanson from Dubuque, and George C. Parsons, Iowa's Northern District deputy Prohibition administrator, based in Fort Dodge. The federal men also brought along Carroll County sheriff Frank Buchheit, for a little local authority.

The carload of Prohibition agents drove past Neppl's house without stopping and parked in front of the hog house. On top of the building, at the ridge formed by its slanting roof and its highest wall, the agents noticed two cupolas. When they slid open the hog house doors and entered, they learned that each cupola hid an exhaust pipe coming off a furnace below and they discovered in each a fire that was still burning, keeping the building warm. Nearby, Parsons counted 110 fifty-gallon barrels of fermenting rye mash and 159 five- and ten-gallon kegs of aging Templeton rye. Distilling equipment seemed to be packed into every inch of the fifteen-hundred-square-foot space. Under each of the two 250-gallon stills was a ten-burner gas stove and stacked nearby were sixteen hundred-pound sugar sacks waiting to be mixed into the next batch of whiskey. Large amounts of fuel and yeast, as well as more distilling equipment, were scattered throughout the room. Parsons would later tell the *Carroll Daily Herald* that the seizure was of "the largest distillery uncovered in the northern Iowa district in recent years."

But it didn't take the federal agents long to realize one ingredient was missing: the actual bootleggers. Knowing that a bust, no matter how spectacular, was of little value without someone to actually arrest, Wilson, Parsons, and Buchheit set out toward Neppl's farmhouse, leaving Burris, Lubbers, and Hanson behind to secure the haul.

Neppl was summoned by Wilson's knock. He was already asleep, or at least was planning to be soon, for he answered the door in his pajamas. Neppl invited the men into his home, then listened as Wilson read him the search warrant issued by H. M. Pratt and announced that he was under arrest. If Neppl hadn't already, he would soon claim the still the men had found was his. None of the officers noted in their depositions whether Neppl protested his arrest or the search of his property. Nor did they say if he seemed surprised by the raid—but the presence of Buchheit among the strange men at his door that night must have provided at least some comfort. Buchheit's was a face well-known throughout Carroll County, and Neppl would have quickly realized that it was at least lawmen and not gangsters out seizing his whiskey. The officers also refrained from tearing through Neppl's house searching for additional whiskey or distilling equipment—a consideration they gave few other suspected lawbreakers. In an effort to find as much evidence as possible they would often overturn a farm site looking for every hidden stash. Wilson never said why Neppl's house was left unsearched—perhaps the officers thought they'd already found enough contraband, or maybe they thought they had already inflicted enough pain on Neppl that they didn't need to add more by disturbing his children.

Once the legal formalities were finished Wilson, Parsons, and Buchheit let Neppl change into more appropriate clothing before they escorted him to the hog house. As they did their boots left prints in the dusting of snow that covered the ground. The clock neared midnight; the raid hadn't yet taken thirty minutes. But it was far from over. Wilson, Buchheit, Parsons, and Neppl returned to the hog house and then waited for, in Parsons's words, "the arrival of others who might be interested in the still."

The men waited in what must have been silence. What could Neppl say as the future of his farm, his family, his freedom consumed his thoughts? And the five lawmen, would they sit around talking shop at 2 AM? Maybe. But they were busy listening. There was no wind that night. The windmill that usually pumped water into the just-raided still wasn't turning—its cyclic whine absent, like the insects, the cicadas and the grasshoppers yet to emerge, that would make such a din on the humid Iowa summer nights to come. In some other era a man might have had a drink to pass the time. Despite all the whiskey surrounding them, that was now impossible. So they smoked. For nearly three hours, the occasional scrape of a match through a matchbook and the subsequent crinkle of a lighting cigarette were all the men heard.

Then at 3 AM a car turned down Neppl's driveway. It followed the same path toward the hog house that Wilson and the other agents had driven hours earlier. Unlike the feds' car, however, this one was new and proceeded almost in silence—the driver had killed the engine at the road and coasted down with the lights off. The precaution was one honed over years of always keeping a low profile, of trying to avoid tipping off the feds and nosy drys and of trying to keep their routine hidden from even the farmers who lived on the land they used for bootlegging. The car stopped within twenty-five feet of the hog house where the agents were hiding. At that point Irlbeck made a crucial mistake: he slammed the door. The agents knew someone was there.

Irlbeck, still unaware he'd tipped off a nest of Prohibition agents, walked up to the building where he expected to find his still undisturbed, and reached to open the door. Before he could, the door opened in front of him and out sailed a tossed cigarette. Then out stepped Agent Parsons.

"Who are you and what are you doing here?" Irlbeck asked. Parsons didn't bother answering. Instead he grabbed Irlbeck and placed him under arrest. As he was fastening the handcuffs, he ripped the flashlight Irlbeck was carrying out of his hand and hurled it into a nearby field, worried that Irlbeck would find some way to use it as a weapon. As he did the car, which had been so silent on its entrance, stuttered to a roar as the driver ignited the engine, threw the vehicle into gear, and spun around in the yard.

Parsons screamed to the rest of the agents to come out, fast. And they did. Once they ran out of the building, two got down on their knees and drew their guns. When the car cut across the yard, they pointed their guns straight at it. Irlbeck claimed the officers opened fire on the vehicle as it sped out of the driveway, shooting "the hell out of the car" as well as a nearby garage. But they failed to hit the driver, Steve Smith, Irlbeck's top lieutenant.

If Neppl's family hadn't been woken during the earlier raid, they certainly would have by now. That is, if Smith really did speed away in a spew of gunfire, as Irlbeck said. Wilson and the rest of the federal agents made no mention of a fusillade in their report. Parsons dryly summed up Smith's escape by writing, "Another person who was in the car which had driven up, escaped by driving the car out of the yard without lights." Agent Lubbers focused not on the headlight infraction but on the fact that whoever was in the car hadn't driven over for a social visit with Neppl at his house:

"The car," he wrote, "was turned around hurriedly and the man therein escaped. The car did not stop at the Neppl residence either when entering or leaving the premises."

There was at least one good reason for the agents to not mention the gunfire: by the time they wrote their report, they had to have realized their evidence against Irlbeck and his mysterious driver was purely circumstantial. All that bootlegging equipment and all that whiskey were found on Neppl's property and Neppl had already claimed it as his own. Unless they could find a witness to connect Irlbeck to the operation, any number of narratives could have explained Irlbeck's and Smith's presence: perhaps they were just nosy trespassers; perhaps they were there to steal livestock feed or to seek a warm place to sleep—it was the Depression, after all. It was better for the officers if their reports gave the distinct impression that the driver was fleeing to avoid being arrested in connection with the massive distillery, without raising the possibility that he retreated because he was being shot at.

Another obvious question the agents left unanswered from that night was how they knew to wait, and why they continued to do so for three hours until someone actually did show up. The decision wasn't without risk: Neppl was being closely watched, but he knew the area better than the officers and could have attempted escape. Also, the agents were on a secluded farm in the middle of the night—they would have had little recourse had the stills' owners mounted an attack. Did the Prohibition agents know for sure that someone else was coming? And if so, who told them? None of them ever said, but perhaps B. F. Wilson's mystery informant, the one who suggested he search Neppl's farm in the first place, also suggested he wait around for Irlbeck to appear.

Also surprising was that Irlbeck even came to the farm that night. He would have known the still wasn't running—the lack of water from the windmill meant there was no way to cool the copper condenser coils. Likely he came to load up whiskey and Wilson got lucky—or Irlbeck was framed. By this point in his investigation, Wilson was already assigning undercover officers to Templeton to attempt to buy whiskey in order to entrap the bootleggers.

After B. F. Wilson raided the farm of Frank Neppl, capturing two 250-gallon stills, 5,500 gallons of mash, and Joe Irlbeck, the still's owner, the *Des Moines Tribune-Capital* printed a photo of the raid along with an optimistic boast. *Copyright Des Moines Register and Tribune Company; used with permission*

Perhaps one of them had placed an order that Irlbeck needed to go to Neppl's to fulfill. Regardless, with Neppl and Irlbeck in custody and the agents convinced the driver had gotten away, they finally began to deal with all their evidence.

Meanwhile, Smith sped into town. He didn't stop until he reached the Irlbeck house. He parked, then ran up to the Irlbecks' bedroom window, where Lauretta, Irlbeck's wife, was asleep inside, and started knocking on the pane. "Get up, get up and come to the back door," he said, his voice weak and shaky.

"Who got him? Who got him?" Lauretta asked.

"I don't know but my guess is that it was the federal men," Smith replied through sobs.

Not long after, the word shot around Templeton: "They got the Beck."

The revenuers found so much equipment and whiskey on Neppl's farm that most of it had to be destroyed on-site. But before doing so, they hauled it all outside. They stacked up the barrels four high, using them as a backdrop to the two stills, squat and domed with the copper coils hanging listlessly off. They then snapped a photo and got to work with their axes. They hacked up the stills and dumped all but one five-gallon keg of moonshine and 1¾ gallons of mash, which they saved for evidence along with the sugar and the coils.

A photo of the haul was sent to the *Des Moines Tribune-Capital*, which published it the next day on the front page, above the fold, under the headline THEY'LL SEE NO MORE TEMPLETON RYE. Either the *Tribune-Capital* had caught the agents' optimism or it didn't quite understand how savvy Irlbeck and his fellow Templetonians were. Templeton rye wasn't going anywhere, and neither was Joe Irlbeck.

Over the next couple of months, Wilson and the federal prosecutors assigned to the case worked on preparing it for trial. Finally, on the steamy day of June 16, 1931, in the US District Court in Fort Dodge, grand jury hearings into case number 1782, the United States of America vs. Frank J. Neppl and Joseph Irlbeck, opened.

Irlbeck and Neppl had been free on bail since their arrest the night of the raid. In their initial arraignment, in front of Commissioner H. M. Pratt in Fort Dodge on the afternoon following the March 4 raid, they were given bail of $1,500 each and told their case would be heard when the Northern District court convened its next session.

The bail was steep, but it didn't seem to cause much difficulty for Irlbeck and Neppl. Their lawyer, Charles E. Reynolds, arrived from Carroll to represent both men in court that afternoon, and he brought along with him a cashier's check to cover the bond. The check was issued in Reynolds's name, but every dollar of it certainly came from Irlbeck. That was, after all, his deal with

Templeton doctor Otis P. Morganthaler, the town's mayor during Templeton rye's most active years, in the late 1920s through the end of Prohibition. He ordered the town's water supply turned on at midnight so bootleggers could fill up their mash tanks and run their stills. He also helped bail out his constituents when they were arrested by the feds.
Courtesy of the Carroll Historical Society

Neppl—to pay all legal costs. Less than a month later the bonds secured by Reynolds's check were replaced with personal bonds cosigned by Irlbeck and Templeton mayor Dr. Otis P. Morganthaler. If federal agents didn't already suspect that Morganthaler, one of the town's most successful and beloved men, was involved with the liquor racket, they soon would.

Neither Irlbeck nor Neppl were allowed in the courtroom on June 16—the grand jury hearing was, as a rule, closed to the defendants. But Irlbeck's lawyers were crafty, and some of the most experienced in Iowa. In addition to Reynolds, who was Carroll's former county attorney and a prominent Republican, Irlbeck was also represented by the accomplished Louis H. Salinger, another partner in one of Carroll's most venerable law firms, Salinger, Reynolds & Meyers.

It was either Salinger or Reynolds who knew the Fort Dodge courthouse well enough to recommend to Irlbeck that he try parking his car outside the courtroom, where he might be able to overhear the proceedings. The recommendation was a smart one on a day when the temperature reached eighty-six degrees; eventually it became so hot on the courthouse's second floor that someone had to open all the windows. Irlbeck could hear many of the voices clearly as they drifted down.

Since Neppl refused to testify against Irlbeck, the prosecution, led by US Attorney Harry M. Reed, was forced to try to establish that Irlbeck was a well-known bootlegger on a grand scale and that, therefore, the distillery operation could be no one's other than his. When Irlbeck was arrested, officers discovered that he was carrying a bank book that showed "a woman relative of Irlbeck had been depositing $500 weekly in a Templeton bank," the *Des Moines Tribune-Capital* reported in its post-raid article. That "woman relative" was his wife, Lauretta. The *Tribune-Capital* also suggested officers planned to investigate Irlbeck for tax evasion, with deputy Prohibition administrator Parsons estimating the bootlegger had earned more than $100,000 in profits over the previous several months.

The tax evasion offense was in vogue that year among prosecutors who found themselves going after bootleggers. On the same day as Neppl and Irlbeck's hearing in Fort Dodge a far more prominent case was on trial in Chicago: the United States vs. Al Capone. Though everyone knew Capone was a gangster, a bootlegger, an extortionist, and likely a murderer, the Justice Department felt the most assured way of sending him to prison was by showing that he was a lavish spender who never paid a penny in income tax. That day, Capone stood in front of Judge James H. Wilkerson, an Iowa native, and pleaded guilty to willfully evading income tax, failing to file tax returns, and violating the National Prohibition Act. Capone's confession wouldn't hold long, as Wilkerson would soon learn something Reed was discovering during his own proceedings that day: big-shot bootleggers had a knack for avoiding convictions.

One of the witnesses Reed called to the stand was Irlbeck's banker, Frank Schreck, of the Peoples Savings Bank in Templeton. Reed proceeded to drill him about the nature of Irlbeck's large and numerous deposits—and tried, on the off chance Schreck wasn't feeling particularly loyal, to get him to admit what everyone in Templeton knew: the source of Irlbeck's wealth was illegal whiskey.

Schreck, thirty-eight and handsome with high cheekbones and a penetrating gaze, first told the grand jury that he didn't think the distillery was Irlbeck's, a statement that astonished the prosecutor, who responded by asking testily, "Didn't you surmise he's a bootlegger coming in here daily with this amount of money? You couldn't help but know the guy is."

"No," Schreck said. "I couldn't say that he is a bootlegger. I've never seen him walk down the street with bottles or anything sticking out of his pocket."

"Well, did you worry about this amount of money coming in here daily? Didn't you wonder how he was arriving at that?"

"Well, gentlemen, I don't know if you are familiar with the banking business or not, but it is not customary for the banker to ask any questions when his customer brings in money. We only ask questions when they want to borrow it." To that the prosecutor could not recover. The coup de grâce delivered, Schreck stepped down, having said nothing to imperil the business interests of his prime client.

Of course, there was no doubt Schreck knew that Irlbeck was a bootlegger, not just because that was something everyone in Templeton knew but because anyone bringing in that much money in a farm community in the early 1930s was indeed suspicious. Farmers across the state were behind on their mortgages and foreclosures were rampant. With few buyers, the seized land was of little value and the bad loans crushed thousands of banks. As the number of bank failures across the country skyrocketed, depositors with money became increasingly fearful that their bank would fail, wiping out their savings (Congress would not found the Federal Deposit Insurance Corporation [FDIC] until 1933). Because of the credit crisis, the bankers at Peoples Savings wouldn't permit Irlbeck to make deposits during the day. Instead he could only bring his money in at night, and then to the back door. Their caution wasn't from fear of the feds but fear that if townspeople learned the bank had such a large influx of capital it would be stampeded by loan seekers.

Irlbeck had discussed the nature of his income even more directly with Schreck one tax season after he had started to make significant money. He had begun to worry that maybe the government would try to come after him on tax evasion charges, the Supreme Court having ruled in 1927 that ill-gotten gains were still subject to the income tax. So he asked Schreck whether he should report his bootlegging earnings.

"Well, let's look at it this way: You're beating them on that," Schreck replied, referring to Irlbeck's ability to violate Prohibition with impunity. "Why not beat them on the other end too?" Regardless of whether Schreck was a natural at aiding and abetting bootleggers, he had learned a few tricks from a fellow banker who worked with an enormous rum-running syndicate based out of Spirit Lake, Iowa, that was operated by five of the Chapman brothers, originally from Carroll.

Maybe the *Des Moines Tribune-Capital* had been trading in unfounded speculation, but despite its earlier report, for some reason prosecutors did not bring tax evasion charges against Irlbeck. Instead they would continue to try to prove he was a bootlegger.

After Frank Schreck's testimony in front of the grand jury, George C. Parsons, the deputy Prohibition administrator who arrested Irlbeck, started to worry the charges against Irlbeck would fail. In an attempt to save the case, he stood up and exclaimed that if none of the witnesses already called would implicate the bootlegger, he would find someone who would. "Before I let this get away from me, I am going to subpoena every merchant in the town of Templeton," he said.

As soon as Irlbeck heard that, he cranked up his car and peeled out of the parking lot. He sped the sixty miles back to Templeton, where he went to every merchant who sold him bootlegging supplies and told them: "Be out of here tomorrow because you might be served with a notice to appear in the court." The next day the investigators came down, but every single store owner was gone.

The tactic worked. On June 17, 1931, the grand jury reconvened, expecting to hear a day full of testimony from the merchants of Templeton. Instead Parsons announced he had no one. As a result, the government's evidence wasn't persuasive enough to convince the grand jury that Irlbeck was a National Prohibition Act violator. There would be no indictment. Irlbeck was free. Judge George C. Scott ordered the return of his $1,500.

Though Parsons realized the day before that the case was unraveling, prior to that point the feds must have felt their evidence was overwhelming. Someone had already prepared the indictment forms, listing as defendants both Irlbeck and Neppl. Now the name "Joseph Irlbeck" had to be scratched out, in pen.

B. F. Wilson had lost the Beck. But he hadn't crawled through a ditch alongside Burris for nothing. The same day the charges against Irlbeck were dropped, Neppl pleaded guilty to manufacturing 1,055 gallons of whiskey. Shortly thereafter Judge Scott delivered his sentence: sixty days in jail and a $1,500 fine, in effect seizing the money that Irlbeck and Mayor Morganthaler had put up for bail.

It is impossible to know if Scott would have given Irlbeck a harsher sentence than he gave Neppl had he been given the chance. But he seemed to at least suspect that Neppl was taking the fall and that Irlbeck was paying the fine, since the financial component of his punishment was far more severe than the incarceration. Compared to the average jail sentence given to Eighteenth Amendment violators nationwide, Neppl was let off easy. Most judges who doled out prison time prescribed sentences closer to seven months. In contrast, Scott set the fine far above normal: the average amount levied for Volstead Act violations in 1931 was just $154.27.

For Wilson, the judgment—the whole case, in fact—was a much different experience than that of his counterparts out in Chicago.

When Capone again entered Judge James H. Wilkerson's packed courtroom on July 30, 1931, he did so expecting to be sentenced to a prison term of just two and a half years. That was what he thought was his agreement with federal prosecutor George E. Q. Johnson and that's what he thought was George E. Q. Johnson's agreement with Wilkerson. But Wilkerson surprised both of them.

"It is utterly impossible," he announced as soon as he took up the case, "to bargain with the court." Though the judge said he understood there was an agreement between Johnson and Capone, he felt that he was under no obligation to follow it. The maximum jail sentence for all of the crimes Capone had pleaded guilty to the previous month was more than three decades. Wilkerson seemed to be implying that the big fellow could get stuck with a significant portion of that.

After a long and animated discussion between Wilkerson and the two sides, the judge finally agreed to allow Capone to change his plea to not guilty. But he also added a few conditions of his own. He wanted the bootlegging conspiracy charge strengthened, so that if Capone was found guilty, he could face the stiffer penalties allowed under the Jones Law. He also demanded that there be no further bargaining between Capone and the federal government. Throughout the case, Johnson had kept most of his evidence against Capone close to the vest. Now the public would finally get a peek.

When the trial opened on October 6, 1931, everything indicated the case's exceptionalism. Again the halls of the federal courthouse in Chicago were teeming to the brink of overflowing. But the first real sign that the case would be unlike any other was the change

Judge Wilkerson made just after starting the proceedings: subtly, and at the last possible moment, he took the list of names from which the trial's jurors were supposed to be drawn and switched it with that of another judge. Word had come from federal investigators that somehow Capone had obtained a list of prospective jurors and in the days before the trial had sent out his cronies to try to bribe or intimidate them, with the hope that they'd have at least one juror in their pocket in case the others wanted to convict.

Once Wilkerson swore in the twelve men chosen as jurors, Johnson and his team of lawyers surveyed the selection and seemed pleased. Capone's lawyers, however, registered a distinctly different reaction: they were horrified. They had wanted men from the city, men who fashioned themselves urbane, cosmopolitan, progressive—men who, of course, drank and who would feel no animosity against Capone simply because he openly violated the liquor laws. What they got was the opposite: a farmer from Clare, a place whose sole distinction was the fact that it actually had a name; a country store owner from the village of Prairie View; a pair of painters and decorators from the small towns of Wilmington and Libertyville. Only one of the jurors was from the city of Chicago. None were younger than forty-five.

Capone's counsel knew enough to not complain about the jury's demographics in open court, but the newspapers summed up what were likely the defense's thoughts the next day. "Capone is to have no trial by his peers," wrote a reporter for the *Chicago Tribune*. Damon Runyon, the writer and reporter who had made his name mining the Prohibition era's characters and colloquialisms, drew an even more disdainful portrait. From the jury, he wrote, he got a "fragrant whiff of green fields and growing rutabagas and parsnips," and saw a slew of "horny-handed tillers of the fruitful soil, small town store-keepers, mechanics, and clerks, who gazed frankly interested at the burly figure of the moon-faced fellow causing all this excitement and said, 'Why, no: we ain't got no prejudice again Al Capone.'" Of course these men were bumpkins and illiterates, he seemed to be saying: they were same type of people who voted in the inane Prohibition law in the first place.

But turning the trial into a referendum on Prohibition was something Johnson wanted to avoid—and accordingly the lawyers working under him focused their arguments on the minute details of a tax case, not the sensationalism that typically filled stories involving "Snorky" Capone.

In his closing argument, Johnson seemed to strive to imbue those arguments with the same sense of gravity that more typically accompanied much more violent crimes. "The government has no more important function, except in the emergency of war, than to enforce the revenue laws, and if the time ever comes when people will pay taxes only when the government seeks to find out what they owe, or when it begins an investigation of their affairs to determine their tax, the government will fail, and organized society will revert to the days of the jungle, where every man will be for himself," he said.

For their part, Capone's lawyers accused the government of going after Capone purely because of the hype and infamy that surrounded him. They implored the jury not to let their client go to jail "merely because his name is Al Capone." "You," one of the lawyers said to the jurors, "are our only bulwark that can resist oppression." In a way, they were asking the jury for the same forbearance the Carroll courts gave their own bootlegger—the forbearance that gave him a pass for violating laws that most people in the community didn't think should be laws to begin with.

On October 17, after both sides rested, the jury went into deliberations. They stayed there for eight hours. When they returned, they announced that they'd found Capone guilty of three felonies and two misdemeanors. The next week, Wilkerson delivered his sentence: eleven years in prison, a $50,000 fine, and court costs amounting to $30,000. The sentence was the most severe ever given to someone convicted of tax fraud.

Generally, the *Chicago Tribune* reported, news of the sentence was "greeted with jubilation" on the streets. "Many expressed regret that the punishment was not more severe. All were unanimous in declaring the sentence to be a reversal of the gang stigma on the city," the paper reported.

Back in Fort Dodge, Iowa, Neppl began his sentence at the Webster County jail on June 20. A week later he asked to be transferred to the Carroll County jail so he could be closer to his family, a request the court quickly granted. For Neppl, the situation could have been a lot worse. He could have received the maximum jail sentence under the Jones Law and been incarcerated for up to five years in a federal penitentiary—convicts from the Midwest were often sent to Leavenworth. Instead he was released on August 18, just in time for harvest. With all the cash he'd earned over the last two years, he could still support his family, even if the corn growing in his fields didn't.

Irlbeck, meanwhile, resumed bootlegging. If anything, he was more confident that he could stay beyond Wilson's reach—the scrutiny of the last few months had done nothing more than convince Joe and Lauretta that the government was ignorant and dumb.

While Wilson was certainly disappointed that his case against Irlbeck, a case that had seemed so tight, had fallen through, he wasn't discouraged. And his associates didn't see him as dumb. A few days after the case closed, Harry M. Reed wrote to George C. Parsons, praising the work of Wilson and Burris over the previous few months. Reed, new to his position as a government prosecutor, said that he had already found the agents working under Parsons to be "efficient and earnest, interested in their work and anxious to do a good job." He added, "I have been very favorably impressed by all of you."

Wilson also didn't wait long to send another reminder to the Templeton bootleggers that he was still hunting them. Exactly a month after the initial grand jury hearing, the agent busted another large Carroll County distillery that would later be associated with Irlbeck. That raid was just the first in what would become an intense crackdown in Carroll County as officers circled closer to Irlbeck.

At some point after the June acquittal, the kingpin and his nemesis met each other on the street by chance. Wilson was coming from a raid. "It's another one just like yours, Joe," he said.

"You didn't find any of my fingerprints on it, did you? Did you, Frank?"

"No, but I will keep trailing you. I will get you sometime."

"Well, I doubt you will, but if you do Frank, it will be on the level, won't it?"

"Oh, yes."

"No stool pigeons, right?"

"Right. I am going to get you and I am going to get you flat-footed."

No stool pigeons. The two men shook hands and parted ways.

11

UPHEAVAL

As Irlbeck was busy dealing with the loss of one of his largest and longest-running distilleries on the farm of Frank Neppl, he was increasingly busy with another crisis with one of his most important partners, Des Moines liquor boss Kenneth Sonderleiter. The trouble had started back in the spring of 1930, when the sordid details of Des Moines's booze-fueled criminal underworld first burst into public view.

Iowa's capital city was certainly not as ridden by violent crime as Chicago, Detroit, or New York: comparatively, it had seemed small-town peaceful. But there had been hints before that the traffic in booze—delivered to guests in their rooms at Hotel Fort Des Moines, to politicians and media men in the city's swankier hangouts, and right to the door of retail customers of every stripe in every neighborhood—was not free of the gangland strife that was Prohibition's most shocking product.

Residents' first glimpse that the liquor trade was controlled by gangsters different only in number from their big-city brethren had come in late 1925, when newspapers reported on injuries sustained by Sonderleiter. Sonderleiter had spent six weeks in the hospital recovering from a fractured leg and internal injuries received in a confrontation with rival bootleggers. It was his second skirmish that year with gangsters trying to usurp his throne.

Several months later, he was present when a shipment of liquor appeared at a battery shop he owned east of downtown. When he later claimed that he at first had no idea where the liquor was from or why it was there, he may have actually been telling the truth. Almost immediately after it arrived he heard a commotion break out outside. Then there was pounding on the door. Then the cops broke in. They filed through the shop and discovered the package of booze.

Sonderleiter was arrested and the evidence turned over to the grand jury. He didn't deny that he had illegal alcohol in his possession, but he claimed he was innocent. The liquor wasn't his, he said; he'd been framed. He speculated that whoever sent it had called the cops as soon as it arrived. Amazingly the grand jury, perhaps out of gross ignorance or pedestrian complicity, believed him. They threw out the case and he went back to bootlegging, apparently as powerful as ever.

For the rest of the decade, Sonderleiter remained at the top of the Des Moines liquor racket, his operation disrupted by no more than a few arrests, a few fines, and a few weeks in jail. But at the start of the new decade, his long streak on top—in an occupation that mostly produced short ones—finally ran out.

The story of his turn of fate was revealed in two headlines, double-stacked and divided by a narrow band of an article covering the most salacious bits, that altogether took up nearly half of the front page of the *Des Moines Tribune-Capital* on Monday, April 28, 1930.

The violence that tantalized the paper's readers had begun a few days earlier, on Thursday, when, for the second time, a load of alcohol being shipped to Sonderleiter from a gang in Chicago was hijacked after it entered Des Moines. Together the two hijacked shipments were worth around $4,000; the Chicago gang was furious.

With no possible recourse to the police, the gangsters resorted to settling the score themselves. As soon as word reached Chicago about the hijacking, the syndicate dispatched two thugs to

Despite being the well-known chief bootlegger of Des Moines, Kenneth Sonderleiter, who regularly brought truckloads of Templeton rye to the capital, managed to mostly stay out of legal trouble. Even when a dispute over a missing shipment of booze turned into a violent public sensation, he avoided conviction on his apparent crimes. *Copyright Des Moines Register and Tribune Company; used with permission*

Des Moines, one of whom was named Clarence Campbell. Their mandate was clear: either return with the liquor or return with the money to pay for it.

When the two Chicago men arrived in Des Moines, they enlisted the help of Sonderleiter, who told them he suspected the culprits were two "widely known" local bootleggers: Jimmy Dickerson and Jack Harris, both of whom the *Tribune-Capital* said had "a reputation of being 'square shooters'" and were "extremely popular among local bootleggers." Opinion on the street was that Harris and Dickerson were innocent. But that didn't stop Sonderleiter and his Chicago accomplices.

On Friday night, the three dressed up as federal Prohibition agents, went out to Dickerson's house in one of the city's fashionable west-side neighborhoods, and knocked on his door. When Dickerson answered it, they barged in. First they searched the entire house—just as Prohibition agents would—but found nothing. Furious, they dropped their cover and confronted Dickerson about the stolen booze shipment. They wanted to know how he was involved, if he knew who took it, where it was currently. In response, all they got was more frustration; Dickerson claimed he had nothing to do with the whole affair. So Sonderleiter and the two thugs informed Dickerson that he was coming with them. They were going to take him for what had already become one of gangsterdom's more euphemistically veiled violent traditions: "a ride."

This ride started out with Dickerson being handcuffed and pushed into the back of a car. He was driven out to an empty lot four miles away and yanked out from the vehicle. Once more, Dickerson denied he knew anything about the stolen booze. One of the three men then grabbed Dickerson, his wrists still bound behind his back, and threw him to the ground. Between kicks to the side of his stomach, his head, his back—whichever surface of his body was facing the assailants' boots as he writhed—he continued to tell them he knew nothing.

Now enraged not just by the theft of the booze but also by Dickerson's refusal to confess, the three men decided a beating was not enough. One flipped Dickerson facedown and stomped on his back while another went back to the car for a rope. When he returned, the men dragged Dickerson under a nearby tree, fastened one end of the rope around his neck and looped the other around a branch, and slowly hoisted him up.

As Dickerson coughed and moaned, Sonderleiter continued grilling him—adamant that he knew something about the hijacking. When Dickerson finally looked like he might pass out, the man heaving him up let go of the rope and let him fall back to the ground, limp. They then circled him and started kicking him again. Campbell also grabbed a pistol, and slammed the butt into Dickerson's jaw.

Still he refused to confess, so they stopped the beating, sat him up, turned him so they were yelling to the back of his head, and told him they had a new game to play. It was called "on the spot." He probably knew it. But in case he'd forgotten they explained the rules again. They were really quite simple: He had until the count of three to confess. If he didn't, he'd be shot in the back of the head.

Campbell stepped a few paces back and aimed his gun at Dickerson's bloodied hair. He counted to one, then two, then three. Still Dickerson remained silent. After a beat, Campbell shot. The bullet struck the side of Dickerson's head, cutting into his flesh but glancing off the side of his skull.

When Sonderleiter, Campbell, and the other Chicago ruffian realized that they hadn't killed him, they looked at each other, confused. They huddled together and in an unnecessary whisper they first agreed that Dickerson was nothing but a liar—a brave liar, but a liar nonetheless. Then they tried to figure out what to do next. They decided that if Dickerson wasn't going to tell them what they wanted to hear, they should try his partner, Jack Harris, instead. But first they had to get to Harris. Dickerson, they realized, was their key.

They went over to the bloody, beaten Dickerson and picked him up. One of the men pulled out a strip of cloth and tied it loosely around his eyes. Then they dragged him back to the car, threw him inside, and drove off. When they arrived at Sonderleiter's palatial home, Dickerson was still conscious and managed to count the number of steps between the ground floor landing and the basement where he was led. Through a crack in the blindfold he noticed a distinctive pattern on the basement's floor. He'd later pass the information on to the police, further evidence connecting Sonderleiter with the crime. For now, though, he was still terrified.

In the basement the threats against Dickerson continued as one of the men passed him a phone and told him to give a call to that man Harris. They ordered him to tell his friend they needed to meet, to tell him it was urgent. Under threat, Dickerson did.

Perhaps Harris could detect the fear in Dickerson's voice, or maybe he'd already heard rumors that some Chicago muscle was in town, or maybe the request was one he never expected from Dickerson. But before he left for the rendezvous, he found another man to go with him for protection. And he took one of his fastest cars.

As Harris and his partner approached the meeting point, they noticed an unfamiliar car—one that didn't look like anything Dickerson ever rode in—pull up in front of them. Harris stepped on the gas and sped away, convinced that something bad had happened to Dickerson. Once he'd lost the other car, Harris drove around Des Moines, dropping in on friends he trusted, friends he knew to be loyal, and told them what had happened. He asked them if they would help find Dickerson. Several of them agreed. And throughout the night and until daybreak they drove up and down the streets of Des Moines looking for anything out of the ordinary. They even pulled over a few suspicious cars and questioned their drivers about whether they had any connection to Dickerson's disappearance or these reputed Windy City hoodlums who were in town. But they didn't manage to find anything.

In the meantime, Sonderleiter and his two associates decided they had gotten all the use out of Dickerson they were going to get; they drove him out to an abandoned lot and threw him out. Despite the severe beating and the gunshot to the head, he managed to walk home.

Cooped up the next day—unable to resume their investigation again until nightfall—Sonderleiter, Campbell, and Campbell's partner were simultaneously furious about Dickerson's lack of cooperation and scared about what would happen if they couldn't come up with either the booze or the money. Twenty minutes after sunset that evening, Dickerson's phone rang. About this thing, let's "arbitrate," the caller said, requesting Dickerson and Harris meet him on another street corner.

Remarkably, the two bootleggers went. When they arrived, Harris opened the driver's-side door and stepped out. Before he could slam the door back shut, the first shots rang out, one of the bullets striking Harris in the back, tearing through his spinal cord. Quickly Dickerson himself jumped out with a shotgun in hand. He spun around and spotted Campbell several yards away and got off a few rounds before he had to duck out of the way of Campbell's bullets. Campbell, crouched on the sidewalk with a row of buildings to his back, seemed trapped.

As the gunfight continued, Campbell made his way to the entrance of a nearby drugstore. With Dickerson closing in, Campbell tried to push his way inside, but before he made it all the way, a hail of buckshot hit his face, one of the balls of lead piercing his cornea. He fell backward into the store, blood covering his face. He then stumbled up and ran behind the clerk's counter. He soon realized that that place wasn't safe enough either, so as soon as he found the door to the basement, he pushed it open and fled down the stairs. Right behind him was a police detective who happened to be in the drugstore running errands.

The detective found Campbell cowering behind a furnace, distraught. He told Campbell he'd agree to try to protect him if he turned over his gun. Campbell, grateful to not be shot at, did.

As the sirens of approaching police and emergency vehicles grew louder, Dickerson charged into the drugstore waving his gun, demanding to know where Campbell was. "He went through the back," one of the clerks replied. Dickerson ran back out.

Before he got far, however, he was stopped by several police officers and arrested. As he was led away in handcuffs, he saw a stretcher hauling Campbell out from the drugstore. Farther away, other emergency workers were attending to Harris, who was in even worse condition. Not long after, Sonderleiter was arrested. The only man to escape without a trip to the hospital or the jail was the second Chicago man, who vanished—possibly returning to his bosses in Chicago, possibly disappearing for good.

Almost immediately news of the shootout spread through both the Des Moines criminal class and the city's more upstanding residents. Meanwhile those who considered themselves "in the know"—fluent in both the lingo of the underworld and the jargon of journalists—predicted that a spate of gunfights worse than the city had ever seen would soon erupt if Harris died of his wounds, in which case, they said, Harris's friends wouldn't settle for anything less than the death of Sonderleiter. It seemed as if an all-out gang war was ready to commence, bringing to Des Moines, Iowa, everything people feared about the gin-fueled violence of the big city.

After surviving the night in the hospital, Harris did die. But by that time Sonderleiter was locked in the county jail, being held on $50,500 bail. He was charged not just for the shooting of Harris but also for the kidnapping of Dickerson and for liquor possession; police had found a quart of alcohol at Sonderleiter's home when they went to arrest him.

Despite the predictions, no large liquor war broke out. Perhaps because he realized he was safer in jail than at home Sonderleiter didn't make bail either. His protection remained the obligation of the state as the case against him and Campbell, who was also being tried for Harris's killing, maneuvered through the court system. Both men pleaded not guilty and Campbell's case came to trial first. Before it began, prosecutors lowered the charge against him to manslaughter. However, the jury's decision did not bode well for Sonderleiter; Campbell was found guilty and quickly sentenced to eight years in prison.

Prosecutors also decided to try Sonderleiter on the lesser manslaughter charge, hoping that with that low bar they could convince a jury that he conspired with Campbell on the murder. But the case took an odd turn soon after both sides finished their opening arguments. Either Sonderleiter had one of the most persuasive attorneys in the county or one of the most sympathetic juries, or something shady had passed behind the scenes, because as soon as the prosecution rested, the defense did as well. They didn't call a single witness.

The jury took just three hours to deliberate before notifying the judge they'd reached a verdict. When everyone returned to the courtroom, the foreman stood up and announced they'd found

Sonderleiter not guilty. But he was also still under arrest for the kidnapping and liquor charges, and despite the jury's pronouncement, he was led away in handcuffs.

Originally the county attorney seemed intent on pushing those two prosecutions forward. But after Sonderleiter was released on bail (which was lowered once he was cleared of the manslaughter charge), the case seemed to fizzle, the government's commitment to his downfall apparently as transitory as that of Harris's friends. As the attention drifted away from Des Moines's rum kingpin and key Templeton rye patron, a more adamant enemy of alcohol trained his sights on Sonderleiter.

John Brown Hammond—descendant of the same family that produced the infamous John Brown who was hanged after raiding the federal arsenal in Harpers Ferry, Virginia, in a failed attempt to procure weapons for the abolitionist movement—was known as "an uncompromising foe of liquor" and credited with drafting nearly every one of Iowa's liquor and vice laws. Capable of directly attacking saloons with Carrie Nation–like passion, in his long career he'd taken on pharmacy liquor-dispensing and drinking by bums in addition to his work against what he saw as the social ills of professional boxing, marathon dancing, and apartment living. But in 1931 his crusade was focused on fighting "near beer" that he thought was a little too near the real thing.

By the time he'd arranged to have fifty cases seized from Sonderleiter in the middle of June, he'd already lost two other court battles on the same issue. Sonderleiter's would be the third. After dragging Des Moines's most renowned bootlegger to court, in front of a jury, a chemist's report revealed that the near beer contained only one-third of 1 percent of alcohol, just below the limit of one half of 1 percent allowed by the Volstead Act. Again a jury released Sonderleiter as a free man.

But as Hammond was busy with his crusade against barely legal beer, Prohibition agents were busy building a case against Sonderleiter that included evidence of him selling liquor that actually was intoxicating. Sometime around April, an undercover Prohibition agent managed to infiltrate Sonderleiter's organization. And over the course of just a few months, he documented the storage, transportation, and sale of hundreds of gallons of whiskey, alcohol, and beer by Sonderleiter, his wife, Faye, and several associates. Combining those findings with evidence from previous investigations dating back to 1929, the federal government, on September 17, 1931, charged Sonderleiter and his associates with conspiracy to violate the Volstead Act. Kenneth and Faye were arrested almost immediately after local authorities learned of the indictment.

The announcement of the arrest sent shockwaves through Des Moines's drinking class, not so much because the city's main bootlegger was now out of business—everyone knew there were plenty of others eager to take his place—but because the federal authorities announced that their undercover agent had recorded, in a little black book, the names of nearly two hundred of Sonderleiter's customers. Among those pages were rumored to be the names of several prominent Des Moines citizens. The feds let it be known that in the event the case came to trial, many of those listed would be subpoenaed to testify.

If the federal prosecutors were trying to intimidate Sonderleiter into pleading guilty to protect his customers, the ploy seemed destined for failure. As the case drew near, the worries of those customers wishing to remain anonymous seemed valid. Sonderleiter pleaded not guilty and let the case proceed to trial.

Perhaps neither he nor his lawyer had any idea how extensive the evidence against him was, or perhaps his customers managed at the last minute to pressure him into keeping their names secret, but after the jury was drawn and the federal prosecutor gave his opening statement, Sonderleiter changed his mind and pleaded guilty. Almost exactly a year after a jury exonerated him of killing Jack Harris, Kenneth Sonderleiter was finally headed to prison.

As he was being led into the courtroom the day of his sentencing, Sonderleiter was stoic—a stark contrast to his wife, who already had tears running down her cheeks as she walked in beside him. Before Judge Charles Dewey delivered the sentences, he heard from the Sonderleiters' lawyer, who argued for leniency for Faye. "She didn't want to get into the liquor business in the first place and she urged Kenneth to drop it several times," he said. He then reminded the court that the Sonderleiters had a three-year-old son, but "no relatives on either side who are in a position to accept responsibility for the boy." As for Kenneth, the lawyer merely stated that he believed his client was finished with bootlegging and wouldn't reenter the racket, no matter what the judge decided.

Perhaps Dewey believed the vow, because though he could have sent Kenneth to jail for seven years and fined him up to $20,000, he settled on just two years in Leavenworth Penitentiary and a $2,000 fine. For Faye, he issued a jail sentence of one year and one day, to be carried out at the new women's reformatory in Alderson, West Virginia. He also fined her $1,000. Dewey's judgment upset Faye even more. As she was led out tears began pouring down her face, and she cried out, "It isn't fair. It's an awful thing to have to face." Her husband simply told onlookers good-bye, adding, "It's a tough break."

Though Sonderleiter told the officer at Leavenworth preparing his intake report that his son could actually stay with his grandparents while he and Faye were in prison, the image of a mother being pulled away in tears from her young child shocked the people of Des Moines.

Just a few days after the Sonderleiters' sentencing, a woman who never revealed her name to court officials delivered to the court clerk a stack of paper for Judge Dewey. In it was a short petition asking for Faye to be paroled on account of her young son, and following were two hundred signatures from people around Des Moines, including, the *Des Moines Tribune* speculated, the "names of some of the city's leading citizens in business, financial, and church circles"—a description that almost perfectly matched earlier ones of the contents of the undercover agent's little black book. But it was too late. Faye was already headed to Alderson.

Kenneth, meanwhile, was at Leavenworth. When the deputy who'd taken him there returned to Des Moines, he said the bootlegger left him with a tip. "Capone's men, of Chicago, they are trying to muscle in on the liquor business in Des Moines," the officer said Sonderleiter had warned. Already they'd been to the city a few times to check things out, Sonderleiter revealed. He told the officer that from his perspective, with him in jail, it seemed like a good moment for them to take over.

For Des Moines's drinkers, the arrest of Sonderleiter came at a poor time. Just as he was being sent to Leavenworth, many across the capital city would have been adding a few extra bottles, maybe even cases, and requests for a few special items to their orders in preparation for the holiday season. Instead of stocking up, however, many past buyers—frightened the feds would come after them next and without a trusted person to buy from anyway—decided to forgo their orders. Demand plummeted 50 percent, but because there was no central force controlling the trade, prices simultaneously spiked at $4.50 to $6.00 a gallon.

Sonderleiter's prediction that someone would try to take over in the void he left proved correct. A few weeks after his organization was dismantled, some gangsters approached the city's remaining bootleggers with a proposition: in exchange for a $1.50 surcharge—one-third of which would even go to a legal defense fund—they'd stabilize prices at $8.50 a gallon. The proposal, the *Des Moines Tribune* reported, threw the city's bootlegging industry even further into chaos. Most bootleggers seemed just fine working on their own, rather than paying some goons a significant portion of their profits. For a while, the syndicate tried the well-honed tactic of violence and intimidation. Deliverymen for bootleggers who hadn't joined were beaten and shot at. But the holdouts stood firm, and in a couple of weeks the police moved in.

The six men they rounded up were run-of-the-mill miscreants, a bank robber, a murderer, and a batterer among them. Most of them were Des Moines residents, when they weren't spending time in prison elsewhere. By all appearances they had no connection to Capone's gang in Chicago, which had become, itself, something of a shamble after George E. Q. Johnson put Scarface Al in jail.

The disruption in the Des Moines liquor market did little in and of itself to slow the business of Templeton's whiskey cookers. By 1931 word of Templeton rye had spread, via word of mouth and press accounts, as well as the little labels bootleggers had at some point started affixing to their bottles once the product became too well known for them ever to hope to hide its place of origin from the feds. Certainly the bootleggers who replaced Kenneth Sonderleiter knew where it could be found, and Irlbeck normally had plenty of other buyers waiting for his booze. Not only did he sell it to large bootleggers like Sonderleiter, but he also did a brisk retail trade out of the parking lot of Templeton's Joyce Lumber Yard, which had been one of the first buildings in town. But sometimes those retail customers didn't stay retail customers.

One day a traveling water pump salesman out from headquarters in Denver stopped in the area with a flatbed truck full of his wares. After spending the afternoon pitching customers throughout Carroll County on his particular brand of centrifugal pumps, he stopped in Templeton to have a bit of Templeton rye. As he was drinking, he got to thinking, and after a glass or two, he got an idea. "By God," he said to Irlbeck, "I am going to take a keg of this along to Denver."

Once the two men loaded it onto his flatbed, he headed off on his six-hundred-mile journey back to the Mile High City. But he didn't stay away for long. When the keg ran dry, he came back for another. And then he returned for an entire load. And shortly thereafter, he decided that he'd been peddling the wrong product all along. After he quit his job at the pump company, he became a full-time rumrunner, hauling loads from Templeton to Denver as often as twice a week.

Though there were several people in town who frequently worked as rumrunners, Joe Irlbeck would occasionally make deliveries himself—hauling a few of his five-gallon cans of whiskey with him when he traveled to Chicago to gamble or attend a baseball game at Wrigley Field. And that booming and diverse Templeton rye trade was now, more than ever, critical to the farmers who were desperate for the money bootlegging brought in—so long as their customers still had money to buy.

The farm crisis of the 1920s had seemed so intractable and so pernicious that when the stock market crash actually came, some Iowans responded with optimism. Finally, they exhaled, after a decade of wild growth in the cities, of the urban riches of the Roaring Twenties denominated as they were in paper stock certificates, sanity would return to the market. Money, people, and focus would return to rural America, where value was concrete and indisputable: the world's most productive land spilling forth bushel upon bushel of grain, the staff of life.

In some, that optimism persisted well into 1930. But as the decade closed in on its first full year, it began, like a seedling in a drought, to wither. By 1931, it had died. Neil Schaffner, owner of an entertainment troupe that traveled through the small towns of Iowa, pegged the date of when everyone realized something truly horrible was wrong at two days after Independence Day 1930. That evening, after a strong summer, he opened a new show and sold almost no tickets.

Others logged their own markers of when the economic situation turned from dire to despairing. In his report on the state of the 1931 crop year, Mark G. Thornburg, Iowa's secretary of agriculture, wrote that there was "no argument necessary to show that it is an impossible situation." But he made that argument anyway: "In 1929 farms had a net income of $2,774; in 1930 a net income of $763; and in 1931, a deficit of $818," he wrote. "The red ink figures were shown despite the fact that farmers raised more pigs per litter, secured more eggs per hen, and tended more crop acres per man than they did in 1930."

Emphasizing the point, a farmer up in the northwest corner of the state noticed that a grain elevator across the border in South Dakota was still buying corn—sort of. Its price: negative three cents. "If you wanted to sell 'em a bushel of corn, you had to bring them three cents," he explained. Meanwhile, agronomists at Iowa State University calculated that to heat their home for a winter, a family would need to raise ten acres of corn. They'd have to burn it, too; coal was too precious. The onset of the Depression also stretched the social fabric of Iowa's communities. In some it was pulled taut into a rigid, impenetrable shell. In many others, it tore. On January 2, 1931, the banner headline space in Carroll's newspaper let up on reporting on liquor busts to cover another crime, locally considered much more serious: animal thefts. Readers learned that four men had been arrested on charges of operating a hog-stealing "ring" that spanned four counties, including Carroll. In the article, Sheriff Frank Buchheit and one of his deputies were lauded for having been "working on the matter day and night for two weeks." Several times they even had to stay out all night on stakeouts, displaying a dedication they had never shown in going after bootleggers. The courts followed their lead: four days later readers learned that three of the men who'd pleaded guilty had already been sentenced. Each was sent to prison for a term of five years.

As the Depression wore on, thieves across the state became more desperate and turned their attention from farm animals to other farm properties, and a rash of violent robberies, especially of elderly couples on isolated farms, broke out. In some cases the criminals made away with several thousand dollars in cash—money the farmers kept at home, because they figured it was safer there than in deposits with the local bank, which always seemed on the verge of failure.

But the Depression also pushed Iowa farm families toward amazing shows of community spirit. Iowa farmers owed twice as much money to creditors as farmers in other parts of the country—carrying more than $1 billion in debt. And through the Depression, the spate of foreclosures that started in the 1920s only increased. In many places, farmers had had enough. In an attempt to strike back against what they saw as unfair foreclosures, they began staging what came to be known as the penny auction.

The premise was simple, if daunting: when it came time to auction a farmer's belongings, his neighbors—hundreds of them—would come out, as they had always done for farm auctions. But unlike before the Depression, when the auctioneer called out the first item, there would be no fervid bidding. In fact, there would be almost no bidding at all. A few may throw out a lowball price, two dollars for a mare worth forty, fifty cents for a mower, a quarter for a cultivator. But those bids were just for solidarity, a door held open for the farmer whose property was being sold off to step through and buy it all back for pocket change. Eventually, though, the protest actions turned violent. As farmers became increasingly desperate for prices that at least covered the cost of production, they set about trying to withhold products from market. The first hint of violence came in February 1931, when farmers in northeast Iowa escalated a long-simmering debate over the testing and condemnation of cattle for tuberculosis. Farmers started gathering in the hundreds to intimidate veterinarians sent out by the state, smashing the officials' windows and slashing their tires and vowing more violence. The governor finally felt that he had no other option but to declare martial law. The farmers set up machine gun battlements and federal troops stormed in to subdue them. Though the event never escalated to killing, it was quickly dubbed the Cow War.

The Cow War presaged the violence that would come later, led by the irascible Milo Reno, an Iowa farmer and clergyman who founded the Farmers' Holiday Association. To protest high taxes, foreclosures, and low commodity prices, farmers who were members of the association vowed to withhold their products from markets until the situation improved. To enforce the strike, they blockaded roads, dumping milk and destroying eggs from trucks trying to pass through. To enforce their checkpoints they wielded guns and pitchforks and were quick with a fistfight. In one place, they hijacked a butter truck and smeared the cargo all over the road, creating an oil slick that sent other vehicles straight into the ditch. But the only death from the movement's protests was that of a young man driving a truck laden with milk cans. He was so eager to not be stopped that he ran a blockade and as he did he was shot. The truck came to a careening halt and the farmers who stopped it jumped on and began pouring out the contents of the milk cans. The odor hit them instantly: the cans were filled with bootleg whiskey. The Farmers' Holiday Association achieved little, at least directly. Prices rose not in the least. But the skirmishes did draw attention to the plight of the farmers, a plight that a writer for the *Nation* who was sent out to check on the situation said was so dire that it was as though a "shadow of peasantry hangs over them." And under that shadow, the country's decade-long obsession with liquor started to seem a bit absurd. For the starving, rag-ridden unemployed, alcohol began to not look very threatening. As the nation's social fabric began to fray, so did the facade of Prohibition.

In 1930, the influential *Literary Digest* magazine sent a poll to its twenty million subscribers asking them whether they favored enforcing the Eighteenth Amendment as it was, modifying it to make it less strict, or repealing it all together. One-quarter of its readership responded and of those who did, nearly 70 percent favored a softening or an ending of the law. Iowans—as they always seemed to be—were more evenly split between enforcement and modification or repeal. Though the results were in no way scientific, and may have been skewed further by a boycott by the drys, they still captured a snapshot of the animosity against strict Prohibition. And similar polls from other publications came to similar results.

There were other signs that support for Prohibition was unraveling. The country's political and especially business elite were increasingly pushing back, arguing that legal alcohol could be taxed and the revenue from that tax could be used to significantly reduce or even eliminate the income tax that they hated so much— or perhaps, as the Depression worsened, bolster the revenue-starved federal government. The Wickersham Commission, convened by

President Hoover to study lawbreaking in America, meanwhile concluded that in regards to Prohibition the nation was far from dry; instead, across the country there was a "virtual local option." Statistics showed just how far from the letter of the law the American public had drifted in its relationship to alcohol. They documented staggering increases in the consumption of corn, sugar, and yeast, which were mingled, doubtlessly, in countless stills—tiny and personal, behemoth- and syndicate-owned—throughout the country.

And then there was that little Christmas decoration that the tiny town of Templeton had strung up over its main street the winter after Sonderleiter and Capone were nabbed.

12

"XMAS SPIRITS"

The holiday season was always the bootleggers' busiest time. People who drank, drank more. Even people who didn't usually drink made an exception for Christmas dinner and the New Year's celebration, or they picked up an extra bottle for that visiting relative who didn't like to pass an evening dry.

Nineteen thirty-one had been a hard year for Templeton's whiskey cookers, starting out with the spectacular arrest of Frank Neppl and worsening with the conviction of one of Templeton rye's main patrons, Kenneth Sonderleiter, and the turmoil caused by his removal from the Des Moines liquor market. And then there was the Great Depression, the ravages of which managed to weaken even the market for booze.

In the weeks before Christmas, Iowa newspapers reported that liquor prices across the state were volatile. A reporter for the *Des Moines Register* wrote that his sources were predicting yuletide prices of $7.50 to $10 a quart at retail, but that actual prices were lower. Others were telling him that "Iowa rye whiskey" could be had at a discount for $4 a quart, but he wrote "a well known drinking dry in Western Iowa informs me it is selling at $4 a gallon."

"Or," he wondered, "is it a bull market?"

Maybe it was this speculation over the possibility of low prices that made Templeton mayor Dr. Otis P. Morganthaler decide that what his town needed was a little advertising for its best-known export. Or maybe he just wanted to remind the bootleggers that after such a difficult year they still had the community's support. Maybe he could see that public sentiment had shifted against Prohibition, or maybe he just thought that in the depths of the Great Depression, people could use something to joke about, something to distract themselves from all the grimness around them. Maybe he just wanted to flaunt the feds' failings. Regardless, as he contemplated that year's town Christmas decorations, he came up with, or someone suggested to him, a clever little pun they could incorporate into the garland they planned to string from lamppost to lamppost across Main Street: a little cardboard cutout of a whiskey jug, identifiable by its fat, round bottom and domed top, with a corked spout directly in the center, next to a little looped handle. Scrawled across the side was XMAS SPIRITS; below, a little Christmas tree. It was innocent yet incriminating.

Jovial, mischievous, round-faced with sparkling eyes, a protracted bachelor (and thought by some to be a bit of skirt chaser), Morganthaler had quickly become one of Templeton's most prominent citizens after he came to town in 1916, twenty-six and just out of the medical school at the Jesuit university of Creighton in Omaha. As his medical practice thrived, he invested some of the money he wasn't spending on fishing poles, guns, or hunting and fishing vacations in southern Canada on property downtown.

When Prohibition began, he was working out of the same building where whiskey cooker Victor Clemens Schwaller used to run his auction business, butcher and whiskey peddler John Kaus used to keep his books, and jeweler Henry Vermeule became so angry about the burgeoning bootleg industry that he decided to write a letter to the attorney general. Morganthaler was one of the few people Vermeule didn't implicate in his letter, but if the doctor wasn't then one of Templeton rye's prime customers and most committed boosters, he soon would be.

Templeton, sitting high along the ridge from which streams flowed on either side to the rivers bordering the state, had suffered, since its founding, a scarcity of one of the three main ingredients needed for whiskey production: water. To conserve that resource, the town's water service was often shut off overnight. But shortly after he became mayor in 1928, Morganthaler decided to reward his constituents by turning the water back on at midnight—right about the time when many of the town's bootleggers would be ready to refill their mash tanks or fire up their stills.

Over time, he also became more involved in the liquor industry—helping bootleggers find buyers and kicking in some money to help with the bail of those arrested. None of that activity drew much notice outside of town. But the Little Brown Jug, as the Christmas decoration came to be called, was a sensation.

For its Sunday-morning edition on December 20, 1931, the *Des Moines Register* sent a reporter and photographer to Templeton to check out what was certainly the most provocative Christmas display in the state. The photographer snapped the image that would go top, center on that day's issue, showing the Little Brown Jug strung up high over downtown. In the street below was parked a car, in apparently good enough condition that it very well may have been paid for with, as the caption stated, "that product that made the town of Templeton, Iowa famous."

The reporter, meanwhile, sauntered up to the locals to dig up a bit of information, and a bit more lore, on Templeton rye. Of course, he had to feign ignorance, affect stealth. Identified only as a "staff writer" in his byline, he began the story by stating that "any conclusion as to the significance of the Little Brown Jug is purely a matter of conjecture, of course, but any visitor too dumb to understand can readily be enlightened by residents here."

"After a visit to Templeton I can say that I know no reason why anyone should be compelled to leave here either thirsty or empty-handed. Roughly speaking, prices are said to be $8 for the aged rye and $5 for raw distilled whiskey, but the first man encountered as I paid my first visit to Templeton informed me that he could get me all the good stuff I could pay for at not to exceed $5 a gallon."

If the reporter—or his informants—were right, that going rate was about equal to what Joe Irlbeck usually charged for a gallon (the man who offered to sell the liquor could have easily been, in fact, either Joe Irlbeck or Steve Smith, both of whom were often seen downtown chatting up customers, even small-volume purchasers). Nonetheless, he stated that Templeton's bootleggers were optimistic going into the holiday season.

"The little brown jug trade is bringing Christmas cheer to those engaged in Templeton's best known industry," he wrote. "Had it not been for a recent upturn in the Templeton rye business cycle, many a child of distiller and bootlegger might have had to go without Christmas toys. But there is a Santa Claus, after all, and the stimulus of purchases by those who want a bit of a nip for holiday cheer has lifted business."

Indeed, if the point of the Little Brown Jug was to advertise Templeton rye, it certainly succeeded in spreading its fame. After the *Register* article, newspapers across the country picked up the story, writing short blurbs about the little Iowa town and its brand-name bootleg. But the decoration's audacity brought more than just Christmas cheer.

The *Chariton Herald-Patriot*, out of a south central Iowa town ten times larger than Templeton, but still small, wrote that Templetonians might be proud of their "sacrilegious bit of yokelry," but "to decent people the effluvium from their cadaverous conception of cleverness is most nauseating."

Charles W. Nelson, Methodist, Republican, future state legislator, from the tinier-than-Templeton town of Packwood, meanwhile, suggested that the governor send in the militia. In response, the *Manning Monitor* printed a sneering, sarcastic column asking why such a solution hadn't been thought of before. For, surely, the column went on, the way to "wipe out booze and crime" in "these Verunreinigen Staaten"—word play on the German "Vereinigte Staaten" (the United States), meaning more-or-less "defiled lands," or, as the paper also wrote, "Templeton, this Sodom and Gomorrah"—was to beg the governor to indeed send in the state militia, and order it "to shoot every man, woman, and child in Templeton" and to not forget "to shoot the little babies and children that

The town of Templeton celebrated Christmas 1931 by stringing up a cutout of a little brown jug of the sort in which they often sold their whiskey in as a decoration over Main Street. After an image of the provocative display was printed in the *Des Moines Register*, outraged drys throughout Iowa called on officers to finally rout Templeton's bootleggers; mostly, though, the brouhaha served to spread word of Templeton rye even farther. *Copyright Des Moines Register and Tribune Company; used with permission*

are born and reared in Templeton, so that they may not carry on the work." The subtext of the *Monitor*'s column was, of course, that wiping out Templeton would hardly do anything to put an end to the rampant Volstead Act violations—the real problem was, as it always had been, demand. But it couldn't come out and say that.

After the harsh backlash, Templeton residents started claiming the Little Brown Jug had been put up purely in jest—a response to all of what they characterized as false rumors floating around the state that Templeton was a bastion of bootlegging. "If a bootlegger from the western part of Iowa is arrested anywhere, the report is: It was found in his possession so many gallons of 'Templeton Rye,' whether it's 'Rhubarb hootch' or whether the fellow arrested knows where Templeton is located or not," another resident from Templeton wrote in complaint, trying to argue that the town was full of nothing but "the spirit of brotherhood, neighborliness, and obedience to the law."

The first two claims were completely legitimate. The last—well, no one was going to buy it, anyway. Especially not the feds. Just as the controversy in the newspapers was dying down, they retaliated. On a cold winter day in the middle of January 1932, twenty-two agents swept into town, as they had done in such large numbers only a few times before. Perhaps they arrived at one of the few times when Irlbeck and the town's other bootleggers, after a busy holiday season, were dry. Or, perhaps, as so frequently happened, someone tipped off the bootleggers. Regardless, for all their show, their only significant arrest was Felix Greteman, the son of grocer Frank Greteman. And all they caught him with was a mere sixteen gallons of bootleg whiskey.

Greteman was arrested with his whiskey in what was known around town as the "White Elephant Building," a massive structure that covered four city lots and was originally built to be a Ford dealership with money from several investors, including the Monsignor Frederick H. Huesmann. The building proved overly ambitious—something the investors learned the winter after they finished construction when they still failed to keep the building heated after burning two entire train-car loads of coal. As a result, they decided instead to subdivide the building and lease it out to a number of different businesses—a repair shop, a cafe, and a temporary barber shop, among them. But none of them would appear to be a magnet for a bootlegger peddling his wares.

Not long before Greteman's arrest, however, a new tenant had moved in, one that perfectly complemented hip flasks and spiked beer: a boxing arena. At least one night a week, men from throughout Carroll County would come out to fight, including one of the town's blacksmiths, Wendell "Weed" Hacker, who not only built some of the finest stills in town but was also a bootlegger himself. Hacker kept his still in a washroom set off the side of his house—a fact everyone learned when, one day, a giant explosion rumbled through town. Flames shot from the building, and Hacker shot through the side boards of the washroom. A few who saw the explosion would later claim he hit a cherry tree as he arced through the air. Fortuitously he landed not far from Dr. Morganthaler's office and was rushed inside. He survived the disaster, but spent the next several weeks in a full-body cast.

It was just one example of Hacker's good luck. In March 1932 he and his family left Templeton to run a cafe in Storm Lake—putting nearly seventy miles between him and his old hometown, at a time when it was just becoming infested with feds. Throughout the summer, federal Prohibition officers, state agents, and Audubon sheriff Fred Clemmensen together busted someone in the whiskey business nearly every week. They went after not just the whiskey cookers but also small-time dealers who had only a pint or two on them when they were arrested. But those arrests were just a sideshow—a display of force, possibly punishment for mocking federal power with the Little Brown Jug.

The real investigation was being carried out by B. F. Wilson—who had made another break in his case against Irlbeck almost as soon as the bootlegger sneaked from his grasp the year before thanks to the loyalty of Frank Neppl, Frank Schreck, and Templeton's businessmen. Exactly one month after the start of that frustrating grand jury hearing that ended with Irlbeck being set free, Wilson had found himself yet again in a hog house on a farm near Templeton, counting barrels of whiskey mash, and searching for gallon jugs of Templeton rye.

July 16, 1931, was another sweltering summer day—the thermometer at Carroll's weather station hit 94 degrees Fahrenheit before it started, ever so slightly, to drop. The meteorologist didn't bother noting whether there was a strong breeze, a light breeze, or no breeze at all. But even the slightest little gust would have been a welcome relief for Wilson and his partners Joe Alberts and J. J. Ingalls as they sat in their car, waiting near the driveway of farmer Adolph Lenz for him to return home.

How they knew he was due back that day from Fremont, Nebraska, they never said. Perhaps Lenz's wife, Anna, or his son Martin, or stepson Alfred had told them the day before—but if one of them did, the officers kept it a secret. Just as they apparently kept secret their knowledge of Lenz's bootlegging operation, once he finally returned and they followed his car down the driveway.

When Alberts, a Prohibition investigator out of St. Paul, Minnesota, questioned Lenz about it, Lenz didn't try to deny it. He immediately confessed, pointing to the nearby hog house, and telling the officers the stills and mash tanks were in there.

Only they weren't. Unbeknownst to Lenz, several hours earlier, Alfred had been shaken awake by Joe Irlbeck. "Hey, kid," Irlbeck said, when Alfred had woken, "I need you to go out to the barn, hitch up a team of horses to the hay rack. Hurry." Alfred jumped out of bed, and once he'd readied the team, he led the horses over to the hog house, where Irlbeck, Steve Smith, and another one of Irlbeck's employees were busy taking apart the stills.

Earlier that morning, Irlbeck's employees had shown up—as they had done several times since they set up the still on the farm in May—with a load of sugar, intending to distill the mash from the fifty barrels they'd mixed up a few days before and while doing so refill those barrels for yet another batch. Except when they arrived, they noticed something suspicious. As a precaution, at each of Irlbeck's still sites, his employees were instructed to place a small sliver of wood or a match above the door before they left, situating it so that it would fall to the ground if anyone opened the door in between their visits. At Lenz's that morning, they noticed that the marker had fallen and concluded that someone must have been snooping around. They went and found Irlbeck and told him they thought someone had been in the building; he ordered them to clear it out.

The stills, one holding six hundred gallons and the other one hundred gallons, they moved a half-mile out into a cornfield; the gas burners from underneath they disassembled and hid in Lenz's house; and their tools and other equipment they gathered up and hid throughout Lenz's farm, wherever each piece looked like it could be for some legitimate purpose. But the twenty-five hundred gallons of fermenting rye and sugar mash presented a problem. Moving so much liquid was next to impossible, especially since Irlbeck did not want to linger and risk getting caught hanging around one of his illegal distilleries again.

They could dump it, taking a loss on a threat they were not totally sure of, but they would still have to take it someplace where it wouldn't be found—the mash, after all, wouldn't just soak into the ground and disappear without leaving some evidence behind. In the end they decided to leave it. If there was a raid, the feds would destroy the mash, but at least they wouldn't find Irlbeck's expensive copper stills and other equipment and destroy them too.

At least that was their plan. The only problem was that Irlbeck and his men failed to cover their tracks. Once Lenz confessed to running a still, Wilson placed him under arrest, and then went with him to the hog house to check out the setup. As they walked past the barrels of mash, which held fifty gallons each, Alberts asked him how much booze he got from each barrel.

"Four to six gallons," Lenz replied.

Alberts continued his questioning when they reached the hog house, expecting to find the stills. "Well, where are they?"

"I don't know. I don't know, they were right here before I took off for Nebraska yesterday," Lenz replied.

"Oh? They were? And yet now they are not," Alberts said.

Remembering the terms of his deal with Irlbeck—that he could, under no circumstances, incriminate his boss—Lenz didn't offer an explanation as to how the two large stills suspiciously disappeared from his own hog house while he wasn't there. Instead he told them that he only just got the stills set up last week. "I haven't even ran a batch of whiskey through them," he told Alberts.

It was an odd claim to make. As if he could insist that he didn't really know anything about the booze business, as if he could believe in his naïveté that maybe that was just something stills did: disappear. Alberts jumped on the statement. "If you haven't ran a batch of whiskey through, then what did you mean when you said a few minutes ago that you got four to six gallons of whiskey from each mash barrel?" he asked.

"Oh, well, I mean, that's what I was told," Lenz stuttered. It was all lies. Irlbeck had actually told him that he'd yield six to eight gallons of Templeton rye from each fifty-gallon barrel of mash; the four to six number Lenz had first offered to the agents was the actual yield—calculated as the average for the 1,488 gallons of booze Irlbeck's men had already produced over five runs of the stills, a figure Lenz knew off-hand because he'd instructed his wife to write down in a ledger each gallon Irlbeck produced.

But at that point, whether Lenz's stills had actually been used didn't really matter. The agents had him with the mash. And, as they walked out of the hog house, Ingalls noticed something else: two tire tracks trailing, seemingly aimlessly, northeast from the hog house out into the middle of a cornfield. Ingalls, with Lenz in tow, followed them until they ended. There they found the two stills, as well as three coils of copper condensing tube. Meanwhile, Wilson followed another set of tracks to a ravine just under a mile from the hog house and there found a dumping ground for some of the spent mash that Lenz claimed was never produced.

Two days after the raid, Lenz was arraigned in the federal courthouse in Fort Dodge, charged with possessing materials for making booze "intended for use by him." Representing him was William Irving Saul, the lawyer who'd begun the Prohibition era as Carroll's county attorney, prosecuting bootleggers like V. C. Schwaller, but had left public service and by the end of the decade formed a partnership with one of the largest rumrunners in the state to build airplanes. Now he was working for the kingpin of Templeton rye. The judge set Lenz's bail at $1,000, but bondsmen were quickly found to cover it and Lenz went free that day.

When his case came to trial in November, Saul instructed him to plead guilty. He did. And the judge fined him $500, which Saul quickly paid—all without Saul billing Lenz a cent. "That deal cost me a lot of money," Irlbeck later told Lenz, when he learned about the judgment. With the cost of the defense, and the fine, and the lost mash and still, it certainly had. But Irlbeck hadn't gotten caught—nowhere in the case filings did Wilson note that he had any evidence suggesting Lenz might be working for Irlbeck or anyone else. Irlbeck's system had worked—or so he thought.

And it didn't turn out too bad for Lenz either. It certainly could have been a lot worse. As it was, he had his freedom and he had the more than $700 he'd earned from Irlbeck. But by the time the case was over, he had other problems to deal with. At the beginning of the year he'd gotten married to Anna. It was a second wedding for each of them. Both of their previous spouses had died a few years earlier—Anna's, the longtime Carroll barber John Beck, in 1928, after a series of heart attacks. Widowed, Anna moved into Lenz's house near Wall Lake, thirty miles north of Templeton, with her two younger children to work as his housekeeper. And within a year or two, a romance had blossomed.

After they were married, they moved onto the farm near Templeton that would be raided later in the year. Anna had objected the very second Adolph told her he'd partnered with Joe Irlbeck to have a still placed in their hog house. But Adolph said it wasn't a decision that was open to discussion. Furthermore he told her she'd have to prepare meals for the whiskey cookers and find a place for them to sleep whenever the still was in operation.

Apparently the argument over the still was just the first of their disagreements as husband and wife. By the middle of December, the marriage was over. Anna was allowed to revert to her old name. As alimony she was given their household goods and $500 cash. She also took with her the knowledge of who really ran her ex-husband's liquor operation.

Was it as a last act of revenge that she went to Wilson with that information? Or did Wilson swoop in to exploit a fraught situation? Or was it Adolph who decided to spill the particulars of his partnership with Irlbeck and hand over that little ledger book (and why hadn't he immediately destroyed it, anyway)? Wilson never made any note in any of his trial records how he got the explosive testimonies from the Lenzes that he managed to take down after their divorce. He included nothing about who approached whom, why they talked, or if he cut them any deal (though if Adolph agreed to one, he didn't agree to very much). All he did was write down detail after detail about who worked for Irlbeck on Lenz's farm, what they did, how much Templeton rye they produced, and when they made it.

Between his interviews with Anna and her son Alfred, and Adolph and his son Martin, he learned the names of four of Irlbeck's main assistants and documented the production of five batches of Templeton rye totaling nearly fifteen thousand gallons of sugar and rye mash. It was an amazing break, the first time since Audubon sheriff Andrew Jorgensen arrested John Schultes in 1927 that one of Irlbeck's partners was willing to actually implicate Irlbeck himself. Perhaps it would have been sufficient to build a case on. But Wilson had been burned enough times, and after nearly a decade of trying to dry out Carroll County, he was finally coming up with leads.

In the same article the *Des Moines Register* published about Templeton's Little Brown Jug decoration and its liquor scene, the reporter burst a popular myth about buying booze in Templeton. Though several of his sources told him that no one would sell him Templeton rye unless he could find another known buyer to vouch for him—to say he was a straight-shooter, not a cop, not a stool pigeon—the reporter found the only introduction he needed was a wad of cash.

Competition, desperation to make a sale in the face of slackening demand because of the Depression, a general lack of vigilance after dodging the feds for so long—all could explain why Templeton's bootleggers were lax. Even Irlbeck wasn't as careful as he should have been. As Millard Lowman told the story, it was the first of December, 1931, and he was at a dance at Terril, Iowa, one hundred miles north of Templeton and a fifth of that from Spirit Lake, standing around with a few other guys talking about liquor. "You know where you can buy the best whiskey," chimed in one man whom Lowman claimed not to know. "Templeton. Yep. I used to live there, it's a fact, Templeton makes the best whiskey you can buy anywhere."

"Oh, really," said Lowman. "You know of anyone I can get some from?"

"Yes, Joe Irlbeck. Go see Joe Irlbeck."

Then the man pulled a small slip of paper out of his pocket, wrote on it "Joe Irlbeck—This man is all right" and, instead of signing his name, made some sort of "peculiar mark" on the note. "Here," he said, handing the note to Lowman. "Take this to the Joyce Lumber Company there in Templeton, say you're there to see Joe Irlbeck, and they will fix you up."

When Lowman and his wife, Geneva, pulled into the lumber yard a few days after the dance in Terril, Millard walked in and was greeted by one of the store's employees. He handed over the card, and said he wanted to talk to Joseph Irlbeck.

"Wait here," the man said. He picked up the phone, told the person he was calling that "there is someone here who wants to see you."

Ten minutes later, Irlbeck pulled up. "Come with me outside," he said. "Where are you from?"

"Wallingford, up near Estherville," Lowman replied.

"All the way up near Minnesota, huh? What do you do up there?"

"Farm."

"And what brings you to Templeton?" Irlbeck asked.

"I want to buy some whiskey, heard you had some for sale," Lowman said. "How much does it cost? Is there a discount if I buy a lot?"

"Five dollars a gallon, any quantity," Irlbeck replied.

"I'll take twenty-five."

Irlbeck then told Lowman to wait around for a bit while he went to go get the liquor. Fifteen minutes later Irlbeck returned and told Lowman to drive around back and pull up alongside his car. When Lowman did he noticed that in Irlbeck's open trunk there were several wooden kegs and about forty one-gallon cans. Irlbeck lifted one of the kegs on top of his car, lined a few cans up along his running board, got out a hose, and began siphoning booze out of the keg and into the cans. When he finished, Lowman handed him $125 and drove away.

If anything during the transaction seemed even the slightest bit strange to Irlbeck, it wasn't enough to make him suspicious that Lowman was anything but a farmer who perhaps peddled a bit of booze on the side. In the next few weeks, Lowman returned to Templeton and purchased a total of ninety gallons of Templeton rye from Irlbeck, paying him $450. Then he went to Wilson with the details.

Lowman was no government man—at least not officially. But in the last years of Prohibition, he'd started working as a snitch. Maybe it was part of the bargain he made a couple of years earlier with the judge who had agreed to suspend his fifteen-year sentence for forging a ten-dollar check. Maybe he'd been arrested in the intervening years on some other charge—before his eventual suicide, he'd add larceny, auto theft, more check forging, and a draft violation to his criminal résumé—and, desperate to not have his probation revoked, said that he could deliver information on some bootleggers. Regardless, the information was critical for Wilson—it gave him evidence that Irlbeck didn't just manufacture whiskey but sold it as well.

Wilson made one other break in his case against Irlbeck, and though it didn't exactly prove anything illegal, or add much directly against Irlbeck, it did help to show just how involved the people of Carroll County were in protecting the lawbreakers. On March 18, 1932, smoke, then flames, started billowing out of a small shed in Templeton. The alarm went out across town and volunteer firemen and neighbors rushed to the scene. When they arrived, they found Irlbeck's assistant Steve Smith reeling in pain, with massive burns covering his body.

As they waited for Dr. Morganthaler to arrive, they watched the building burn to the ground—powerless to stop the fierce fire raging inside. Morganthaler rushed Smith to the Wyatt Hospital in Manning. The doctors stabilized Smith, bandaged his wounds, gave him some painkillers, and let him rest a bit. Then one of the hospital's employees came by his room to ask him questions for the form required of all patients. But Smith refused to answer nearly all the questions. He wouldn't give the hospital much of his medical history, or details about the injuries. He even refused to tell them his nationality. And he continued to do so over the next two weeks he spent there recovering.

But plenty of people around Templeton already knew exactly what had happened. As demand for Templeton rye increased, and storing large amounts of whiskey became riskier, Irlbeck had started looking for ways to speed up the aging of his liquor. The solution he came up with was terrifying: Over a roaring flame, he hung a barrel of booze from chains and let it swing back and forth. The sloshing and the heat he believed made the whiskey develop the flavor of a high-quality aged product far quicker than if he just let it sit around. It certainly imparted more of the flavor from oak barrels than a solution other bootleggers used, mingling rusty nails in with their unaged liquor to give it color. But it was far riskier (and also would have resulted in significant evaporation, as bootleggers around the country learned when they devised their own variations on the process).

Wilson found one reluctant Carroll County resident who said he was willing to testify in front of a grand jury that the building was, in fact, used as an aging plant, but the man refused to sign any statement and was hesitant to actually talk to anyone other than Wilson. Wilson ran into even more trouble when he contacted the state fire marshal's office for the report that every local fire department was supposed to submit detailing the cause and damage done by any fire in their district. The report was missing, and seemed as though it had probably never been filed.

When Wilson asked Templeton's fire chief about the incident directly, he learned that the chief had indeed interviewed Smith about the fire. Smith told him the fire started because of gas that pooled on the floor from a leak in the fuel line, and that eventually the puddle grew so big it reached the burner and ignited. But the chief apparently never asked Smith about what, exactly, he was doing with an open burner and so much fuel in the tiny little shed. Finally, in the middle of June, Wilson managed to secure a search warrant for the property where he believed the plant had been. When he arrived he found a newly built garage. When he inspected the ground around it, he saw what to him looked like charred remnants of an earlier building. Upon entering he found a few whiskey kegs of the type used by Templeton's bootlegger and a bill with Steve Smith's name on it that had been left lying about.

He considered going to Dr. Morganthaler with the evidence and asking him what exactly he knew about the incident—but by then he'd already figured out that no operation as big as Irlbeck's could operate in a place as small as Templeton without permission from the top. If he was going to get any information from Morganthaler, he decided, it would have to be when the mayor was in front of a grand jury, under oath. He added the notes to his file, satisfied that he finally had enough to press the case forward.

Early in December 1932, Wilson sat at his desk, typing up his findings, struggling a bit with the spelling and the grammar—a fault that had plagued him his entire career, but one that others now rarely noted; his fellow agents, in their periodic evaluations, were much more likely to comment on his thoroughness and accuracy. He wove together a story of Irlbeck's operation, starting with the arrest of John Schultes in 1927 and bringing up the case at Neppl's, in addition to the testimony from the Lenzes, Millard Lowman, and witnesses to the explosion at the suspected aging plant.

As he wrote down the details of his investigation, he could probably see a few of the weaknesses already. He couldn't, for one, put an exact figure on the amount of alcohol Irlbeck produced, or the number of farmers with whom Irlbeck had worked. Really, he realized, he couldn't say for sure that Irlbeck wholly owned the stills—only that he did so "at least in part." He probably wished he could keep the investigation open, wished he could go out and find more stills, more buyers, more evidence to strengthen his case. But he also knew that he didn't have much time. As he signed his name at the bottom of the report, he knew, as everyone across the nation knew, that it was time for Prohibition's last call.

Whether the case would be enough to finally nab Irlbeck would depend on the federal prosecutor, the grand jury, and the judge.

13

A SHORELESS SEA

On October 4, 1932, President Herbert Hoover stood in front of a "heckle-proof" crowd of ten thousand carefully selected Iowa Republicans in the Des Moines Coliseum. His first term was almost up. The election that could bring him a second was just a month and a few days away. He'd delayed formally starting his campaign as long as he could, arguing that the nation's economic crisis demanded his unbroken attention, but with his opponent, New York governor Franklin Delano Roosevelt, rallying countless supporters around the country, he finally decided it was time to enter the race.

Though the crowd applauded when it was meant to and looked on intently when it was supposed to be silent, Hoover's speech would be considered by many to be droll, pedantic, and defiant—haunted as it was by the comment he had made a little more than four years earlier, when he was merely the newly minted Republican nominee for president. "We in America today are nearer to the final triumph over poverty than ever before," he had declared in those more optimistic days. "The poorhouse is vanishing from among us."

On the other side of the Coliseum's walls, out on the streets of Des Moines, the proof of just how disastrously wrong he had been was the more interesting spectacle. There, nearly two thousand Iowa farmers and wage laborers, their wives, and their children, attired in tarnished overalls and worn work clothes, drove in rusted-out pickup trucks, chanting and holding signs protesting Hoover's response to the Great Depression that had so quickly set in and destroyed so many of their lives.

Just how much the nation had changed during Hoover's four years as president was captured, in part, by the leaders of the rally: Iowa Republican senator Smith Wildman Brookhart, among the country's most outspoken drys, and Milo Reno, leader of the borderline militant, fiercely populist Farmers' Holiday Association.

Noticeably absent was attention to either side of the liquor question. Prohibition was still an issue; the election again offered a wet candidate and a dry candidate. And Hoover was undoubtedly the dry candidate, even though he had stated previously that he was opposed to Prohibition as it currently stood, and that he planned to bring back beer if elected. It was just that, as Brookhart's presence in the rally against the president showed, the economy, not Prohibition, was the defining issue of the election. And it doomed Hoover.

The returns on Election Day, November 8, 1932, came in quickly and were overwhelming. In a record national vote, county after county, throughout nearly all the country but the Northeast, voted for Roosevelt.

The New York Times called the election a "political cataclysm," as strongholds of the Republicans fell to the Democrats. Among them was Iowa, which voted against its native son by a margin of almost 20 percent. The returns in Eden Township, which never cared much for Hoover in the first place, were even more stark: of the 460 votes cast, all but 14 were for Roosevelt. And it wasn't just in the presidential election that Democrats swept the state. The party won at all levels of government, from the governorship on down.

The wets responded, as expected, with jubilation. Many had noticed that the results were so strongly in their favor that not just a weakening of the Volstead Act but its outright repeal was now a possibility. In one of the more colorful phrases uttered during the Prohibition era, Morris Sheppard, the US senator from Texas who'd authored the Eighteenth Amendment, had declared toward the end of 1930 that "there is as much a chance of repealing the Eighteenth Amendment as there is for a hummingbird to fly to the planet Mars with the Washington Monument tied to its tail." The wets, it would seem, were poised to achieve rocketry. But Prohibition wasn't over yet.

As the rest of the nation obsessed about Roosevelt's plans for ending the Great Depression and repealing Prohibition, Wilson didn't waver from his job. With his case against Irlbeck still working its way through his superiors, he was back out in the field. He even had a new job title: in January, he'd been appointed the acting deputy administrator for Iowa, replacing George C. Parsons.

As if to pay homage to the start of his career fighting bootleggers as a small-town sheriff, the career that had taken him to the top of the dry forces in Iowa, he returned to Audubon a few weeks after receiving his promotion to bust a few stills. On February 13, 1933, Wilson, along with two of his partners on the Neppl raid, F. H. Burris and Oscar Hanson, as well as Audubon sheriff Fred Clemmensen, drove toward the farm of Frank Thielen, a few miles east of the small town of Brayton, in southern Audubon County. As they pulled alongside Thielen's driveway, they stopped and rolled down their windows. They sniffed the air and would later claim they could smell the odor of fermenting mash. Whoever was driving then stepped on the gas and sped down the driveway.

The officials burst out of the car and ran toward a barn on the property. Knocking quickly, they pushed through the door. Immediately they were hit with an intense odor of not just distilling whiskey but nearly thirty thousand gallons of fermenting mash. They also startled twenty-four-year-old Carl Tacke, who said he was from Breda. Once they arrested Tacke, they began to catalog the equipment. In addition to the massive amount of mash, they found nearly a ton of corn sugar and close to one thousand gallons of recently distilled liquor. To process it all: a behemoth still. They estimated it was capable of producing around eight hundred gallons of alcohol a day. Altogether the contraband, they told newspaper reporters, was worth around $15,000. It was one of the largest raids ever in Iowa.

Normally, once the government was done with such property and had finished their investigation into the case, they would destroy it. But a month later, Clemmensen announced that he'd arranged to have the still and some of the other seized property transferred from federal custody into the possession of Audubon County. Two of the large vats were set up outside a county-owned farm to be used for grain storage and wooden boards confiscated from the operation were used to build storage bins for potatoes. Continuing with their clever streak of Depression-era resourcefulness, the county officials even managed to find a use for the still: they repurposed it as a giant boiler and used it later that year to can tomatoes from a community garden.

In earlier years, a raid that size would have been splashed across the front pages of area newspapers, just as the Neppl raid had been not that long ago. But in February 1933, all attention was on Washington. Exactly a day after the raid, Senate drys were in a desperate scramble to stop the anti-Prohibition amendment from moving through Congress. With Brookhart working behind the scenes, ready to take over, Senator Morris Sheppard began a filibuster that afternoon against the legislation. He rambled on in a slow, dry, monotone about the League of Nations for over eight hours. But eventually the drys' efforts failed and on February 16, the Senate voted to send the repeal amendment to the states. Brookhart was joined in voting against it by Iowa's other senator, Republican Lester Dickinson. The next week the House approved it, and government printers rushed the amendment off. As had been the case with the Eighteenth Amendment fourteen years earlier, the repeal amendment would take the next several months to be passed by two-thirds of the states. But Americans wouldn't have to wait so long for a legal drink.

Roosevelt took office on March 4, 1933, with a promise of action. In his inauguration speech that day, he talked mostly about finding a way to move the country out of the Great Depression. But implementing the policies to do that would take time. It was in regard to beer that the nation would see how swiftly he could move.

Within two weeks he'd pushed through legislation to raise the definition of intoxicating liquor in the Volstead Act from a strict 0.5 percent to 3.2 percent, high enough to permit beer. In another three weeks the law would go into effect. In Iowa, the bill provoked fretting. The fear wasn't over concern that the state would soon be awash in drunkards, nor that legal beer would put an end to one of the state's more profitable exports, Templeton rye, but, conversely, that legal beer would deprive Iowans of their beverage of choice since the start of Prohibition: near beer, which they liked to spike with bootleg whiskey. Once real beer returned to many other parts of the nation, Iowa would remain legally dry, as state prohibition was still ensconced in liquor laws enacted before the Eighteenth Amendment. And some drinkers worried that the brewers would give up producing near beer once they could sell real beer to much of the rest of the country. It was a non-problem, idle speculation at most, but that it would be talked about publicly at all showed just how anxious people had become for a drink.

April 7 was the day the change in the definition of intoxicating beverages was set to go into effect. Despite a straw poll from the *Des Moines Register* that found that Iowans, or at least those *Register* readers motivated enough to respond, supported beer legalization by nearly three to one, the state legislature still hadn't managed to pass a bill undoing the old prohibition laws in time. So once again the bootleggers stepped in. Reporters from many cities stated that 3.2 beer smuggled in from outside the state would be available for six dollars a case.

But for those who were tired of dealing with bootleggers, or who wanted to celebrate for once out in the open, without the worry, no matter how remote, of a raid, there were plenty of other options. Prospective revelers needed to only look at one of the maps printed in the newspapers around that time to notice that of the six states that bordered Iowa, four of them would be immediately selling legal beer. Apparently plenty did. And many of them noticed that the tiny community of Lineville, which straddled the Iowa-Missouri border almost directly south of Des Moines, wasn't really all that far away.

The first shipment of legal 3.2 beer arrived on the Missouri side of Lineville just after nine in the morning, consigned to the bar Jack Craney hastily set up just five hundred feet from the Iowa border. The place had a few long tables, a few four-tops, and no bar—the last a stipulation of Missouri law, which, in an effort to try to prevent the return of the saloon, banned not just that infernal piece of furniture, but singing and music as well. Patrons were informed they must remain seated at all times while drinking— another Missouri rule—but other than that there were few restrictions. The state hadn't even enacted a closing time and Craney announced he planned to hire two shifts and keep his bar open around the clock.

Most people didn't expect the shipment of beer to arrive as early as it did, thinking the brewers would be too backed up to deliver on time, so the first seventy-five cases weren't gulped down immediately. But Craney said he expected that by Saturday and Sunday he'd have well over one thousand customers, many of them from Iowa. Once they were soused and had had their fill, Craney would even sell them a case of beer to take back home for just $4.80.

Meanwhile, Iowa lieutenant governor Nelson Kraschel, eyeing the $400,000 to $500,000 in tax revenue legal beer was expected to bring in, announced that he would push through a beer bill as fast as he could. He was, he said, "sick of the prohibitionists." Not that they had ever managed to give him all that much trouble.

Kraschel was one of the Democrats who'd ridden the anti-Republican wave to office in November and prior to taking the job had been a livestock breeder and auctioneer in Harlan, located in the county adjacent to Carroll to the southwest. As it happened, Kraschel knew through his work Joe Irlbeck's older brother Frank, a specialist in valuing thoroughbred Poland China hogs.

When Kraschel realized that he and his running mate, soon-to-be Iowa governor Clyde Herring, were on their way to winning the election, he contacted Frank about purchasing a keg of Templeton rye to stock the Democratic party headquarters at Hotel Fort Des Moines. Frank passed the order along to Joe, and Joe, a committed Democrat, obliged—dispatching Steve Smith to personally deliver the whiskey.

Within a week of legal beer coming to the country, Kraschel had made good on his promise and cleared the way for it to flow into Iowa as well. As soon as they could, the Carroll city council opened a special session to approve the first nine applicants for licenses to sell beer by the bottle. They approved the first applications shortly after seven in the evening on Tuesday, April 18, and immediately afterward beer wholesalers began their deliveries. By midnight drinkers across the city were blowing foam off their steins of Country Club beer—the only brand initially available. Overall reports on the quality of the brew were favorable—though a few of the more seasoned drinkers found they still needed to break out a pint of Templeton rye to boost the potency a bit.

By the end of week, revelries in Carroll began to take on a pre-Prohibition tone. On Friday a group of musicians revived the old tradition of the "little German band"—a roving musical group that would go from bar to bar playing German folk songs. The only difference, the *Carroll Daily Herald* reported, was that "in this instance the band turned out to be quite a sizable organization instead of the customary six or eight pieces. Perhaps the possibility of 'treat' swelled the ranks.

"However the band members didn't trust their capacity or the power of the 3.2 because they were all afoot instead of afloat when the band ceased its labors."

On the first of June, the day the indictment was filed in Wilson's case against Irlbeck, New Jersey became just the fifth state to ratify the repeal amendment. If Irlbeck had been hoping that the law he was accused of breaking would no longer be on the books by the time his case wound up in court, he was going to have to find a different strategy.

In addition to Irlbeck, the indictment named Steve Smith, Adolph Lenz, Frank Neppl, Lawrence Long, and Ollie Weber, Wilson having found evidence that the last two were still hands. Together they were indicted on charges of conspiracy to violate the Volstead Act, rather than on any specific instances of their crimes, in part because both Neppl and Lenz had already pleaded guilty to the violations that made up the bulk of the case. Within days, arrest warrants went out for every one of the men except Lenz. He was confined to a hospital room, where he was recovering from a serious accident with a train. Again Irlbeck's talented defense lawyer William I. Saul had them all out on bail before they'd even spent a single night in jail.

Saul was known to be indefatigable. For the previous few weeks he had been feeling sickly, afflicted by a persistent cough and wheezing. But he also had more experience defending bootleggers than any other lawyer in the area and Irlbeck relied on him.

As he reviewed the indictment, Saul immediately saw ample room for attack. Despite all of the evidence from the two raids and his informants, Wilson still had only a hazy idea as to how, exactly, the conspiracy worked, exactly how large it had been, to whom it actually sold all its booze, and how long it had been in existence. Wilson had noted in his case report that the first time Irlbeck was implicated in a bootlegging case was in 1927 when he was arrested alongside John Schultes, but the conspiracy indictment failed to include that detail. Saul noted that the government couldn't even say whether the conspiracy was formed at a time when making booze under federal law was actually illegal. Furthermore it lacked the specific dates that Ollie Weber and Lawrence Long actually ran the stills, and didn't provide even a general estimate as to how much booze was produced on the farms of Neppl and Lenz. About the only solid details were a couple of documented sales to Millard Lowman, a man Saul wanted more information on.

As Saul was mounting his defense, the repeal amendment continued gathering momentum. Unlike the Eighteenth Amendment, when the question of ratification was decided in state legislatures, the Twenty-First Amendment was to be voted on by specially called state conventions—in part to diminish the outsized power rural politicians still held in many parts of the country. In Iowa the process worked like that of the Electoral College in presidential elections. First each county selected two delegates, one for repeal, the other against, then a popular vote was held to determine which slate of candidates would cast the official votes in the state convention.

The lead-up to the June 20 popular vote was a repeat of the campaigns preceding so many elections on the liquor question in Iowa. Only this time it was the wets who were fighting for change. When the vote was held, turnout blew away expectations, with 611,303 Iowans casting a ballot. Of those, 368,691 voted for the repeal candidates. In Carroll the margin countywide was well over double that of the state at large; in Eden Township it was significantly higher than even that: there were 403 votes for repeal, 11 against. Templeton mayor Dr. Otis P. Morganthaler, when asked about the result, said he was puzzled. Four of the anti-repeal votes he could account for; the other seven, though, were completely unexpected. "Confusion in voting," he guessed. He didn't even try to address the even more interesting question of why Templetonians would vote to overturn the very law they made so much money violating. Perhaps the answer was that they didn't see repeal as a threat at all. Maybe they figured that Iowa would never completely shed the dry yoke and hard liquor would remain illegal there, keeping their market open, but without the meddlesome feds. Or perhaps they had finally tired of all the attention from the public and from the agents like Wilson that Templeton rye had brought there.

Iowa, at the forefront with Maine and Ohio of the temperance movement for nearly a hundred years before the Eighteenth Amendment, was the first of those three states to support repeal. Even though the amendment was only halfway to passing, Prohibition enforcement was already waning. At the beginning of July, the Prohibition Bureau, facing a severe budget shortfall, furloughed hundreds of employees. Among them was B. F. Wilson, who was cut despite his offer to take a demotion and a lower salary.

Almost immediately after the bureau's announcement of Wilson's termination, letters from police officers, lawyers, and prosecutors throughout the state arrived at the desks of Wilson's bosses, informing them they had made a mistake. The very first letter to arrive came from Carroll sheriff Frank Buchheit. "It is not my place to tell you what to do," he wrote to Attorney General Homer Cummings, under whose Justice Department the Prohibition Bureau had been transferred, "but I can tell you that he is the best you ever had in the northern district of Iowa, and I believe, the best in the state. Even in this county, where sentiment is very strong against Prohibition, B. F. Wilson has had more success than any other agent, and still he is highly respected here. I never knew him to be unfair to any man." Despite all the other similar letters, the pleas were not enough to convince the bureau to immediately reinstate Wilson.

As Wilson was helping his longtime partner F. H. Burris take over some of his duties overseeing Iowa's Prohibition office, Saul was getting sicker. Over the weekend of July 8 and 9, Saul took a break from trying to press the government to hand over more evidence and went with his wife to Indiana to visit their daughter. As they were driving back on Monday, the delegates in Des Moines were casting their official ballots on the repeal amendment. Voting with them was the Sauls' fellow Carroll County resident, Dr. Morganthaler. By the time the Sauls returned home late on Monday, William was exhausted. He went to bed. In the middle of the night he was awoken by an excruciating pain in his head. His wife called a doctor and he passed out. For the next week he remained unconscious in the hospital. On Saturday he died.

The headline for the newspaper article announcing his death spanned the entire top of the front page of the *Carroll Daily Herald*, a distinction often reserved for only the most important of national news, or the most dramatic liquor raids. At just forty-six, Saul hadn't lost a bit of his boyish handsomeness, despite a life that could only be described as grueling. Before age twenty he was studying electrical engineering at Iowa State College. At twenty-four he was an editor at the weekly *Carroll Herald*; at twenty-five the owner of the *Breda News*. By the time he was twenty-six he was working as a clerk in his father's law firm, and he passed the bar two years later, all while managing a theater his father owned—a position he kept until he became county attorney in his midthirties. And he hadn't slowed down a bit by the time of his death. In addition to handling Irlbeck's liquor conspiracy case, he was representing Les and Barney Chapman in a similar case also being prosecuted on evidence obtained by B. F. Wilson.

The case against the Chapmans portrayed the brothers as operating a syndicate modeled after their counterparts in the big city. They seemed to care little about what they sold. Some bottles they filled with booze from stills they ran in Carroll and elsewhere in western Iowa, others they bought from bootleggers in Wisconsin and Illinois. Some of it was industrial alcohol that Les bought under the pretense of needing it as antifreeze for his auto business. Always, their booze was cheap—sometimes they sold it for nearly half what Irlbeck sold his for; often it was bad (and at times so bad that buyers refused to purchase any after trying a sample).

When they thought Millard Lowman, who also snitched on them for Wilson, stole $140 worth of their liquor, they kidnapped him. They drove him around in a Buick sedan, a sawed-off shotgun pointed as his face, demanding he pay for the liquor. If he didn't, they said, they'd kill him and dump his body in a nearby lake, shoving it under a sheet of ice for it to lie frozen until spring. In the end, however, they left the future key witness against them facedown in a cornfield at 4 AM, alive and unhurt.

Their organization proved to be nowhere near as close-knit as that of the Templeton bootleggers. While Irlbeck was indicted with just a few of his employees and a couple of his associates, the Chapmans' case touched four dozen, with even more willing to testify in detail against them.

With Saul's death, the case against the Chapmans was interrupted just as the one against Irlbeck was. Over the rest of the summer and into the fall, Lou Salinger, who replaced Saul as defense attorney in both cases, worked to catch up. As he did, ratification of the repeal amendment accelerated—winning approval in state conventions faster than anyone had guessed it would.

By November, when both Irlbeck and the Chapmans' cases again started to move forward, the amendment needed just over a half dozen more states for ratification. On November 20, Salinger filed a brief in Irlbeck's case expanding on the slew of deficiencies Saul had found in the government's case prior to his death. In fifty-six pages, Salinger attacked every aspect of the indictment. He harped on its lack of details, claiming the dates were so vague that the charges violated the defendants' Fifth Amendment rights against double jeopardy because the government could potentially charge them again, using specific dates in the new charge. He also attacked the government for its inability to provide even a general estimate as to how much booze Irlbeck's organization produced. Instead, the prosecutors relied on terms such as "large quantities," which he said were all but meaningless. Overall, the indictment was nothing but a "shoreless sea of generalities; a desert of conclusions barren of the smallest oasis of individualizing fact," he concluded.

Four days later, Irlbeck's case was called to trial and the defendants were asked how they cared to enter their pleas. Irlbeck and

Smith both pleaded no contest to the charges. Once they did, US Attorney Harry Reed dismissed the charges against Adolph Lenz, Ollie Weber, Lawrence Long, and Frank Neppl. Irlbeck was charged $750, Smith $250. It was the wholesale value of two hundred gallons of Templeton rye—about one-fifth of the booze the feds happened to find lying around on Neppl's farm when they raided it two years earlier. By all appearances, Reed could see Salinger had a point about the weakness of his case and cut a deal with Irlbeck and Smith.

The Chapmans didn't fare much worse. When Les and Barney, along with their brother Len and an associate in a separate case, pleaded guilty they were sentenced with fines that totaled $1,600. But the feds weren't done with them—another case was building, this one involving the breaking of a law that wasn't even remotely at risk of being repealed. They'd be back in court soon. As would Irlbeck.

But first the nation had a party to attend.

On December 5, the improbable state of Utah, the stronghold of the decidedly dry Mormons, ratified the repeal amendment. For the first time ever, one constitutional amendment had overturned another. No hummingbird went to Mars. But for drinkers the change brought by ratification was almost as remarkable. The jig with the bootleggers was up—gone were the days of having to be vouched for to make a purchase and of worrying that the liquor might be adulterated, toxic, or vile. One could enter a bar and really relax, knowing that the risk of federal agents bursting through a door, even if it had been slight before, was now nonexistent. And mobsters stopped killing each other over booze. Of course they didn't stop killing each other for good, but they were forced to move on to less morally acceptable sources of income.

Iowans were again hobbled by state law when it came to buying liquor, as they had been in regard to beer a few months earlier. But again there was an oasis just across the river. On December 6, an Illinois liquor distributor announced he would have a fleet of trucks waiting just at the base of the MacArthur Bridge, connecting the states at the ever-wet city of Burlington. They would all be full of liquor for parched Iowans. Toll collectors, meanwhile, were waiting for a swell of business like the one that accompanied legal beer, when receipts increased threefold.

But government-sanctioned booze came with a price. For thirteen years, drinkers had become used to buying booze tax free. And some weren't quite ready to give the government a cut.

14

THE BOOTLEGGERS' HANGOVER

As America notched off the months toward its first full year in over a decade as a normal liquor- and beer- and wine-drinking country, the saloon did not return. Abandoned little girls did not fill the streets as their fathers swilled away the family's bread money in the tavern. Booze-filled brothels did not invade the hollowed-out shells of abandoned churches.

Mostly a river of money just flowed straight into the federal government's coffers, at a rate that in 1934 averaged nearly three-quarters of a million dollars a day.

But in Iowa reports started noting that not everyone was embracing the new state-run liquor stores. One headline from a newspaper in northern Iowa summed up the problem, declaring, ONLY THE RICH CAN AFFORD LIQUOR. Liquor from the state-run stores, that was. As result, the article declared, "Templeton rye is being made in the state as usual and is being sold all over Iowa."

If anything, Templeton rye became more attractive after repeal, when the price started to fall, eventually settling between $3.00 and $3.60 a gallon. "Testimonials from old-time booze hounds as well as some of the younger amateur drinkers are to the effect that the Templeton product has the dollar and dollar and a half a pint state brands beaten by a mile," wrote a reporter for the *Audubon Advocate-Republican*.

Proof that Templeton rye was still flowing out of Joe Irlbeck's stills came that summer, when top assistant Steve Smith was arrested at a distilling operation about ten miles from Templeton with forty-five gallons of Templeton rye and three thousand gallons of rye mash. The crime was no longer producing the actual liquor, but doing so without paying any tax. Enforcing the new federal tax laws required, of course, a new federal division—the Alcohol Tax Unit, which scooped up many of the investigators from the obsolete Prohibition Bureau, including B. F. Wilson. On April 9, 1934, he was back on the government payroll, his new job not that different from what he'd been doing for the past decade.

Though he now did little investigating of his own, he oversaw the team that continued to track Irlbeck and his men. As they did, he also must have watched with interest the new case winding its way through the courts against the Chapmans. Shortly after being fined late in November 1933 for liquor charges, Len Chapman was indicted again, along with his brother Henry this time. The two were charged with jury tampering, accused of paying a juror $200 to stymie a conviction in an earlier bootlegging trial. Apparently, they were successful.

In the summer of 1934, however, they were found guilty on those tampering charges and given a sentence far harsher than the one they probably would have received for the original bootlegging charges. In addition to a $1,000 fine, they were also sentenced to a year in jail apiece. The juror whom they bribed was dealt with even more harshly: he was given a prison sentence double theirs.

While they were in jail, their brother, Les Chapman, continued on in the vice business. After Prohibition he established a network of cigarette vending machines across the state. To that business he brought with him the tenaciousness that had served him well as a bootlegger. He was even willing to fight parent-teacher organizations to make way for his machines.

Kenneth Sonderleiter, having served his time at Leavenworth, became even more infamous in his post-Prohibition life. After legal beer came to the state, he started a beer distributorship and quickly made use of the advantages of being in a legal industry.

A few years after repeal, he brought charges against a competing beer distributor, accusing the other man of trying to start a monopoly in the city by charging his customers a ten-cent-a-case "protection fee." He alleged that his competitor told his customers that in return they could operate on Sunday, in violation of the state's closing laws. If they were caught, he'd use his influence with state officials, garnered through large campaign contributions, to make the fines go away.

The chief of the Des Moines police dismissed the charges, however. "You usually hear those rumors when a fellow begins to develop a pretty good business," he said. "As soon as he starts to sell more beer than the rest, rumors that you have to buy his beer 'or else' fly thick and fast. Personally, I don't take much stock in them."

And neither, apparently, did the grand jury charged with investigating them. For the next half decade Sonderleiter continued to harass the police department, once even complaining that the city ought to go after the bootleggers dealing in tax-free booze that were cutting into his business. If they wouldn't, he said, he'd do it himself, and he filed papers to run as the city's public safety commissioner.

If his previous transgressions weren't enough, what he did next showed just how unfit he was for that job. He decided to start a zoo. He bought three monkeys, three armadillos, four opossums, two baby eagles, a squirrel, and some white mice. He planned to fund it with proceeds from the penny arcade he ran next door. At some point not long after opening, he realized that the zoo was a bit heavy on rodents and birds and quite lacking in things that people actually go to zoos to see, such as lions. So he bought two lions. As winter approached, the nation was embroiled in the Second World War. And though Sonderleiter wanted to build a shelter to keep the lions (Dolly and Nero) warm during the winter, the War Production Board denied him the materials to do so.

Heartbroken, he said, over the thought of them suffering through one of Iowa's frigid, windy winters, he threatened to kill them instead. In the spirit of not letting anything go to waste, however, he vowed not to just throw their corpses out. Instead, he said he planned to turn them into the zoo's newest attraction and money-making scheme: lion burgers, grilled fresh. What actually happened to the lions that winter went unrecorded. But Sonderleiter's zoo continued for another decade, acquiring over two thousand animals, including a black panther with a habit of escaping. Finally the operation overwhelmed him and he wanted to be rid of it. He asked the city of Des Moines to take it over. When the request was refused, he threatened to cage all the animals and dump them on the steps of City Hall. Still the councilors never relented. He eventually closed it down.

Joe Irlbeck was arrested for the last time on November 11, 1936. He was in a garage in downtown Templeton with ten gallons of Templeton rye. The law, it seemed, had finally caught up with him directly—this time there was no one for him to hide behind, no one to claim the alcohol wasn't actually his. "You are going to have to do at least a year in jail," one of the officers involved in the arrest told him. "For the time you've gotten by, you are looking at a year to five."

Irlbeck was terrified that now that the government finally had an unmuddled case against him, it would use the opportunity to treat him harshly as recompense for all those years when he got off with just a couple of fines. When he went to his father for advice about what to do, his father told him it was time to get out of the business. It was time to go legal. "There's a tavern for sale here in Dedham," he told him. "Why don't you buy that? If you need money, there is money here for you."

As Irlbeck thought it over, he realized his father was right. Even if he did sit through a year in jail and go back to bootlegging, how much longer could it last? How much longer would people keep buying bootleg whiskey? He now had a family, was a father himself. He and his wife, Lauretta, had adopted a daughter a few years earlier. How much longer could he keep taking risks? He decided he had to find a way out.

In the meantime, the last of the bootleggers' stocks of Templeton rye began to run out. Just before Christmas that year, the *Des Moines Register* decided to send a correspondent to Templeton to find out why. Just as his colleague had done five years earlier, when he came to gawk at the Little Brown Jug, the reporter cast about the town, asking about their famous product. What he discovered was just how much the place had changed. "The once mighty flood has been reduced to a forlorn gurgle," he wrote. "Gone is the merry song of corks popping from the little brown jugs of Templeton rye. If you ask for whiskey in Templeton they refer you to the state liquor store at Manning." Irlbeck had stayed in the business longer than most other bootleggers and now, without his booze, the town, likely for the first time ever, was without a place to buy hard drink—at least for outsiders.

"'Templeton rye,' once the much-counterfeited symbol of bootleg quality, has been relegated to the back country from which it sprang to national fame during Prohibition."

One day while Irlbeck was free on bail, he came up with an idea as to how he might beat the charge. He went to visit the sheriff in Carroll. "Does Agent Wilson ever come around here, or do you know how to get a hold of him?" he asked.

The sheriff offered to call Wilson up right then, and when he did and Wilson heard that Joe Irlbeck of Templeton wanted to talk to him, he agreed to come down the next day. Irlbeck figured that Wilson thought he was going to try to cut a deal with the government, to rat out a few of the other bootleggers he had worked with over the years. But Irlbeck was no snitch.

"Look," Irlbeck said when the two men finally met, "I got a chance to get out of Templeton and I want to get away from this racket all together. I've got a chance to buy this tavern, but I think I have to do some time on this arrest. And I am afraid I am going to have to pass up the opportunity to get out."

"Joe," Wilson replied. "If you got a chance to buy that tavern, you go ahead and buy it. I know once you quit you are going to be through with it. As far as doing time, when your plea hearing comes up, I'll be there and I'll take you into the district attorney's and the judge's offices and tell them about how you are all cleaned up and done with the bootlegging business." He asked if Irlbeck could stand to pay a $200 fine.

"Yeah," Irlbeck replied. "I think I can."

During the late winter months and into the spring, Irlbeck worked readying his bar to open. He installed new floors and ordered his stocks of beer.

Then on June 8, 1937, Irlbeck showed up at the federal courthouse in Fort Dodge to learn whether he had been right to trust Wilson and go ahead and buy the bar. When he walked in, Wilson was sitting on one of the benches out front. He jumped up when Irlbeck entered.

"Come with me," Wilson said. He took him into the county attorney's and judge's chambers and, just as he'd promised, told the officials that Irlbeck was all right, that he had promised to go clean. In more than a decade of chasing the bootlegger, Wilson knew one thing: that Irlbeck's word was good.

Irlbeck then waited around outside the courthouse until case number 1990, the United States of America vs. Joe Irlbeck, was called. He went in, stood up, and was asked how he pleaded.

For the first time ever, he gave a straightforward, unequivocal answer. "Guilty," he said.

"Two hundred dollars and costs," the judge announced. He struck his gavel. The court adjourned.

Irlbeck hurried out and headed home. He had no time to wait around. It was almost evening; his neighbors in Dedham would be leaving work soon, going out for a bite to eat and then, maybe, a drink. And he had a bar to tend.

EPILOGUE

When the United States Patent and Trademark Office released its list of registered marks awarded in 1934, there was one, in the section for beverages, that was granted to a Julius A. Tacke of Carroll, Iowa. It was for "Templeton Rye" and intended, of course, to be used on bottles of whiskey.

Among all the stories to come out of Prohibition, that of Templeton rye was a rarity. Famous bootleggers, famous speakeasies, famous flappers, and louts, and wits—those thirteen dry years minted them all. But what it did not do was propel many varieties of bootleg to renown. And the ones it did were usually notable not because their purchasers went back for more, but because they went to their graves.

The *Chicago Tribune* dedicated its article acknowledging the thirteenth anniversary of Prohibition on January 16, 1933, by foretelling its end. To do so, it quoted the going rate of a few well-known regional drinks. It listed Georgia and Texas corn whiskey, Idaho potato whiskey, raisin wine from Kansas. Then it went to Iowa. There it could not just check in on the price of any generic whiskey. Instead it reported on the "renowned Templeton rye," a quart of which, it found, could be had for a dollar. Pricey compared to its competitors, it was still a relative bargain.

Forays into etymology are never easy, particularly when the term in question is one that leaves little documentation. Who first coined the term Templeton rye was a question I always hoped to find the answer to, but never did. Was it Joe Irlbeck, or Kenneth Sonderleiter, or B. F. Wilson? Was it bestowed by a newspaper reporter or chosen by Dr. Otis P. Morganthaler, the mayor who was always keen on promoting one of his town's largest moneymakers? Up until the last years of the 1920s, none of them appeared to have used the name. Then they all did. And within a couple more years, the complaint went out that it was being abused by bootleggers who were located nowhere near Carroll County and producing nothing nearly as palatable as Templeton rye. The reason for its rise is clear: it was a much admired, much trusted name brand.

That Tacke, a Carroll developer, realized as much immediately after Prohibition is no surprise. Just as it is no surprise that my father—thinking of whatever one thinks about after too many hours in a combine and with too many more to go, one harvest season some seventy years after repeal—also realized it. Tacke probably came to the idea too early: his trademark was never used and eventually expired. By the time my father was granted the trademark, things had changed. Built on the allure of Prohibition-era authenticity and spiked with the romance of the rural Midwest, modern-day Templeton Rye has been one of the leaders of the American rye whiskey renaissance. (My father left the company many years before this book was even the slightest idea.)

What's often left glossed over in its story, however, is that making it was a flat-out crime. Few laws are as clear as the Eighteenth Amendment's prohibition against making and selling alcohol. Fewer still are as ensconced in such a hallowed document as the United States Constitution. The Eighteenth Amendment was nestled right between two that today we cherish as true expressions of the American Idea.

My bias in favor of Templeton's bootleggers throughout this book is, I think, clear. President Herbert Hoover was right when he called Prohibition "a great social and economic experiment, noble in motive and far-reaching in purpose." Few could doubt the earnestness of those early temperance activists. When Iowa's territorial governor Robert Lucas vowed to appoint no one as a public employee whom he knew to be a drinker, he was doing so not to carry out some sinister plot but with the belief that this new domain of his—soon to be a state—could rise above all those depravities many were convinced had already befouled so much of the nation. It was a startlingly ignorant idea and it turned into a terrible law. Drinking is one of life's better pleasures. The history of human experience overflows with evidence for the, if not essential, then almost universal, desire for some form of intoxication. I can't help but root for anyone who makes the experience that much more enjoyable.

Certainly fine drink was what motivated Templeton's earliest bootleggers, including Joe Irlbeck, to take up the craft. That the first batches of Templeton rye were not created to make money, but simply because their makers wanted a drink when few could be found, is one of the legends surrounding the stuff that is supported by historical evidence. But that it not only turned out to make money at a time when few other things did, but turned out to make quite a great deal of money, certainly also explains its rise to become the town's most important industry. Without it, Templetonians probably wouldn't have starved, but their Depression-era story would be much more dismal—much more like that of the rest of the state, where the suffering was insidious rather than acute, born as it was from the anxieties of losing the land one's parents and grandparents had worked so hard to acquire, and with it that attachment to the lifestyle and communities they adored.

In 1935, when the state compiled statistics on the percentage of land in each county held by corporations—a measure of farm foreclosure activity—the counties with the most farm failures had more than a quarter of their land owned by companies. Even in the better-off counties like Audubon or Des Moines's Polk, the rate was still at 10 and 7 percent. The lowest, however, was a mere fraction of that—Carroll County was at just under 3 percent. More evidence of the positive impact Templeton rye had on the area's economic health came from Templeton's Peoples Savings Bank. Like banks across the country, Peoples found its finances so perilous that it had to declare bankruptcy. Unlike most banks, it remarkably managed to pay out to depositors every penny they were owed. During the worst of the Depression, it even seems possible that it was Irlbeck's deposits alone that kept the bank liquid.

Joe Irlbeck never held onto much of his money. He was one of those men as good at spending as he was at earning. He couldn't refuse a friend or a neighbor who in a pinch needed a charitable loan, just as he could not refuse a good game of craps. He stayed behind the bar at his tavern only a few years before tiring of having to police his occasionally rowdy patrons, especially after the world neared another great war and tempers among those with varying national allegiances escalated. Instead, like Sonderleiter, he moved into beer distribution. Previously convicted bootleggers had to stay out of trouble for several years before qualifying for a distributor's license, but Sonderleiter managed to obtain a pardon from President Franklin Delano Roosevelt himself. Irlbeck, who came from a large family of committed Democrats, tried to work his political connections as well, but he failed. So he applied in his wife's name instead. When the regulators again refused the application, he, Lauretta, and his lawyer headed off to St. Paul to appeal the decision in court.

The Irlbecks' lawyer laid out his argument: Lauretta had a right to earn a living, yet her association with Joe prevented her from getting the license to do so. Therefore, he wanted to know if the government "would recommend a divorce in this case."

The judge almost cut him off, "Oh no!" he exclaimed. "This court will go on record as having no part of separating any family."

With that, the license was granted. And once more Joe worked hard to keep the glasses of area drinkers full. In his off time, he sipped from his stash of Templeton rye, a stash which he occasionally restocked using the tiny little still he kept in his garage.

Benjamin Franklin Wilson remained committed to the liquor laws. For nearly twenty years after Prohibition ended, he stayed in Iowa working to enforce the new alcohol tax laws, eventually rising to head the tax unit in Des Moines. He retired in 1952 after thirty-one years on the force. He died eleven years later, when he rear-ended another driver. It was in that same year, 1963, that Iowa finally permitted again the sale of liquor by the drink.

ACKNOWLEDGMENTS

During this project's transformation from an idea to a book, three people without whom I would have lacked the foundation to create it died. They were my grandfather Vic Bauer (a rare German-Methodist), who taught me the value of taking pride in one's work; Chuck Manatt, who taught me not to be scared of ambition nor intimidated by first steps; and Louis Lauritsen, who taught me the joy of a life well lived and a story well told.

Had Dan Manatt not invited me to work on the documentary film that also tells this story, I would never have known the Templeton rye story as anything more than an intriguing anecdote. Even if I had, without his guidance and backing I would have been at a loss where to begin and how to proceed.

The support of Elaine Schwaller and her family, especially Rhonda Schwaller, was critical. Without it and the invaluable research done by her late husband, Lambert, this project would have lacked all the texture that made it a story. My indebtedness extends to all the people of Templeton, Carroll County, and Audubon County who graciously provided their stories and knowledge. Among them: Meryl Kerkhoff, Fay Irlbeck, Ken Behrens, Rich Danner, Helen David, Brent and Janis Gehling, Tom Greteman, Eugene Heithoff, William Horbach, Merlyn Irlbeck, Sam and Lois Kauffman, Keith Kerkhoff, Joan Kerkhoff, Ruth Kisgen, Alma Klocke, Cliff Romey, Gus Schroeder, Hilda Steffes, and Gene Wiese. In addition, Joyce Burner and Dylan Kuhlman at the National Archives in Kansas City graciously culled from an accumulated decade of federal case files the most essential. Their counterparts in Washington, DC—especially Christina Jones—Chicago, and St. Louis provided crucial help. The office of Senator Tom Harkin provided essential assistance in securing the release of key records. Jonathan Eig, Bill Friedricks, Lisa Ossian, David Pickerell, Gary Regan, and Dorothy Schwieder shared their vast knowledge of the place, the era, and the context.

I am also grateful to a number of institutions as a whole, including the New York Public Library, the Queens Library, the Library of Congress, both branches of the State Historical Society of Iowa and in particular Charles Scott, the Des Moines Public Library, the Carroll County Historical Society, the Carroll Public Library, and Humanities Iowa.

Without the early and continued support of my agent Adriann Ranta and the guidance, forbearance, and discipline provided by my editor Yuval Taylor, this project would have remained much less than even an ambitious file on my computer. Also, Devon Freeny and everyone at Chicago Review Press provided so much invaluable input.

Catherine Hull led me through many crises, textual and psychological. Margaret Poe's insight, to say nothing of her near-decade of vital friendship, was as essential to forming this book in its earliest stages as it was to reaching the end.

For both professional growth and personal development, I owe much gratitude to University of Iowa professors David Schoenbaum, who showed me to think but first to look, and Jennifer Seter Wagner, who nurtured some of my earliest writing. At Sarah Lawrence College, Jo Ann Beard helped me understand what I was trying to do craft-wise long before I had a clue myself and has provided steady guidance and inspiration ever since. Rachel Cohen taught me focus. Vijay Seshadri told me "to just write a book."

My cousin Alex Ryan Bauer, a talented writer himself, has given me so much comprehension and camaraderie throughout so much of our lives.

Finally, to my parents I can say little more than thanks. You've granted me more inspiration and encouragement than any two people can be expected to give in a thousand lifetimes.

To those that I've forgotten, my deepest apologies.

ON SOURCES AND ABBREVIATIONS

SOURCES

Some quotes have been elided or modified for style, tense, or clarity. Others were created from paraphrase. Such instances are marked only in the source notes. For this reason, those wishing to reprint material quoted in this book should consult the original work. Newspapers are cited in source notes only, as are records from the US Census (digital copies were obtained from Ancestry.com and FamilySearch). All places are in Iowa unless otherwise specified. Dorothy Schwieder's *Iowa: The Middle Land*, Daniel Okrent's *Last Call*, Jonathan Eig's *Get Capone*, and Gary Regan and Mardee Haidin Regan's *Book of Bourbon* provided significant domain knowledge not fully reflected here. Additionally, invaluable contextual information was provided by the residents of Carroll and Audubon Counties in formal and informal interviews over the course of nearly a decade. Their names can be found in the acknowledgments.

ABBREVIATIONS

AA	*Audubon Advocate*
BWOPF	Benjamin Franklin Wilson, official personnel folder
CB	City of Templeton centennial book, *A Century of Memories*
CDH	*Carroll Daily Herald*
CH	*Carroll Herald*
CT	*Carroll Times*
DMR	*Des Moines Register*
DMT	*Des Moines Tribune* (variously *Des Moines Tribune-Capital*; *Des Moines Evening Tribune*)

IIR   US Bureau of Prohibition, Irlbeck investigation report

JII   Recorded interview between Joe and Lauretta Irlbeck and Elaine and Lambert Schwaller

MM   *Manning Monitor*

NYT   *New York Times*

USC   United States Census (year indicated)

IYBA   *Iowa Year Book of Agriculture* (year indicated)

SOURCE NOTES

1. JUNE 16, 1931

taxi . . . "Voice Unresentful as Gang Czar Says 'Guilty' 3 Times," *Chicago Herald-Examiner*, June 17, 1931.

Model T . . . JII.

Lexington Hotel . . . "Voice Unresentful."

headed toward . . . JII.

entire life . . . CB, 575.

same age . . . Eig, *Get Capone*, 20; CB, 575.

values associated with rural America . . . Mennel, "Prohibition"; see Eagles, *Democracy Delayed* for further discussion of urban-rural conflict.

Of medium height . . . US Selective Service System, Joe Irlbeck WWI draft registration card.

December 1899 . . . *Dedham* . . . *Bavaria* . . . CB, 575.

"legalizing . . ." Okrent, *Last Call*, 108.

operation had grown . . . JII.

"far-famed . . ." "'Little Brown Jug' Swings High in Templeton Street," *DMR*, December 20, 1931.

Benjamin Franklin Wilson . . . BWOPF.

The still . . . "They'll See No More Templeton Rye," *DMT*, March 6, 1931.

rent Neppl earned . . . JII.

The June 16 hearing . . . US v. Neppl, Frank J.

eavesdropped . . . *What he overheard* . . . *town banker* . . . JII.

"furors" . . . *"cheap Brooklyn* . . ." "Capone's 'Guilty' Pleas Mark End of Thug's Rule," *Hartford Courant*, June 17, 1931.

stunning . . . "Cell to End Capone Power," *Chicago Tribune*, June 17, 1931.

"I plead guilty" . . . *just "guilty"* . . . "Capone's 'Guilty' Pleas."

three minutes . . . "Capone's Pleas of Guilty May Lighten Term," *Washington Post*, June 17, 1931.

"a monarch . . ." Ibid.

2. EDEN'S OASIS

announced in a newspaper ad . . . CB, 20.

Like its competitors . . . Chicago, Milwaukee, and St. Paul Railway Company, map of the railroad and extensions.

On June 27 . . . Clark, "Liquor Legislation 1878–1908," 524–25.

Templeton was perched . . . Maclean, *History of Carroll County*, vol. 1, 19–20, 211; Natural Resources Conservation Service, "Iowa Soil Regions Map."

Prior to Templeton's founding . . . Executive Council of Iowa, *Thirteenth State Census of Iowa*, 11.

surged to nearly 900 . . . Secretary of State of Iowa, *Census of Iowa for the Year 1885*, 12.

At the turn of the century . . . USC 1900.

Even as pioneers . . . CB, 194–95.

a pound of butter cost . . . Derks, *Value of a Dollar*, 51, 52, 57.

cost $33,000 . . . CB, 194–95.

Catholics weren't . . . Ibid., 267.

the wife . . . Ibid., 52, 613–14.

immigrants from Germany . . . Unfortunately, township-level data on heritage is not available. However, in the 1895 Iowa State Census, 72 percent of Templetonians had at least one foreign-born parent, and the 1900 US Census showed that for the people in Carroll County with foreign parentage, 80 percent of those parents came from Germany. Ultimately, the excellent Templeton centennial book, *A Century of Memories*, places the percentage of people with German heritage at more than 95 percent and also gives specific origin for many.

"Does all of Germany . . ." "German Families Arrive in Carroll, 1882," *Der Carroll Demokrat*, March 3, 1882, trans. David Reineke, IAGenWeb Project, 2007, www.iagenweb.org/boards/carroll/documents/index.cgi?read= 157416.

fondness for beer . . . Tolzmann, *German-American Experience*, 234.

Unless he'd shaven . . . Iowa Legislature official website, "Orlando H. Manning."

opponents of alcohol . . . Ibid.

Manning was born . . . Ibid.; *Biographical and Historical Record of Greene and Carroll Counties, Iowa*, 332–33.

At the age . . . Iowa Legislature official website, "Orlando H. Manning."

bastion . . . Maclean, *History of Carroll County*, vol. 1, 80.

more often Democrats . . . Ibid., 79.

1883 Republican State Convention . . . "Iowa Republicans," *Burlington Weekly Hawkeye*, July 5, 1883.

Manning rose . . . Clark, "Liquor Legislation 1878–1908," 536–37.

he declared . . . Ibid.

"uproarious . . ." Ibid.

From the Iowa chapter . . . "Floral School House" postcard.

left Iowa and made a fortune . . . Clark, "Liquor Legislation 1878–1908," 187–89.

three times . . . "O.H. Manning's Death," *Jefferson Bee*, September 29, 1909.

"the longest bar . . ." History Book Committee of Manning, *We Can Remember*, 206.

foul dens . . . Okrent, *Last Call*, 13.

Indicative . . . "Advertisement of an Honest Rumseller."

Though at the time of Manning's speech . . . *Americans were drinking* . . . *forty years* . . . Lender, *Drinking in America*, 205.

In 1880 . . . *In Chicago* . . . *In San Francisco* . . . Rose, *American Women*, 17

In Des Moines . . . "Prohibition Iowa," *Chicago Daily Tribune*, December 11, 1885; the *Tribune* article lists Des Moines's population as 37,000, while the Census gives it as 32,469, which is the number used to calculate here the bar-to-person ratio.

Jim Himes's place . . . "John Barleycorn's Career in Des Moines Runs to Extremes," *DMR*, July 1, 1919.

"liquor is brought . . ." Clark, "Liquor Legislation 1846–1861," 80.

built atop skids . . . *Bootleggers roamed* . . . Maclean, *History of Carroll County*, vol. 1, 148–49.

profession took its name . . . Carr, *Second Oldest Profession*, 27–28.

entire side street . . . Maclean, *History of Carroll County*, vol. 1, 148–49.

Camaraderie . . . Okrent, *Last Call*, 28; Rose, *American Women*, 17–18.

The trebling of the saloons . . . Lender, *Drinking in America*, 96–97.

"double distilled . . ." Sunday, *Water Wagon*, 7.

"Famous Booze . . ." Bruns, *Preacher*, 166.

"sworn, eternal . . ." . . . "'run for its money'" . . . Sunday, *Water Wagon*, 3.

Born William Ashley Sunday . . . Bruns, *Preacher*, 22; Wheaton College, "Papers of William Ashley 'Billy' Sunday."

"whiskey-soaked . . ." Bruns, *Preacher*, 13.

drank moderately . . . Ibid., 43.

His conversion . . . Ibid., 43–45; Denison, "Billy Sunday and His War."

Sunday didn't immediately . . . Wheaton College, "Papers of William Ashley 'Billy' Sunday."

As his first assignment . . . Bruns, *Preacher*, 30.

When he left baseball . . . Bruns, *Preacher*, 57; cf. Denison, "Billy Sunday and His War" ("$500 a month").

"he began by slapping . . ." Denison, "Billy Sunday and His War."

The number he brought . . . 1,118 . . . Fairfield . . . Ibid.

When Sunday proclaimed . . . Sunday, *Water Wagon*, 4.

"Influence of sermons . . ." Denison, "Billy Sunday and His War."

3. PATRIOTIC MURDER

April 2, 1917 . . . "belligerent . . ." . . . "The world . . ." . . . "We have no quarrel . . ." "President Calls for War Declaration," NYT, April 3, 1917.

Cobb . . . "Once lead . . ." Cobb, *Cobb of "The World,"* 267–70.

Creel . . . "fear . . ." Okrent, *Last Call*, 101.

Unwilling . . . Kennedy, *Over Here*, 104–5.

"spirit . . ." Ibid., 119.

Hoover was born . . . Burner, *Herbert Hoover*, 8–11.

120,000 Americans . . . Ibid., 73.

"Food . . ." Ibid., 96.

rather than forcing . . . pledge to "wheatless" . . . Kennedy, *Over Here*, 118.

vastly increase . . . tractors . . . IYBA 1917, v.

as much a German country . . . Tolzmann, *German-American Experience*, 268.

"ludicrous" . . . "fat old . . ." Tuchmann, *Guns of August*, 313.

term "Hun" . . . Ibid., 8.

EAT LESS WHEAT . . . US Food Administration, "Defeat the Kaiser."

CAN VEGETABLES . . . National War Garden Commission, "Can Vegetables, Fruit, and the Kaiser Too."

GERMAN SLAVERY . . . "German Slavery or Liberty Bonds."

language was taught . . . Wrede, "Americanization of Scott County."

"traitors" . . . Kennedy, *Over Here*, 84.

cohort did in Denison . . . "Pupils Burn Hun Books," DMR, April 29, 1918.

Babel Proclamation . . . Derr, "Babel Proclamation."

"Plank" . . . Untitled item under Brief News Notes from Many Points, CT, October 23, 1919.

German Savings Bank . . . measles . . . Derr, "Babel Proclamation."

murder was "patriotic" . . . Okrent, *Last Call*, 101.

In Davenport . . . Wrede, "Americanization of Scott County."

December 26, 1917 . . . "Two Men Are Almost Lynched," CT, January 3, 1918; "Some Doings at Audubon," *Anita Record*, January 3, 1918 (reprint of article from the *Audubon Advocate*); "Near Hanging for Kaiserites," CH, January 2, 1918 (all information on near-lynchings is from one of these three newspapers unless otherwise noted).

legal basis . . . Allen, "Anti-German Sentiments"; Wrede, "Americanization of Scott County."

Robert C. Spencer . . . "Mob Attacks Pro-Germans," *Oxford Leader*, January 10, 1918; Andrews, *History of Audubon County*, 352–54.

Ernest J. W. Starck . . . Andrews, *History of Audubon County*, 652–53.

Tennigkeit . . . Rec. fr. USC 1930, Kit Carson County, CO; Leroy Township, plat map, 1921.

already seen as a traitor . . . "Ordered to Stop Preaching in German," *Le Mars Sentinel*, September 14, 1917.

"inciting . . ." "Seek German Preacher," *Le Mars Semi-weekly Sentinel*, March 1, 1918.

First National Bank . . . Tennigkeit v. Wilson.

hundred sent around back . . . "Audubon Pro-Germans Given Scare by Citizens," *Fayette County Leader*, January 17, 1918.

socializing . . . *"I'd just* . . ." "Jury Returns Verdict Against Fred Tennigkeit," *Atlantic News-Telegraph*, November 10, 1921.

The weather . . . National Environmental Satellite, Data, and Information Service, "Record of Climatological Observation, Station: AUDUBON, IA, US."

"excited" . . . *"hatred* . . ." Tennigkeit v. Wilson.

"Give me a gun . . ." "Plaintiff Rests in Tennigkeit Damage Suit," *Atlantic News-Telegraph*, November 9, 1921.

only option . . . Ibid.

"I have already . . ." "Plaintiff Rests" (quote from paraphrase).

"Come here . . ." "Two Men Are Almost Lynched" (curse omitted from original; "son of a bitch" inserted on assumption).

willingly turned him over . . . "Plaintiff Rests"; Tennigkeit v. Wilson.

"All right" . . . "Two Men Are Almost Lynched."

he confiscated . . . "Audubon Pro-Germans Given Scare."

injunction . . . "Ordered to Stop Preaching in German."

came screaming . . . "Narrowly Escape Lynching," *Le Mars Semi-weekly Sentinel*, January 1, 1918.

men rushed . . . Untitled item under Iowa News, *Marble Rock Journal*, January 10, 1918.

By February 1918 . . . "Search Made in Chicago for Starck," *Atlantic News-Telegraph*, February 28, 1918; "Federal Court Is Asked to Return Pro-German Preacher," *Waterloo Evening Courier*, April 19, 1918; Untitled item under Brief News Notes From Many Points, *CT*, April 15, 1918.

arrested in Chicago . . . "Federal Court Is Asked."

October 1919 . . . "Mrs. Starck Dead," *Le Mars Sentinel*, October 17, 1919.

Liberty Bonds at the pulpit . . . Bruns, *Preacher*, 256.

"Thou knowest . . ." Ibid., 255 (quote elided).

"in defense . . ." . . . *"every plot* . . ." Sunday, *Water Wagon*, 3, 17.

"We have German . . ." Okrent, *Last Call*, 100.

Hoover's Food Administration . . . Kennedy, *Over Here*, 123.

quota . . . limited . . . Okrent, *Last Call*, 99.

possibly get drunk . . . Bruns, *Preacher*, 218.

coming too fast . . . "Iowa Will Be Late Joining Dry Column," *DMT*, January 14, 1919.

11:30 AM . . . "Iowa Ratifies National Dry Amendment." *DMT*, January 15, 1919.

its house voted unanimously . . . Today Nebraska has a unicameral legislature, but at the time of the amendment it was divided into a senate and a house of representatives.

personal cellars . . . Okrent, *Last Call*, 111.

Lanseboro . . . Untitled item under Brief Notes from Many Points, *CT*, February 13, 1919.

fifth-largest . . . Okrent, *Last Call*, 3.

Andrew J. Volstead . . . US Congress, "Volstead, Andrew John, (1860–1947)"; Okrent, *Last Call*, 112–13.

The brewing industry . . . Behr, *Prohibition*, 48.

"liberty cabbage" . . . Okrent, *Last Call*, 101, 111.

"Police say" . . . "Cops Hold 'Wake' for Jawn Barleycorn; Recall Days of Unchecked Rivers of Booze," *DMR*, January 17, 1920.

"The party staged . . ." "'Riotous Orgy' Not Like the Old Days," *CT*, June 19, 1919.

Sunday . . . Norfolk . . . "The reign . . ." Behr, *Prohibition*, 82.

Der Carroll Demokrat . . . passing . . . "The *Demokrat* Has Ceased Publication," *CT*, June 14, 1923.

4. STEADY GAZE

Vast quantities . . . Behr, *Prohibition*, 80.

Residents of Windsor . . . Okrent, *Last Call*, 124.

the cars rolling . . . Ibid., 94; Behr, *Prohibition*, 81, 92–102.

Late in December 1920 . . . "Mr. Tennigkeit Is Heard From Again," *Atlantic News-Telegraph*, October 16, 1919; "Audubon German in Trouble Again," *CH*, October 22, 1919.

strong anti-German temper . . . Tolzmann, *German-American Experience*, 298–99.

readers of the Atlantic News-Telegraph . . . "Plaintiff Rests in Tennigkeit Damage Suit," *Atlantic News-Telegraph*, November 9, 1921.

Prior to the start . . . Ibid.

"in violation . . ." Tennigkeit v. Wilson.

"gathering" . . . "Plaintiff Rests."

"continued to mingle . . ." Tennigkeit v. Wilson.

But Wilson's lawyer . . . "Plaintiff Rests."

The entirety of Wilson's . . . Tennigkeit v. Wilson.

At 4:25 PM . . . "Jury Returns Verdict Against Fred Tennigkeit," *Atlantic News-Telegraph,* November 10, 1921.

After hearing the verdict . . . Tennigkeit v. Wilson.

Wilson was of average . . . BWOPF.

twenty-six-year-old . . . Rec. fr. USC 1900, Audubon County.

Henry Hagedorn . . . *Almost immediately* . . . *Within hours* . . . *"Carroll county offender"* . . . *"If the Carroll sheriff* . . ." "Sheriff Uncovers Bootlegging Ring," *AA,* September 30, 1919.

Two weeks later . . . "No Evidence in That Case of Bootlegging," *CT,* October 9, 1919.

"will stick close . . ." . . . *"he finds* . . ." "Divorce, Booze, and Farming," *DMR,* October 21, 1919.

Several months later . . . "Sheriff Gets Three Moon Shiners Here," *AA,* July 8, 1920; rec. fr. USC 1920, Carroll County.

a bouquet . . . "Wilson and Conway Get Bouquet from Inspector," *AA,* September 23, 1920.

renomination papers . . . "Little Interest in Primary Election," *AA,* June 3, 1920.

little surprise . . . *lost* . . . "Mantz and Jorgensen Win in County," *AA,* June 10, 1920; "G.O.P. Gets Every Office in County," *AA,* November 14, 1920.

dropped out . . . BWOPF.

study . . . *fingerprinting* . . . "G.O.P Gets Every Office."

In addition to the countless . . . Schmeckebier, *Bureau of Prohibition,* 174–228.

Congress appropriated . . . US Industrial Alcohol Bureau, *Statistics Concerning Intoxicating Liquors, December, 1930.*

At the job . . . Behr, *Prohibition,* 80; BWOPF; "Dry Law Will Be Rigidly Enforced," *DMR,* December 28, 1919.

railway wage laborer . . . Derks, *Value of a Dollar,* 150, 154.

Methodist . . . Rec. fr. Iowa State Census 1915, Audubon County, via FamilySearch, www.familysearch.org/learn/wiki/en/Iowa_Census.

didn't require passing . . . Okrent, *Last Call,* 134.

"Do you use . . ." BWOPF.

Representative William Green's . . . Ibid.

a practical necessity . . . Behr, *Prohibition,* 83.

On the first of February 1922 . . . BWOPF.

extreme southern Iowa . . . "Wilson Gets Job as Federal Prohibition Agent," *AA,* February 2, 1922.

officials at the Prohibition Bureau . . . *aware* . . . Vermeule, letters to Attorney General Palmer.

It was a trend . . . "Sheriff Gets Three Moon Shiners."

5. ANYPLACE BUT THE RECTORY

The weather was slightly cooler . . . IYBA 1920, 622.

Irlbeck . . . went to work . . . wages . . . JII.

Max Kastl . . . ten dollars a gallon . . . Ibid.

cost of a pack of cigarettes . . . Derks, *Value of a Dollar*, 171.

Henry Ford and John D. Rockefeller . . . Lender, *Drinking in America*, 108.

In Chicago . . . Behr, *Prohibition*, 84.

And across the country . . . Ibid., 87–89.

Ernest Hemingway . . . "Canuck Whiskey Pouring into U.S.," *Toronto Star Weekly*, June 5, 1920.

A week earlier . . . "Flying 'Legger' Here from Canada," *DMR*, May 25, 1920.

Around the same time . . . "'Bob' Cassidy Goes on Long 'Still' Hunt," *CT*, June 17, 1920.

born in Ohio . . . Rec. fr. USC 1920, Carroll County.

Civil War veteran . . . Find a Grave, "Elijah Hoover (1822–1900)."

Herbert Junior's middle name . . . Ancestry.com, "Herbert Clark Hoover," in California death index.

For most of his life . . . History Book Committee of Manning, *We Can Remember*, 71.

including Templeton . . . CB, 87.

"I am the Village Blacksmith . . ." History Book Committee of Manning, *We Can Remember*, 71.

process has been modified little . . . Connelly, "Science and Art of Whiskey Making."

Hoover spent two years . . . "Will Village's Citizens Carry On?" (see note in bibliography).

small frame building . . . "Twenty Gallon Still Captured," *MM*, July 27, 1922.

pickle barrel . . . coffeepot . . . Untitled history of Templeton Rye.

Occasionally tapping . . . Carr, *Second Oldest Profession*, 75–83.

75 percent . . . David Pickerell, e-mail with author.

More advanced stills . . . Carr, *Second Oldest Profession*, 75–83.

By 1922 . . . "Twenty Gallon Still Captured"; untitled history of Templeton Rye.

automobile dealer . . . "May Be Copper for Still," *CT*, April 8, 1920.

Irlbeck never said . . . Irlbeck and his accomplice . . . a few days . . . mash was ready . . . nearly a minute . . . Trecker's worries . . . last drop of booze dripped . . . JII.

Shortly after the first Europeans . . . Carr, *Second Oldest Profession*, 9.

Many of the homesteaders . . . Ibid., 11.

The grain was one of the first . . . Ibid., 16.

dominant liquor . . . Clarke, "The Comeback Kid."

Made by George Washington . . . Mount Vernon official website. "George Washington's Distillery."

among the many crops planted . . . Maclean, *History of Carroll County*, vol. 1, 24.

replaced by corn . . . Secretary of State of Iowa, *Census of Iowa for the Year 1895*, 461.

Within months . . . Behr, *Prohibition*, 187; Okrent, *Last Call*, 128.

On a smaller scale . . . Behr, *Prohibition*, 86.

Henry, Leonard, Claude, and Leslie Chapman . . . "Albert Chapman, Father of Local People, Is Dead," *CDH*, January 6, 1933; rec. fr. USC 1900, Crawford County; US Selective Service System, Henry E. Chapman WWI draft registration card.

Glidden . . . Ibid.; Maclean, *History of Carroll County*, vol. 1, 82.

clothing salesman . . . US Selective Service System, Leonard E. Chapman WWI draft registration card.

farm laborer . . . US Selective Service System, Claude V. Chapman WWI draft registration card.

"Triad" . . . "Organization Saul Aircraft Co. Now Being Effected," *CT*, January 9, 1929.

other ventures . . . US v. Chapman, Les R.

Len moved . . . *cottage* . . . US v. Chapman, C. V., and Chapman, L. E.; US Bureau of Prohibition, Chapmans of Carroll first investigation file.

massive stills . . . Ibid.

a bitter chemical . . . Agency for Toxic Substances & Disease Registry, "Public Health Statement: Diethyl Phthalate."

Chapmans argued . . . US v. Chapman, C. V., and Chapman, L. E.

Three months later . . . "Three Guilty on Charges of Liquor Law Violations," *Humboldt Independent*, January 24, 1924.

Len vowed . . . "Liquor Law Violators Fined $200 and $300," *Humboldt Independent*, January 31, 1924.

US attorney filed . . . US v. Chapman, C. V., and Chapman, L. E.; US Bureau of Prohibition, Chapmans of Carroll second investigation file; "Liquor Law Violators Fined"; "District Court Deal Justice with Firm Hand," *Humboldt Independent*, January 15, 1925.

government opened 7,291 . . . *29,114* . . . *to climb* . . . US Industrial Alcohol Bureau, *Statistics Concerning Intoxicating Liquors*, December, 1930.

"indulged . . ." . . . *"if the Anti-Saloon . . ."* "Prohibition," *CT*, January 23, 1919; "Hiding His 'Hootch' Gets Man into Court, *CT*, December 15, 1921 (quote elided).

Consumption did fall . . . Miron and Zweibel, "Alcohol Consumption During Prohibition."

local market . . . Eig, *Get Capone,* 14.

By the start of Prohibition . . . "Bootleggers Could Lift Sugar Famine in America," *DMR,* November 23, 1919; Carr, *Second Oldest Profession,* 94–95.

William and Frank Greteman . . . CB, 554.

When Frank was twenty . . . Ibid., 554–55.

Greteman charged just five dollars . . . Untitled history of Templeton Rye.

For yeast . . . JII.

Nearby William Greteman . . . CB, 60, 557.

The ruse . . . Untitled history of Templeton Rye.

"see that house . . ." Ibid. ("Mister" added).

6. THIS NEFARIOUS BUSINESS

Assistant Attorney General . . . City of Chattanooga official website, "1901–1905 William Little Frierson."

a Sioux City man . . . "Iowa Is Not Dry All the Time Is Proven," *CT,* April 15, 1920.

In a slight endorsement . . . "H.V. Janssen to Succeed Himself," *CT,* April 15, 1920.

More evidence . . . "Sheriff Uncovers Small Distillery," *AA,* December 30, 1920; "Here's Reason Why Raisins Are Scarce," *CH,* January 5, 1921.

drawn to a farm . . . "Sheriff Uncovers Small Distillery."

found two stills . . . US v. Hagedorn, Herman, and Heuerman, Amos.

feds deliberately . . . "Reason Why Raisins Are Scarce."

owned by Henry's relative . . . Familial connection speculative, would go back to Germany; rec. fr. USC 1910, Audubon County; rec. fr. USC 1900, Carroll County.

first-time violators . . . Okrent, *Last Call,* 317.

June 14, 1921 . . . US v. Hagedorn, Herman, and Heuerman, Amos; US v. Hagedorn, Herman (states second offense pleaded guilty).

profitable farming operation . . . Rec. fr. Iowa State Census 1915, Carroll County, via FamilySearch, www.familysearch.org/learn/wiki/en/Iowa_Census.

"The raisin market . . ." "Reason Why Raisins Are Scarce."

"near beer" . . . Okrent, *Last Call,* 250.

most popular . . . Ossian, "Prohibition Possibly Prohibited," 229; "13th Year Finds Prohibition at Death's Door," *Chicago Tribune,* January 16, 1933.

Over two days . . . "Agents Getting Many Stills in Carroll County," *AA,* January 6, 1921.

Prohibition Bureau's budget for 1921 . . . US Industrial Alcohol Bureau, *Statistics Concerning Intoxicating Liquors, December, 1930.*

Brookhart proposed . . . Ossian, "Prohibition Possibly Prohibited," 234.

following day's newspaper . . . "Agents Getting Many Stills."

Janssen beat . . . "5,679 Voters Smash Primary Predictions," *CT*, June 8, 1922; "Has No Opposition But Asks for Votes," *CT*, November 2, 1922 (a misprint in the banner of the November 2, 1922, issue of the *Carroll Times* gives the year as 1921, causing it to appear, at least in the NewspaperArchive.com database, out of order).

"golden era . . ." Ossian, *Depression Dilemmas*, 172.

advent of Armistice . . . Burner, *Herbert Hoover*, 249.

before the war was over . . . Ossian, *Depression Dilemmas*, 30, 109.

Ireland and Appalachia . . . Thompson, *Spirits of Just Men*, 68–71.

hundreds of thousands of people . . . *work in the city* . . Perlman, "Recent Recession of Farm Population and Farm Land"; "Farms Don't Pay, Watson Admits," *CT*, June 21, 1923.

"For the last two . . ." *IYBA* 1922, 73 ("the farmer's" added for clarity).

Cameron then called . . . Ibid., 33.

Reverend J. M. Lowe . . . "Many Attended Public Klan Lecture," *AA*, September 4, 1924.

1920 Census . . . Eagles, *Democracy Delayed*, 3.

Lowe had . . . "Many Attended Public Klan Lecture."

uncomfortably hot . . . National Environmental Satellite, Data, and Information Service, "Record of Climatological Observation, Station: AUDUBON, IA, US."

four hundred . . . Untitled brief under masthead, *CT*, August 23, 1923.

Their membership was alleged . . . "Klan Injected in Audubon Election; Territory Results," *Atlantic News-Telegraph*, April 1, 1924.

"The Ku Klux Klan . . ." "Many Attended Public Klan Lecture" (quote elided; "while" added for clarity).

the second Klan arose . . . *Simmons* . . . *offer of empowerment* . . . *undermining the traditional* . . . Schwieder, "A Farmer and the Ku Klux Klan"; Neymeyer, "In the Full Light of Day"; Coben, "Ordinary White Protestants."

The Klan reached . . . Schwieder, "A Farmer and the Ku Klux Klan"; cf. Neymeyer, "In the Full Light of Day" ("40,000").

One Klan member . . . *"We have a Klan sheriff* . . ." . . . *the Marathon Flaming Circle* . . . "A Farmer and the Ku Klux Klan."

If the Flaming Circle's members . . . Goldberg, "Unmasking the Ku Klux Klan"; "'Red Knights' Form to Oppose Ku Klux," *NYT*, September 7, 1923.

By 1925 . . . Schwieder, "A Farmer and the Ku Klux Klan."

In September 1924 . . . "Klukers Organizing," *CT*, September 25, 1924; "Firemen Stop Klan Meet," *Cedar Valley Daily Times*, September 27, 1924.

In July 1920 . . . "'Dry' Officers Here Draw Net Tighter Around Bonded Whisky Smugglers," *DMR*, July 24, 1920.

fleshy and dog-eyed . . . "Koolbeck, Ben, Agent Badge."

"People are finding . . ." "'Dry' Officers Here Draw Net Tighter."

more Americans were drinking . . . Miron and Zweibel, "Alcohol Consumption During Prohibition"; Okrent, *Last Call*, 249.

$1-billion-a-year industry . . . *$4 billion* . . . Behr, *Prohibition*, 147, 158 (see sources for date).

his original appointment . . . BWOPF.

By May 1922 . . . "Western Iowa's Oasis Raided Yesterday," *Atlantic News-Telegraph*, June 27, 1922; "Federal Men Make Sensational Raid on Templeton," *CH*, June 28, 1922.

7. STORMING EDEN

Late in the morning . . . *"heart of* . . ." "Federal Men Make Sensational Raid on Templeton," *CH*, June 28, 1922.

thirty-eight . . . Ibid; "State, Federal, and County Officers Make Gigantic Haul in Booze Raid," *AA*, June 29, 1922.

"put up . . ." "State, Federal, and County Officers Make Gigantic Haul."

chicken coop . . . "Federal Men Make Sensational Raid."

Jake Duwell . . . Details from *AA*, June 29, 1922; name spelling from *CT*, June 29, 1922, and *CH*, June 28, 1922.

three gallons . . . "$50,000 in Liquor, 22 Persons Taken in Big Booze Raid," *CT*, June 29, 1922.

Clarence Bengford . . . "State, Federal, and County Officers Make Gigantic Haul"; "Federal Men Make Sensational Raid."

caramel coloring . . . US v. Lang, Herman.

John Steffes . . . US v. Steffes, John.

hot, cloudy . . . National Environmental Satellite, Data, and Information Service, "Record of Climatological Observation, Station: CARROLL."

Altogether . . . "State, Federal, and County Officers Make Gigantic Haul"; "Federal Men Make Sensational Raid"; "Federal Officers Raid Templeton and Dedham," *MM*, June 29, 1922.

seven . . . *found nothing* . . . "State, Federal, and County Officers Make Gigantic Haul"; "Federal Men Make Sensational Raid."

Even more evidence . . . "Federal Men Make Sensational Raid."

Born in 1857, Schwaller . . . CB, 656.

November 1876 . . . "Shooting Affray," *CH*, December 6, 1876.

Hillsdale . . . Reineke, *German Heritage of Carroll County*, chapter 4.

almost been wiped . . . Maclean, *History of Carroll County*, vol. 1, 75.

Schwaller was yearning . . . "Shooting Affray"; "Premeditated Murder," *CH*, January 24, 1877.

entire population . . . Reineke, *German Heritage of Carroll County*, chapter 4.

Frank Hoelker . . . Spelling from ibid.

The bullet passed . . . *fester* . . . *trio of doctors* . . . *death* . . . "Premeditated Murder."

Despite the doctors' . . . *further helped* . . . *Manning* . . . *self-defense* . . . *refused to indict* . . . "Shooting Affray"; "Premeditated Murder"; "Released on Bail," under Local News, *CH*, January 31, 1877; "District Court," *CH*, April 11, 1877.

raid on Schwaller's . . . US v. Schwaller, Victor C.

prepared to file charges . . . "Will Determine Raid's Legality," *MM*, July 20, 1922.

Emmons . . . *prejudiced* . . . US v. Schwaller, Victor C.

new judge . . . "Will Determine Raid's Legality."

William Irving Saul . . . Maclean, *History of Carroll County*, vol. 1, 67–68, 164–65.

Throughout his fight . . . *complaint* . . . *still as evidence* . . . US v. Schwaller, Victor C.

hand it back . . . *"swill"* . . . *"the Prohibition* . . ." "Schwaller Gains Possession of His Swill," *AA*, August 8, 1922.

state chemist . . . *bail* . . . US v. Schwaller, Victor C.

On November 14 . . . "Victims of Booze Raids Pay Heavy Fines," *AA*, November 23, 1922; US v. Schwaller, Victor C.; "State, Federal, and County Officers Make Gigantic Haul."

Herbert Hoover . . . *"very crude* . . ." . . . *"all steamed* . . ." . . . *brush* . . . "Twenty Gallon Still Captured," *MM*, July 27, 1922.

near town . . . Ewolt and Warren Township, plat map, 1923.

Herman's wife . . . CB, 606–7.

"very confidently" . . . *"he was* . . ." . . . "Twenty Gallon Still Captured."

left Templeton . . . CB, 432.

A few weeks before Christmas . . . "Much Hootch Destroyed," *Audubon Republican*, December 7, 1922.

8. "THE TREASURE CHEST"

Short . . . *his driver* . . . JII.

deliver . . . *aging* . . . US v. Irlbeck, Joe, et al.

hauled equipment . . . IIR.

Easter . . . Untitled item under Templeton, *CDH*, April 22, 1933.

In front of him was the truck . . . JII.

Five foot nine . . . fleshy cheeks . . . left school . . . beverage business . . . scar . . .
Leavenworth Penitentiary, "Kenneth Sonderleiter," inmate case file.

Sonderleiter was busted . . . Ibid; "Rum Syndicate Focused Light on Bootlegging," *DMT,* December 31, 1931.

After he was released . . . consolidating . . . DIAL 5-6350 . . . Templeton rye . . .
"Rum Syndicate Focused Light"; US v. Sonderleiter, Kenneth.

Hotel Fort Des Moines . . . JII.

1919 . . . cost . . . Jim Pollock, "Venerable Fort Nears 75," *DMR,* August 9, 1994, reprinted at Hotel Fort Des Moines official website, www
.hotelfortdesmoines.com/history/hotel_story.php.

best speakeasies . . . JII.

But Sonderleiter wanted a cut . . . Irlbeck . . . accepted . . . Ibid.

*Smith was posted . . . Ed Reicher . . . small syringe . . . Before the next keg . . .
$52.50 . . . The idea . . . thirty-two hundred gallons . . . Chicago . . .* JII;
"E.J. Reicher Dies; Chief of Police," *Carroll Daily Times Herald,* September 14, 1955.

bootleggers in Chicago . . . "Rum Syndicate Focused Light."

all night . . . JII.

Lincoln Highway . . . Hokanson, *Lincoln Highway,* 14.

stories horrifying . . . See, for example, "Mud Forces Carroll Man to Abandon Car on Lincoln Highway," *CT,* April 13, 1922.

Henry A. Wallace . . . Ossian, *Depression Dilemmas,* 5–6.

Three years earlier . . . "Chicago People in Smashup Last Week" and "The Chicago Tribune Says About Accident," *CT,* February 4, 1926; "Alterie Slightly Hurt When Auto Crashes in Iowa," *Chicago Tribune,* January 31, 1926.

To disguise . . . Anselm . . . Fords . . . Merlyn Irlbeck, interview with Dan Manatt.

Joe Kohorst . . . CB, 602.

"lady attendant" . . . See, for example, "J. H. Kohorst, Funeral Director" (advertisement), *CT,* February 15, 1928.

new hearse . . . "Announcement" (advertisement), *CT,* August 5, 1926.

his wife . . . Untitled history of Templeton Rye.

six hundred gallons of 40-proof liquor . . . Lender, *Drinking in America,* 205; USC 1930.

a thousand gallons of liquor a day . . . JII.

Irlbeck thought even . . . Ibid.

"numerous" . . . "large quantities" . . . IIR.

two of Trecker's neighbors . . . JII.

tolerated in his jurisdiction . . . "Mallonee Hits Blow at Booze," *AA,* April 7, 1921.

Mallonee arrived . . . Iowa Legislature official website, "Standard Form for Members of the Legislature: L. Dee Mallonee"; rec. fr. USC 1900, Guthrie County.

In March 1922 . . . "Audubon Lady Is Freed Booze Case," *Atlantic News-Telegraph*, February 21, 1923.

thirty-eight . . . US Selective Service System, Fred Ceranek WWI draft registration card.

When the case . . . "Audubon Lady"; "Ceranek Declared Guilty by Jury on the Third Hearing," *AA*, December 20, 1923.

Ceranek's second trial . . . "Trial of Ceranek Case Now Before Court Will Be Last," *AA*, May 3, 1923.

In December 1923 . . . Ibid; "Audubon Lady"; "Ceranek Gets Jail Term for 'Legging,'" *AA*, December 27, 1923; "Audubon Legger Convicted at Trial; $1,200 Expended," *Atlantic News-Telegraph*, December 15, 1923.

late 1924 . . . "Thirty-One Indicted for Bootlegging by Cass County Jury," *AA*, October 16, 1924.

Half a decade later . . . "Agent Says Rum Causes Most Crime," *DMT*, February 25, 1929 (actual day, "January 24, 1929," quoted in original, was removed and replaced by the phrase "for this one particular day").

federal level . . . Okrent, *Last Call*, 112.

Emory Roy Buckner . . . Ibid., 253–55; *Dictionary of American Biography*, under "Emory Roy Buckner."

June 1923 . . . "Iowa Is Leading in Dry Law Enforcement," *DMT*, June 12, 1923.

Bureau had concluded . . . US Bureau of Prohibition, "Southern District Problem Enforcement."

Predisposed . . . Okrent, *Last Call*, 137, 140

"It is very . . ." US Bureau of Prohibition, "Southern District Problem Enforcement."

Charles C. Kennedy . . . "Sheriff Gets Many 'Leggers,'" *AA*, December 27, 1923.

state conference . . . "Code Revision Urged by Dry Confab," *DMR*, November 8, 1923.

"too ridiculous . . ." "Still Passing the Buck," *Jefferson Bee*, November 28, 1923.

"mean" . . . Untitled brief under masthead, *CT*, November 22, 1923.

a few more interesting questions . . . "Still Passing the Buck."

"juries . . ." Okrent, *Last Call*, 253.

a veritable army . . . "State Agents in Great Flocks Swoop Down on Carroll County," *CT*, December 25, 1924.

"astonishing" . . . Ibid.

next several days . . . "Busy Session of District Court to Start Monday," *CT*, January 1, 1925.

In January . . . "Entered Pleas of Not Guilty Before Judge," *CT*, January 22, 1925.

thirty-one-year-old . . . US Selective Service System, Will Heires WWI draft registration card.

Germany . . . *Kentucky* . . . Rec. fr. Iowa State Census 1895, Carroll County, via FamilySearch, www.familysearch.org/learn/wiki/en/Iowa_Census.

William I. Saul . . . "W. Irving Saul Taken by Death This Morning," *CDH*, July 15, 1933.

Over the next day and a half . . . *By Tuesday* . . . "Jury in First Booze Case Disagrees—and Is Discharged," *CT*, March 19, 1923.

jurisdictions across the nation . . . Okrent, *Last Call*, 253.

The summer before . . . "Federal and State Agents Swoop Down on Carroll Stills," *CT*, June 12, 1924.

Prosecutions . . . "Court Hands Moonshiners Stiff Fine," *AA*, June 26, 1924.

Beebe's case . . . US v. Beebe, Ulysses S.

agents fired . . . Behr, *Prohibition*, 153.

Fort Dodge lawyer . . . *"You need . . ."* . . . *hackles* . . . *handkerchiefs* . . . *chemist's report* . . . *"is the best . . ."* . . . *"most assuredly . . ."* . . . *he revealed* . . . BWOPF.

Meanwhile the bootlegger . . . E-mails between author and Joyce Burner regarding federal case US v. Seevers, Grover C., May 28 and 29, 2013.

most of the 1920s . . . US Industrial Alcohol Bureau, *Statistics Concerning Intoxicating Liquors, December, 1932.*

September 1926 . . . "Brunson to Go After Bootleg Barons with New 'Undercover Men,'" *DMT*, September 28, 1928.

Starting with New York State . . . Behr, *Prohibition*, 166; Okrent, *Last Call*, 256–57.

first half of June 1927 . . . "Visit by Sheriff to Farm Locates 60 Gallon Still," *AA*, June 23, 1927.

northeast corner . . . Viola Township, plat map, 1921.

John Schultes . . . US Selective Service System, John Schultes WWI draft registration card (*AA* rounded up Schultes's age to thirty-six from thirty-five years and eight months).

"make a lot . . ." . . . *Irlbeck hauled* . . . IIR.

June 17 . . . "Visit by Sheriff."

Irlbeck, he thought . . . IIR.

arrested him . . . "Visit by Sheriff."

negotiations . . . "Joe is in . . ." JII.

terms . . . "Visit by Sheriff."

baseball game . . . "Anniversary Was Celebrated Sunday," *CT*, June 29, 1927.

9. CLOSING IN ON THE GOLDEN GOOSE

acceptance speech . . . "Full Text of Hoover's Speech Accepting Party's Nomination for the Presidency," *NYT*, August 12, 1928.

"a great social . . ." Ibid.

personally didn't . . . evening cocktails . . . Burner, *Herbert Hoover*, 203, 218.

tacked differently . . . Behr, *Prohibition*, 226.

wholesale return . . . "The cure . . ." Ibid., 227–28.

"cocktail President" . . . Ibid., 225.

"a vassal . . ." Okrent, *Last Call*, 306.

"the kind . . ." Behr, *Prohibition*, 227.

Heflin . . . Okrent, *Last Call*, 306.

Over vast swaths . . . Ibid., 308, 327.

Election Day . . . Peters, "1928 Presidential Election."

On April 20, 1928 . . . "Carroll County Democrats Select Eighteen Delegates and Instruct for Al. Smith," *CT*, April 11, 1928; "Schmich Sweeps the County for Sheriff—Election Results," *CT*, June 5, 1924; "Light Vote Cast in Party Primary Election Monday," *CT*, June 6, 1928.

something remarkable . . . "Official Returns for All Precincts in Carroll County," *CT*, November 21, 1928.

cluster . . . Wikimedia Commons, "Presidential Election Results by County (1928)."

"broom for . . ." Bergreen, *Capone*, 141.

a weapon . . . Kobler, *Capone*, 97.

terrorize the public . . . Ibid.

"the chopper" . . . Eig, *Get Capone*, 52.

businessmen . . . Ibid., 128.

Valentine's Day . . . Ibid., 187–91, 193; images from the St. Valentine's Day Murder.

Hoover announced . . . ballistics experts . . . Eig, *Get Capone*, 194, 216.

radios . . . Joint Congressional Committee on Inaugural Ceremonies, "Herbert Hoover, 1929."

the "home folks" . . . Ossian, *Depression Dilemmas*, 1.

themes . . . "There would . . ." Hoover, inaugural address.

before seven . . . "Former Carroll Business Man Died Last Saturday at Dubuque—Templeton Youth Killed by Carbon Monoxide—Other Deaths," *CT*, March 6, 1929; rec. fr. USC 1920, Carroll County.

portrayed bootleggers . . . Hoover, inaugural address.

Statistics . . . Ossian, *Depression Dilemmas*, 10.

Funeral services . . . Untitled item under Templeton, *CT*, March 13, 1929.

dozen men . . . "Government Men Raid Templeton," *Coon Rapids Enterprise*, March 15, 1929.

black ribbon . . . *agents debated* . . . *"if you* . . ." . . . *Reicks's basement* . . . JII.

"The federal . . ." "Government Men Raid Templeton."

Buchheit, who'd replaced . . . "Light Vote Cast"; "Official Returns for All Precincts."

hat . . . Untitled history of Templeton Rye.

nab . . . "Government Men Raid Templeton"

former city councilman . . . CB, 133.

honeymooned . . . JII.

county court . . . "Government Men Raid Templeton."

Calvin Coolidge . . . "Two Arrested at Capital Under New Law," *NYT*, March 3, 1929.

Increased Penalties Act . . . Okrent, *Last Call*, 317–20.

The same afternoon . . . JII.

The summer . . . *"Sign that* . . ." . . . *"I know* . . ." . . . *what evidence* . . .

relented . . . Ibid.

"Dear Joe" . . . Mallonee, letter to Joe Irlbeck.

land now worth less . . . Ossian, *Depression Dilemmas*, 12–14.

Thousands of other farmers . . . Ibid., 9–10.

their children . . . CB, 312.

automobile ownership . . . Ossian, *Depression Dilemmas*, 22.

California . . . "Iowa Still Second in Per Capita Car Ownership in U.S.," *CT*, March 23, 1927.

paved roads . . . Ossian, *Depression Dilemmas*, 31.

new Chevy . . . *Michigan* . . . JII.

Others bought . . . CB, 312.

Huesmann had arrived . . . Ibid., 200.

May 1929 . . . *June 25* . . . *one thousand guests* . . . *Madeline Schwaller* . . . *banquet* . . . *Kohorst* . . . *band* . . . "Throngs Honor Templeton Priest—Bishop Invests Monsignor Huesmann with Robes at Pontifical High Mass," *CT*, June 16, 1929.

bottles to visitors . . . *stow* . . . JII.

many Catholic clergy . . . Watman, *Chasing the White Dog*, 106; Okrent, *Last Call*, 186–87.

promoted from a deputy . . . "Clemmensen Is New Sheriff of County," *AA*, January 19, 1928.

Buchheit and another . . . "*Stueve's . . .*" "Seize Two Stills and 2500 Gallons Mash, Templeton," *AA*, June 27, 1929.

volume of sell orders . . . Individual Iowans . . . Ossian, *Depression Dilemmas*, 25–30.

warning about dangerous speculation . . . Burner, *Herbert Hoover*, 245–47.

urban equivalent . . . Ossian, *Depression Dilemmas*, 31–32.

"*I want the goose . . .*" "Letters to Santa Claus," *CT*, December 18, 1929.

uncle John . . . CB, 520.

10. WILSON GETS THE BECK

Neppl and his family . . . Rec. fr. USC 1930, Carroll County.

160-acre . . . Roselle Township, plat map, 1923.

blue-eyed . . . US Selective Service System, Frank Neppl WWI draft registration card.

Neppl's parents . . . Rec. fr. USC 1900, Carroll County.

one day in 1929 . . . JII.

Neppl's farm . . . Roselle Township, plat map, 1923; US v. Neppl, Frank J.

filled the building . . . Ibid.

rent he received . . . JII.

February 1931 . . . IIR.

March 3 . . . crawled . . . IIR; US v. Neppl, Frank J.

sun had set . . . US Naval Observatory, "Complete Sun and Moon Data for One Day."

the temperature . . . National Environmental Satellite, Data, and Information Service, "Record of Climatological Observation, Station: CARROLL."

smell it . . . big whiff . . . redolence . . . "*positive . . .*" . . . *Pratt . . . hunch . . .* IIR; US v. Neppl, Frank J.

half million dollars . . . US Industrial Alcohol Bureau, *Statistics Concerning Intoxicating Liquors, December, 1932.*

Moonlight . . . fourteen degrees . . . US Naval Observatory, "Complete Sun and Moon Data for One Day"; National Environmental Satellite, Data, and Information Service, "Record of Climatological Observation, Station: CARROLL."

At 11:35 . . . without stopping . . . Parsons counted . . . IIR.

"*the largest . . .*" "Rum Raid Nets Federal Agents Two Big Stills," *CDH*, March 5, 1931.

set out toward Neppl's farmhouse . . . knock . . . pajamas . . . Buchheit . . . refrained . . . formalities were finished . . . escorted . . . "*the arrival . . .*" . . . *silence . . . wind . . .* IIR.

windmill . . . smoked . . . JII.

3 AM . . . silence . . . twenty-five feet . . . IIR.

slammed . . . cigarette . . . JII.

"Who are you . . ." . . . grabbed . . . flashlight . . . IIR.

screamed . . . guns . . . "the hell . . ." JII.

"Another person . . ." . . . "was turned . . ." IIR (latter quote elided).

circumstantial . . . IIR; US v. Neppl, Frank J.

mystery informant . . . Ibid.

"Get up . . ." . . . "Who got . . ." . . . "I don't know . . ." . . . "They got . . ." JII.

destroyed . . . above the fold . . . "They'll See No More Templeton Rye," *DMT*, March 6, 1931.

preparing it for trial . . . IIR.

June 16, 1931 . . . bail . . .$1,500 . . . Reynolds . . . Morganthaler . . . US v. Neppl, Frank J.

outside the courtroom . . . JII.

eighty-six degrees . . . National Environmental Satellite, Data, and Information Service, "Record of Climatological Observations, Station: FORT DODGE 5 NNW."

Irlbeck could hear . . . JII.

Reed . . . US v. Neppl, Frank J.

"a woman relative . . ." "They'll See No More Templeton Rye."

Lauretta . . . JII.

United States vs. Al Capone . . . Eig, *Get Capone*, 332.

Wilkerson . . . Longden, "Famous Iowans—George E. Q. Johnson."

Reed was discovering . . . US v. Neppl, Frank J.

Schreck . . . CB, 653.

"Didn't you surmise . . ." . . . "Well, gentlemen . . ." JII.

no doubt . . . bankers . . . Ibid.

Supreme Court . . . Eig, *Get Capone*, 174.

"Well, let's look . . ." . . . "Before I let . . ." . . . peeled out . . . "Be out . . ." JII.

tactic worked . . . Scott ordered . . . scratched out . . . seizing . . . US v. Neppl, Frank J.

average jail sentence . . . average amount levied . . . US Industrial Alcohol Bureau, *Statistics Concerning Intoxicating Liquors, December, 1932.*

July 30, 1931 . . . "It is utterly . . ." Eig, *Get Capone*, 332.

animated discussion . . . "Capone 'Deal' Ruling Today," *Chicago Tribune*, July 31, 1931.

trial opened . . . teeming . . . bribe . . . Eig, *Get Capone*, 344-45.

pleased . . . horrified . . . "U.S. to Begin Its Capone Evidence Today," *Chicago Tribune*, October 7, 1931.

What they got . . . "Capone is to . . ." Ibid.

Damon Runyon . . . referendum . . . Bergreen, *Capone*, 443; Eig, *Get Capone*, 347.

"The government . . ." Johnson, closing arguments in Capone case (quote elided).

"merely because . . ." . . . "bulwark . . ." "Fate of Capone Rests with the Jury Today," *Chicago Tribune*, October 17, 1931.

three felonies . . . Eig, *Get Capone*, 367.

eleven years . . . Kobler, *Capone*, 342.

"greeted . . ." . . . "stigma . . ." "Hail Sentence of Capone as Public Victory," *Chicago Tribune*, October 25, 1931.

Neppl began . . . transferred . . . August 18 . . . US v. Neppl, Frank J.

Reed wrote . . . BWOPF.

Exactly a month . . . "Adolph Lenz Farm Near Templeton Is Raided on Thursday," *CDH*, July 17, 1931.

"It's another one . . ." JII.

11. UPHEAVAL

Residents' first glimpse . . . "Bootleggers Seek Revenge," *Iowa City Press-Citizen*, December 30, 1925.

grand jury . . . Leavenworth Penitentiary, "Kenneth Sonderleiter," inmate case file.

The story . . . "Sonderleiter's Bond Set at $50,500; Bootleg King May Be 'Put on Spot,'" *DMT*, April 28, 1930.

The violence . . . had begun . . . Clarence Campbell . . . Jimmy Dickerson and Jack Harris . . . Ibid.

"extremely . . ." Ibid. ("local" added for clarity).

innocent . . . Friday night . . . "a ride" . . . Dickerson denied . . . hoisted him up . . . slammed the butt . . . "on the spot" . . . bullet struck . . . Sonderleiter's palatial home . . . noticed a distinctive pattern . . . In the basement . . . sped away . . . drove up and down the streets . . . abandoned lot . . . Ibid.

sunset . . . US Naval Observatory, "Complete Sun and Moon Data for One Day."

"arbitrate" . . . "Sonderleiter's Bond Set at $50,500."

spinal cord . . . "Capital Gangster Dies of Wounds," *Ames Daily Tribune*, April 29, 1930.

jumped out with a shotgun . . . hail of buckshot . . . police detective . . . Dickerson charged . . . man to escape . . . spate of gunfights . . . gang war . . . "Sonderleiter's Bond Set at $50,500."

Harris did die . . . "Capital Gangster Dies of Wounds."

not guilty . . . "Not Guilty Plea 'Filed' by Kenneth," *DMT*, May 17, 1930.

lowered the charge . . . "Sonderleiter Trial Continues Today in Des Moines Court," *Atlantic News-Telegraph*, November 25, 1930.

three hours . . . *not guilty* . . . *kidnapping* . . . "Is Freed of Manslaughter," *Charles City Press*, December 2, 1930.

John Brown Hammond . . . *"an uncompromising* . . .*"* Ossian, "Prohibition Possibly Prohibited," 236–37.

the third . . . "Hammond Beat Again in Battle Against Near Beer," *Ames Daily Tribune*, July 22, 1931.

undercover Prohibition agent . . . *charged* . . . "Man of Mystery in Bootlegging Case Steals Limelight," *Muscatine Journal and New Tribune*, September 21, 1931; US v. Sonderleiter, Kenneth.

Kenneth . . . *arrested* . . . Untitled article, *Atlantic News-Telegraph*, September 19, 1931.

shockwaves . . . *black book* . . . "Man of Mystery"; "Can Breathe Easier," *CDH*, December 4, 1931.

not guilty . . . *changed his mind* . . . Leavenworth Penitentiary, "Kenneth Sonderleiter," inmate case file.

stoic . . . *tears* . . . *Dewey* . . . *"She didn't want* . . .*"* . . . *"no relatives* . . .*"* "Kenneth Is Given 2-Year Term in Prison and Fine," *DMT*, December 12, 1931.

seven years . . . "Sonderleiter Up Saturday," *DMT*, December 11, 1931.

Leavenworth . . . *For Faye* . . . *"It's a tough break"* . . . "Kenneth Is Given 2-Year Term."

told the officer . . . Leavenworth Penitentiary, "Kenneth Sonderleiter," inmate case file.

Just a few days . . . *"names of some* . . .*"* . . . *too late* . . . *"Capone's men* . . .*"* "Parole Asked for Woman," *DMT*, December 15, 1931.

Demand plummeted . . . *gangsters* . . . *Most bootleggers* . . . *holdouts* . . . "Rum Syndicate Focused Light on Bootlegging," *DMT*, December 31, 1931.

six men . . . "Six Men Jailed in Drive Upon Rum Syndicate; Jury's Report Awaited," *DMT*, December 30, 1931.

brisk retail trade . . . IIR.

Joyce Lumber . . . CB, 80.

water pump salesman . . . *"I am going* . . .*"* . . . *full-time rumrunner* . . . *make deliveries himself* . . . JII.

focus would return to rural America . . . Ossian, *Depression Dilemmas*, 32–33.

Neil Schaffner . . . Terkel, *Hard Times*, 368–71.

1931 crop year . . . *"no argument* . . .*"* . . . *"In 1929 farms* . . .*"* IYBA 1931, 7.

"The red ink . . .*"* Ibid. (quote elided).

negative three cents . . . "If you wanted . . ." Terkel, *Hard Times*, 218–19.

calculated that to heat . . . Ossian, *Depression Dilemmas*, 100.

hog-stealing "ring" . . . "Fourth Member of Hog Stealing Ring Taken," *CDH*, January 2, 1931; "Two More Hog Stealing Suspects Behind Bars," *CDH*, January 6, 1931.

rash of violent robberies . . . Ossian, *Depression Dilemmas*, 125–27.

penny auction . . . premise . . . lowball price . . . Nuhn, "The Farmer Learns Direct Action"; Ossian, *Depression Dilemmas*, 120.

February 1931 . . . Schwieder, *Iowa*, 257–59; Ossian, *Depression Dilemmas*, 121.

To protest . . . Schwieder, *Iowa*, 259–61.

achieved little . . . "shadow . . ." Nuhn, "The Farmer Learns Direct Action."

influential Literary Digest . . . Ossian, "Prohibition Possibly Prohibited," 229–30; "Iowa's Vote in Prohibition Poll Is Now 17,543 for Change and 12,960 for Enforcement," *DMT*, March 20, 1930; Behr, *Prohibition*, 233.

business elite . . . Okrent, *Last Call*, 331–33.

"virtual . . ." Ibid., 334.

staggering increases . . . Thompson, *Spirits of Just Men*, 56.

12. "XMAS SPIRITS"

yuletide prices . . . Untitled brief, *DMR*, December 16, 1931.

came to town in 1916 . . . "Dr. Morganthaler, 85, Dies in Florida," *Carroll Daily Times Herald*, December 8, 1975.

invested . . . CB, 61, 75, 322.

Prohibition began . . . Ibid., 75.

water back on . . . Ibid., 311.

Sunday-morning edition . . . "After a visit . . ." . . . "The little . . ." "'Little Brown Jug' Swings High in Templeton Street," *DMR*, December 20, 1931.

newspapers across . . . See, for example, "Gives Name to Whisky," *Salt Lake Tribune*, December 21, 1931.

"sacrilegious . . ." "A Jug Instead of a Star," *Chariton Herald-Patriot*, December 24, 1931.

Nelson . . . Iowa Legislature official website, "Standard Form for Members of the Legislature: Charles Wesley Nelson"; USC 1930.

militia . . . sneering, sarcastic . . . "Templeton/Brown Jug," *MM*, January 14, 1932.

word play . . . Translation and interpretation provided to author by Wolfram Anders.

"Sodom . . . little babies . . ." "Templeton/Brown Jug."

"If a bootlegger . . ." "Templeton," *MM*, January 7, 1932.

retaliated . . . Untitled history of Templeton Rye.

Felix Greteman . . . US v. Greteman, Felix.

son . . . CB, 554.

failed to keep . . . Ibid., 68.

family left . . . Untitled item under Templeton, *CDH*, March 19, 1932.

pint or two . . . "Arrests Made Here During County Fair," *AA*, September 22, 1932.

sweltering . . . National Environmental Satellite, Data, and Information Service, "Record of Climatological Observations, Station: CARROLL."

Wilson and his partners . . . IIR.

followed his car . . . *confessed* . . . *weren't* . . . "Hey, kid" . . . *Alfred jumped* . . . *load of sugar* . . . *noticed* . . . Ibid.

As a precaution . . . JII.

The stills . . . US v. Lenz, Adolph.

they moved . . . IIR.

cover their tracks . . . *confessed* . . . *Alberts asked* . . . Ibid.

"*Four to six* . . ." . . . "*Well* . . ." "*I don't know* . . ." "*Oh?* . . ." . . . *lies* . . . *been used* . . . *tire tracks* . . . *followed* . . . Ibid. (quotes from paraphrase; some details speculative).

three coils . . . US v. Lenz, Adolph.

Wilson followed another . . . IIR.

arraigned . . . *Saul* . . . US v. Lenz, Adolph.

working for the kingpin . . . IIR.

Lenz's bail . . . *guilty* . . . $500 . . . US v. Lenz, Adolph.

"*That deal* . . ." IIR.

married to Anna . . . "Carroll Woman Marrys Wall Lake Man," *CDH*, February 4, 1931.

previous spouses . . . Rec. fr. USC 1920, Crawford County; rec. fr. USC 1920, Carroll County; rec. fr. USC 1930, Sac County; "John J. Beck Died from Heart Attack Thursday Morning," *CT*, May 2, 1928.

Anna had objected . . . IIR.

marriage was over . . . Untitled item under Courthouse Happenings, *CDH*, December 17, 1931.

interviews . . . IIR.

As Millard Lowman told the story . . . IIR (quotes from paraphrase).

wife, Geneva . . . Rec. fr. USC 1930, Hancock County.

few days after . . . "*Wait here* . . ." . . . *Fifteen minutes* . . . *Lowman returned* . . . IIR (quotes from paraphrase).

fifteen-year sentence . . . "Millard Lowman Sentenced," *Emmetsburg Democrat*, November 1, 1928.

suicide . . . "Farmer Takes His Life by Hanging," *Waterloo Daily Courier*, March 31, 1955.

larceny . . . "Forgery Suspect Is Returned Here to Be Arraigned," *Carroll Daily Times Herald*, June 5, 1943.

March 18, 1932 . . . *Morganthaler* . . . *refused to answer* . . . IIR.

roaring flame . . . Rich Danner, interview with author (description of aging system).

significant evaporation . . . Carr, *Second Oldest Profession*, 112–13.

Wilson found one . . . *state fire marshal's office* . . . *fire chief* . . . *newly built garage* . . . *bill* . . . *permission from the top* . . . *under oath* . . . IIR.

Early in December . . . Ibid.

spelling . . . BWOPF.

He wove . . . IIR.

13. A SHORELESS SEA

October 4, 1932 . . . Ossian, *Depression Dilemmas*, 156–65.

"We in America . . ." Burner, *Herbert Hoover*, 201.

nearly two thousand . . . Ossian, *Depression Dilemmas*, 160.

dry candidate . . . "Hoover for Dry Law Change," *DMR*, August 12, 1932.

"political cataclysm" . . . "Sweep Is National," *NYT*, November 9, 1932.

returns in Eden . . . "How Carroll Voted on State, National Tickets," *CDH*, November 9, 1932.

outright repeal . . . "Sweep Is National."

"hummingbird . . ." Okrent, *Last Call*, 330.

new job title . . . BWOPF.

February 13, 1933 . . . *Thielen* . . . *odor* . . . *thirty thousand gallons* . . . *Tacke* . . . *one thousand gallons* . . . *behemoth still* . . . $15,000 . . . "1,000 Gal. Still Is Found on Brayton Farm; Man Jailed," *DMR*, February 14, 1933; "Mammoth Alcohol Still Is Seized East of Brayton," *AA*, February 16, 1933; "Thielen Is Free On $1,500 Bond," *AA*, February 23, 1933.

Clemmensen announced . . . "Sheriff Donates Still to County," *AA*, March 16, 1933; "Indict Thielen, Carl Tacke on Liquor Charges," *AA*, October 12, 1933.

Exactly a day . . . "Filibuster on Repeal Checked After 8-Hour Siege," *NYT*, February 15, 1933; "Resolution Passes 63-23," *NYT*, February 17, 1933.

inauguration speech . . . "Text of the Inaugural Address; President for Vigorous Action," *NYT*, March 5, 1933.

raise the definition . . . Okrent, *Last Call*, 352.

provoked fretting . . . "Beer Law May Make Iowa Dry," *CDH*, March 15, 1933.

straw poll . . . "For Beer, 61,230; Against, 22,610," *DMR*, April 2, 1933.

Reporters from many cities . . . "What! No Beer? Not In Iowa," *CDH*, April 6, 1933.

one of the maps . . . "Beer to Be Available Immediately in 23 States," *CDH*, March 17, 1933.

Lineville . . . "Beer on Sale 500 Ft. South of Iowa Line," *DMR*, April 7, 1933; "First of 3.2 Beer at 'Oasis' 500 Feet From Iowa Line," *DMR*, April 8, 1933.

"sick . . ." "Open War for Beer Called by Kraschel," *DMR*, April 8, 1933.

prior to taking the job . . . Rec. fr. USC 1910, Shelby County.

contacted Frank . . . JII.

special session . . . "Twelve Licenses to Sell Beer Are Issued," *CDH*, April 19, 1933.

"in this instance . . ." "German Band in Great Form for Beer Serenades," *CDH*, April 22, 1933.

the indictment . . . *arrest warrants* . . . US v. Irlbeck, Joe, et al.

indefatigable . . . "W. Irving Saul Taken by Death This Morning," *CDH*, July 15, 1933.

As he reviewed . . . US v. Irlbeck, Joe, et al.

diminish the outsized power . . . Okrent, *Last Call*, 35.

expectations . . . "Wets, Drys Battle in Iowa Tomorrow," *CDH*, April 22, 1933.

ballot . . . "No Saloon Pledge Is Presented," *CDH*, July 11, 1933.

margin countywide . . . *Eden* . . . *"Confusion* . . ." "Carroll County Votes 4 to 1 for Repeal," *CDH*, June 21, 1933.

Wilson, who was cut . . . BWOPF.

"It is not . . ." . . . *"but I can tell you* . . ." Ibid. (quote elided).

Saul took a break . . . "W. Irving Saul Taken."

Sauls returned . . . *pain* . . . Ibid.

representing Les and Barney . . . US v. Chapman, Les R.

case against the Chapmans . . . US Bureau of Prohibition, Chapmans of Carroll first investigation file.

On November 20 . . . US v. Irlbeck, Joe, et al.

Four days later . . . IIR.

The Chapmans . . . *pleaded guilty* . . . "Federal Judge Sentences Six" (see note in bibliography).

Illinois liquor distributor . . . "Whisky Trucks Await Iowans," *DMR*, December 7, 1933.

14. THE BOOTLEGGERS' HANGOVER

three-quarters of a million dollars . . . Okrent, *Last Call*, 361.

ONLY THE RICH . . . "Only the Rich Can Afford Liquor," *Algona Upper Des Moines*, August 2, 1934.

price started to fall . . . *"Testimonials* . . ." "Free Advertising for New Liquor
  Stores," *Cedar Rapids Times*, July 7, 1934 (reprint of original article).
Steve Smith was arrested . . . "Federal Men Seize Whisky and Stills," *Daily
  Hawk Eye Gazette*, July 17, 1934.
back on the government payroll . . . BWOPF.
indicted again . . . *found guilty* . . . *juror whom they bribed* . . . "Bedell and
  Chapmans Are Guilty," *CDH*, June 16, 1934; "Chapmans Refused Stay of
  Sentence," *CDH*, October 1, 1935.
network of cigarette . . . "Informations Filed Against 50 Druggists," *CDH*,
  April 20, 1938.
Sonderleiter . . . *"You usually hear* . . ." "Charges Move to Control Beer
  Trade," *DMT*, December 2, 1936.
next half decade . . . "Jury to Hear Sonderleiter," *DMT*, December 26, 1940;
  untitled article, *DMT*, July 12, 1941.
start a zoo . . . *bought two lions* . . . *lion burgers* . . . Ibid.
asked the city . . . "Zoo Goes A-Begging," *NYT*, November 30, 1950.
closed it down . . . "Des Moines Zoo Owner Is Dead," *Muscatine Journal*,
  August 26, 1959.
November 11, 1936 . . . US v. Irlbeck, Joe, and Lang, Lambert.
"You are going . . ." JII.
Just before Christmas . . . CB, 314.
free on bail . . . *"Does Agent* . . ." JII (author's note: Irlbeck says $250 but is
  fined only $200 per US v. Irlbeck, Joe, and Lang, Lambert, quote modified,
  on assumption his recollection was mistaken).
Wilson was sitting . . . *"Come with* . . ." JII.
case number 1990 . . . US v. Irlbeck, Joe, and Lang, Lambert.
bar to tend . . . Untitled item under Dedham local news, *CDH*, May 12, 1937.

EPILOGUE

marks awarded in 1934 . . . US Patent and Trademark Office, *Official Gazette*,
  442.
"renowned Templeton . . ." "13th Year Finds Prohibition at Death's Door,"
  Chicago Tribune, January 16, 1933.
Robert Lucas vowed . . . Clark, "Beginnings of Liquor Legislation in Iowa,"
  198.
percentage of land . . . *held by corporations* . . . IYBA 1934, 237.
Peoples Savings Bank . . . "Templeton Bank Depositors to Be Paid In Full,"
  CDH, July 24, 1936.
Joe Irlbeck . . . Rich Danner, interview with author.

beer distribution . . . JII.

Sonderleiter . . . *pardon* . . . US v. Sonderleiter, Kenneth.

political connections . . . *his wife's name* . . . *right to earn a living* . . . "Oh no . . ."
. . . *granted* . . . JII.

head the tax unit . . . *retired in 1952* . . . BWOPF.

died . . . "B. F. Wilson," *Carroll Daily Times Herald*, June 25, 1963.

BIBLIOGRAPHY

Sources that lack a discernible author are alphabetized by subject or title. As federal investigation files have no titles, they appear here under designations given by the author. Court cases are alphabetized by parties. Some federal court cases were transferred from one division or district to another; in such cases, the designation listed here is where the case was adjudicated.

UNPUBLISHED SOURCES

Ancestry.com. "Herbert Clark Hoover." In California death index, 1940–1997. http://search.ancestry.com/search/db.aspx?dbid=5180.

Danner, Rich, and Fay Irlbeck. Interview with author.

Iowa Legislature official website. "Standard Form for Members of the Legislature: Charles Wesley Nelson." www.legis.iowa.gov/DOCS/LSA /History_Docs/47th%20GA/Nelson,%20Charles%20W.pdf.

———. "Standard Form for Members of the Legislature: L. Dee Mallonee." www.legis.iowa.gov/DOCS/LSA/History_Docs/54th%20GA/Mallonee,%20 Louis%20D.pdf.

Irlbeck, Joe and Lauretta. Recorded interview with Lambert and Elaine Schwaller. Courtesy of Elaine Schwaller.

Irlbeck, Merlyn. Interview with Dan Manatt.

Johnson, George E. Q. Closing arguments in Capone case. Federal records created by George E. Q. Johnson. Via National Archives, Chicago, IL.

"Koolbeck, Ben, Agent Badge." Via National Archives, College Park, MD, RG 58, entry 330, "Identification Cards Folders of Prohibition Agents 1921– 1925," folder title 6047.

Leavenworth Penitentiary. "Kenneth Sonderleiter," inmate case file #40243. Via National Archives, Kansas City, MO.

Mallonee, L. Dee. Letter to Joe Irlbeck. Copy courtesy of Elaine Schwaller.

National Environmental Satellite, Data, and Information Service. "Record of Climatological Observations, Station: AUDUBON, IA, US." US Department of Commerce, National Oceanic & Atmospheric Administration. Retrieved for author, 1917–33.

———. "Record of Climatological Observations, Station: CARROLL." US Department of Commerce, National Oceanic & Atmospheric Administration. Retrieved for author, 1920–35.

———. "Record of Climatological Observations, Station: FORT DODGE 5 NNW." US Department of Commerce, National Oceanic & Atmospheric Administration. Retrieved for author, 1920–35.

Pickerell, David. E-mail with author about production capacity, April 1, 2012.

Tennigkeit v. Wilson. S. Dist. IA, W. Div., no. 125-Law

Untitled history of Templeton Rye (four pages). Provided to the author by the Romey family.

US Bureau of Prohibition. Chapmans of Carroll first investigation file. Via National Archives, College Park, MD, RG 60, 665 23-27-31.

———. Chapmans of Carroll second investigation file. Via National Archives, College Park, MD, RG 60, 668 23-27-108.

———. Irlbeck investigation report. Via National Archives, College Park, MD, RG 60, 675 23-28-110.

———. "Southern District Problem Enforcement." Via National Archives, College Park, MD, RG 60, 667 23-28-3.

US Naval Observatory. "Complete Sun and Moon Data for One Day." Astronomical Applications Department website. http://aa.usno.navy.mil/data/docs/RS_OneDay.php.

US Selective Service System. Claude V. Chapman WWI draft registration card. Via United States World War I Draft Registration Cards, 1917–1918, by FamilySearch. https://familysearch.org/search/collection/1968530.

———. Frank Neppl WWI draft registration card. Via U.S., World War I Draft Registration Cards, 1917–1918, by Ancestry.com. http://search.ancestry.com/search/DB.aspx?dbid=6482.

———. Fred Ceranek WWI draft registration card. Via United States World War I Draft Registration Cards, 1917–1918, by FamilySearch. https://familysearch.org/search/collection/1968530.

———. Henry E. Chapman WWI draft registration card. Via United States World War I Draft Registration Cards, 1917–1918, by FamilySearch. https://familysearch.org/search/collection/1968530.

———. Joe Irlbeck WWI draft registration card. Via U.S., World War I Draft Registration Cards, 1917–1918, by Ancestry.com. http://search.ancestry.com/search/DB.aspx?dbid=6482.

———. John Schultes WWI draft registration card. Via United States World War I Draft Registration Cards, 1917–1918, by FamilySearch. https://familysearch.org/search/collection/1968530.

———. Leonard E. Chapman WWI draft registration card. Via United States World War I Draft Registration Cards, 1917–1918, by FamilySearch. https://familysearch.org/search/collection/1968530.

———. Will Heires WWI draft registration card. Via United States World War I Draft Registration Cards, 1917–1918, by FamilySearch. https:// familysearch.org/search/collection/1968530.

US v. Beebe, Ulysses S. N. Dist. IA, C. Div., no. 1454.

US v. Chapman, C. V., and Chapman, L. E. N. Dist. IA., C. Div., no. 1472.

US v. Chapman, Les R., et al. N. Dist. IA, W. Div., no. 3456.

US v. Greteman, Felix. N. Dist. IA, C. Div., no. 1853.

US v. Hagedorn, Herman. N. Dist. IA, C. Div., no. 1501.

US v. Hagedorn, Herman, and Heuerman, Amos. N. Dist. IA, C. Div., no. 1253.

US v. Irlbeck, Joe, et al. N. Dist. IA, C. Div., no. 1881.

US v. Irlbeck, Joe, and Lang, Lambert. N. Dist. IA, C. Div., no. 1990.

US v. Lang, Herman. N. Dist. IA, C. Div., no. 1336.

US v. Lenz, Adolph. N. Dist. IA, C. Div., no. 1820.

US v. Neppl, Frank J., et al. N. Dist. IA, C. Div., no. 1782.

US v. Schwaller, Victor C. N. Dist. IA, C. Div., no. 1345.

US v. Sonderleiter, Kenneth, et. al. S. Dist. IA, C. Div., no. 3998.

US v. Steffes, John. N. Dist. IA, C. Div., no. 1341.

Vermeule, H. F. Letters to Attorney General Palmer, March 3 and April 26, 1920. Via National Archives, College Park, MD, RG 60, 664 23-27-0.

Wilson, Benjamin Franklin. Official personnel folder. Via Civilian Personnel Records Center, National Archives, St. Louis, MO.

PUBLISHED SOURCES

"Advertisement of an Honest Rumseller as It Should Be!" Via National Archives, Still Pictures Division, College Park, MD, RG 58, GHF-4-4.

Agency for Toxic Substances & Disease Registry. "Public Health Statement: Diethyl Phthalate." US Centers for Disease Control, June 1995. www.atsdr .cdc.gov/phs/phs.asp?id=601&tid=112.

Allen, Leola. "Anti-German Sentiments in Iowa During World War I." *Annals of Iowa* 42 (1975).

Andrews, H. F. *History of Audubon County, Iowa.* Indianapolis: B. F. Bowers, 1915.

Behr, Edward. *Prohibition: Thirteen Years That Changed America.* New York: Arcade Publishing, 2011.

Bergreen, Laurence. *Capone: The Man and the Era*. New York: Simon & Schuster, 1994.

Biographical and Historical Record of Greene and Carroll Counties, Iowa. Chicago: The Lewis Publishing Co., 1887.

Bruns, Roger. *Preacher: Billy Sunday and Big-Time American Evangelism*. Urbana, IL: University of Illinois Press, 2002.

Burner, David. *Herbert Hoover: A Public Life*. New York: Knopf, 1979.

Carr, Jess. *The Second Oldest Profession: An Informal History of Moonshining in America*. Englewood Cliffs, NJ: Prentice-Hall, 1972.

Chicago, Milwaukee, and St. Paul Railway Company. Map of the railroad and extensions, 1881. Via Library of Congress. Call no. G4061.P3 1881.G2.

City of Chattanooga official website. "1901–1905 William Little Frierson." In History of Mayors. www.chattanooga.gov/about-chattanooga/history-of -mayors/1901-1905-william-little-frierson.

City of Templeton. *A Century of Memories: Templeton, Iowa, 1882–1982*. City of Templeton, 1982.

Clark, Dan Elbert. "The Beginnings of Liquor Legislation in Iowa." *Iowa Journal of History and Politics* 5, no. 2 (April 1907). Digital copy via Internet Archive. www.archive.org/details/iowajournalofhis05stat.

———. "The History of Liquor Legislation in Iowa 1846–1861." *Iowa Journal of History and Politics* 6, no. 1 (January 1908). Digital copy via Internet Archive. www.archive.org/details/iowajournalofhis06stat.

———. "The History of Liquor Legislation in Iowa 1878–1908." *Iowa Journal of History and Politics* 6, no. 3 (July 1908). Digital copy via Internet Archive. www.archive.org/details/iowajournalofhis06stat.

Clarke, Paul. "The Comeback Kid." *Imbibe Magazine*, January/February 2007.

Cobb, Frank Irving. *Cobb of "The World": A Leader in Liberalism*. New York: E. P. Dutton, 1924.

Coben, Stanley. "Ordinary White Protestants: The KKK of the 1920s." *Journal of Social History* 28, no. 1 (August 1994).

Connelly, Andy. "The Science and Art of Whiskey Making." Theguardian.com, August 27, 2010. www.theguardian.com/science/blog/2010/aug/23/science -art-whisky-making.

Denison, Lindsay. "The Rev. Billy Sunday and His War on the Devil." *American Magazine* 65, no. 5 (September, 1907).

Derks, Scott. *The Value of a Dollar: Prices and Incomes in the United States, 1860–2004*. Millerton, NY: Grey House Publishing, 2004.

Derr, Nancy. "The Babel Proclamation." *Palimpsest* 60 (1979).

Dictionary of American Biography, under "Emory Roy Buckner." New York: Charles Scribner's Sons, 1973. Accessed via Biography in Context online database, May 16, 2013.

Eagles, Charles W. *Democracy Delayed: Congressional Reapportionment and Urban-Rural Conflict in the 1920s*. Athens, GA: University of Georgia Press, 1990.

Eig, Jonathan. *Get Capone: The Secret Plot That Captured America's Most Wanted Gangster*. New York: Simon & Schuster, 2010.

Ewolt and Warren Township (Carroll County). Plat map, 1923. Des Moines: Anderson Publishing. Via the archives of the State Historical Society of Iowa, Iowa City.

Executive Council of Iowa. *Thirteenth State Census of Iowa*. Des Moines: R. P. Clarkson, State Printer, 1875. www.statelibraryofiowa.org/datacenter /Publications/iowa1875.pdf.

"Federal Judge Sentences Six." Newspaper unknown (possibly *Des Moines Register*), exact publication date unknown (around Prohibition's repeal). This article was one of several clippings provided courtesy of Elaine Schwaller; unfortunately, citation information was not included.

Find a Grave. "Elijah Hoover (1822–1900)." www.findagrave.com/cgi-bin /fg.cgi?page=gr&GRid=96604115.

"Floral School House Presented to Hon. Lieut. Gov. O. H. Manning" postcard, provided by David Kusel.

"German Slavery or Liberty Bonds" WWI poster. Via Library of Congress. www.loc.gov/pictures/item/2002695589/.

Goldberg, David J. "Unmasking the Ku Klux Klan." *Journal of American Ethnic History* 15, no. 4 (Summer 1996).

History Book Committee of Manning. *We Can Remember: A History of Manning's First 100 Years*. Odeboldt: Odebolt Chronicle Print, 1981. Digitized by David Kusel. www.davidkusel.com/centennial/.

Hokanson, Drake. *The Lincoln Highway: Main Street Across America*. Iowa City: University of Iowa Press, 1988.

Hoover, Herbert. Inaugural address. Via Herbert Hoover Presidential Library Association. http://www.hooverassociation.org/hoover/speeches/inaugural _address.php.

Iowa Legislature official website. "Orlando H. Manning." www.legis.iowa.gov /DOCS/LSA/History_Docs/17th%20GA/Manning,%20Orlando%20H.pdf.

Iowa State Department of Agriculture. *Iowa Year Book of Agriculture*. Des Moines: State of Iowa, 1917.

———. *Twenty-First Annual Iowa Year Book of Agriculture*. Des Moines: State of Iowa, 1920.

———. *Twenty-Third Annual Iowa Year Book of Agriculture*. Des Moines: State of Iowa, 1922.

———. *Thirty-Second Annual Iowa Year Book of Agriculture*. Des Moines: State of Iowa, 1931.

———. *Thirty-Fifth Annual Iowa Year Book of Agriculture.* Des Moines: State of Iowa, 1934.

Joint Congressional Committee on Inaugural Ceremonies. "Herbert Hoover, 1929." www.inaugural.senate.gov/swearing-in/event/herbert-hoover-1929.

Kennedy, David M. *Over Here: The First World War and American Society.* Oxford: Oxford University Press, 2004.

Kobler, John. *Capone: The Life and World of Al Capone.* New York: Putnam, 1971.

Lender, Mark Edward. *Drinking in America: A History.* New York: Free Press, 1987.

Leroy Township (Audubon County). Plat map, 1921. Des Moines: Anderson Publishing. Via the archives of the State Historical Society of Iowa, Iowa City.

Longden, Tom. "Famous Iowans—George E. Q. Johnson," DesMoinesRegister. com. http://data.desmoinesregister.com/dmr/famous-iowans/george-eq -johnson.

Maclean, Paul. *History of Carroll County Iowa.* Vol. 1. Chicago: S. J. Clark Publishing Company, 1912.

Mennel, S. J. "Prohibition: A Sociological View." *Journal of American Studies* 3, no. 2 (December 1969).

Miron, Jeffrey A., and Jeffrey Zweibel. "Alcohol Consumption During Prohibition." *American Economic Review,* May 1991.

Mount Vernon official website. "George Washington's Distillery." www.mountvernon.org/distillery.

National War Garden Commission. "Can Vegetables, Fruit, and the Kaiser Too" WWI poster. Via Library of Congress. www.loc.gov/pictures /item/2003652822/.

Natural Resources Conservation Service. "Iowa Soil Regions Map." US Department of Agriculture. ftp://ftp-fc.sc.egov.usda.gov/IA/technical /IowaSoilRegionsMap.html.

Neymeyer, Robert J. "In the Full Light of Day: The Ku Klux Klan in 1920s Iowa." *Palimpsest,* Summer 1995.

Nuhn, Ferner. "The Farmer Learns Direct Action." *Nation* 136, no. 3531 (March 8, 1933).

Okrent, Daniel. *Last Call: The Rise and Fall of Prohibition.* New York: Scribner, 2010.

Ossian, Lisa L. *The Depression Dilemmas of Rural Iowa, 1929–1933.* Columbia, MO: University of Missouri Press, 2011.

———. "Prohibition Possibly Prohibited." *The Social History of Alcohol and Drugs* 20, no. 2 (Spring 2006).

Perlman, Jacob. "The Recent Recession of Farm Population and Farm Land." *Journal of Land & Public Utility Economics* 4, no. 1 (February 1928).

Peters, Gehard. "1928 Presidential Election." American Presidency Project. University of California, Santa Barbara. www.presidency.ucsb.edu /showelection.php?year=1928.

Regan, Gary, and Mardee Haidin Regan. *The Book of Bourbon and Other Fine American Whiskeys.* Cheltenham, UK: Mixellany Limited, 2009.

Reineke, David. *The German Heritage of Carroll County, Iowa.* IAGenWeb Project. www.rootsweb.ancestry.com/~iacarrol/reineke/book/germimmindx .htm.

Rose, Kenneth D. *American Women and the Repeal of Prohibition.* New York: New York University Press, 1996.

Roselle Township (Carroll County). Plat map, 1923. Des Moines: Anderson Publishing. Via the archives of the State Historical Society of Iowa, Iowa City.

Schmeckebier, Laurence F. *The Bureau of Prohibition: Its History, Activities, and Organization.* Washington, DC: Brookings Institution, 1929.

Schwieder, Dorothy. "A Farmer and the Ku Klux Klan in Northwest Iowa." *Annals of Iowa* 61, no. 3 (Summer 2002).

———. *Iowa: The Middle Land.* Iowa City: University of Iowa Press, 1996.

Secretary of State of Iowa. *Census of Iowa for the Year 1885.* Des Moines: Geo. E. Roberts, State Printer, 1885. www.statelibraryofiowa.org/datacenter /Publications/iowa1885.pdf

———. *Census of Iowa for the Year 1895.* Des Moines: F. R. Conaway, State Printer, 1895. www.statelibraryofiowa.org/datacenter/Publications /iowa1895.pdf.

Sunday, Rev. William Ashley. *Get on the Water Wagon.* Sturgis, MI: Journal Publishing Company, 1915.

Terkel, Studs. *Hard Times: An Oral History of the Great Depression.* New York: New Press, 2011.

Thompson, Charles Dillard, Jr. *Spirits of Just Men: Mountaineers, Liquor Bosses, and Lawmen in the Moonshine Capital of the World.* Urbana, IL: University of Illinois Press, 2011.

Tolzmann, Don Heinrich. *The German-American Experience.* Amherst, NY: Humanity Books, 2000.

Tuchmann, Barbara Wertheim. *The Guns of August.* New York: Ballantine/ Presidio Press, 2004.

US Congress. "Volstead, Andrew John, (1860–1947)." In *Biographical Directory of the United States Congress.* http://bioguide.congress.gov /scripts/biodisplay.pl?index=V000114.

US Food Administration. "Defeat the Kaiser and His U-Boats." Via American
    War Posters, University of North Texas Digital Library. http://digital.library
    .unt.edu/ark:/67531/metadc418/.

US Industrial Alcohol Bureau. *Statistics Concerning Intoxicating Liquors,
    December, 1930.* Washington, DC: Government Printing Office, 1931.

————. *Statistics Concerning Intoxicating Liquors, December, 1932.*
    Washington, DC: Government Printing Office, 1932.

US Patent and Trademark Office. *Official Gazette* 442 (1934).

Viola Township (Audubon County). Plat map, 1921. Des Moines, Iowa:
    Anderson Publishing. Via the archives of the State Historical Society of
    Iowa, Iowa City.

Watman, Max. *Chasing the White Dog: An Amateur Outlaw's Adventures in
    Moonshine.* New York: Simon & Schuster, 2010.

Wheaton College official website. "Papers of William Ashley 'Billy' Sunday and
    Helen Amelia (Thompson) Sunday—Collection 61." http://www2.wheaton
    .edu/bgc/archives/GUIDES/061.htm.

Wikimedia Commons. "Presidential Election Results by County (1928)."
    http://en.wikipedia.org/wiki/File:PresidentialCounty1928Colorbrewer.gif

"Will Village's Citizens Carry On Its Fame?" Newspaper unknown (possibly
    Des Moines Register), exact publication date unknown (around
    Prohibition's repeal). This article was one of several clippings provided
    courtesy of Elaine Schwaller; unfortunately, citation information was not
    included.

Wrede, Steven. "The Americanization of Scott County, 1914–1918." *Annals of
    Iowa* 44 (1979).

INDEX